ALMANAC OF THE AMERICAN PEOPLE

ALMANAC

of the

AMERICAN

PEOPLE

TOM and NANCY BIRACREE

Facts On File®

New York • Oxford

Almanac of the American People

Library of Congress Cataloging-in-Publication Data

Biracree, Tom, 1947–
    Almanac of the American people.

    Bibliography: p.
    Includes index.
    1. United States—Economic conditions—1981–
Statistics.   2. United States—Social conditions—
1980–   —Statistics.   I. Biracree, Nancy.   II. Title.
HC106.8.B57   1988   330.973'0927   88-3882
ISBN 0-8160-1821-9 (HC)
ISBN 0-8160-2329-8 (PB)

British CIP data available on request
Printed in the United States of America
10 9 8 7 6 5 4 3 2

To our wonderful son, Ryan,
and the rest of America's children.
Embodied in you
are all of our hopes
and dreams
for what America
can and should be.

ACKNOWLEDGMENTS

First, our thanks to Jay Acton, who urged us to expand our research into this book, and to Jane Dystel, who skillfully guided the project to a safe haven while providing us with lots of good advice and moral support. Gerry Helferich, editor and friend, has the magical ability to make the process of writing and producing a book both profitable and fun. Ernie Haim, the designer of this book, is not only talented, but a consummate professional who continually provided invaluable guidance.

Secondly, we'd like to express our appreciation for some of this country's most valuable and most unappreciated people— America's demographers and market researchers. Their work produces not dry statistics, but an invaluable and fascinating portrait of who we are.

Finally, we'd like to thank our family and friends for their help and moral support during the long research, writing, and production process. In particular, we appreciate the efforts of Keith Peitler, a fine young man who befriended Ryan and freed many extra hours for us to work on this book.

TABLE OF CONTENTS

INTRODUCTION

THE ALMANAC OF THE AMERICAN PEOPLE is a unique and important book about every aspect of the everyday lives of you and your fellow Americans. This book combines the most up to date and accurate information with text that interprets these facts and relates them to each other. This almanac is not only a valuable reference volume, but also a fascinating narrative of American life.

For example, in our section titled "Your Money," you'll find detailed information about exactly how much money people make, the sources of that income, how much they spend and what they spend it on, how much they pay in taxes, how much they save, how much they owe, and even how much cash they carry around in their pockets. The result is a fascinating portrait of the financial lives of Americans, rich, poor, and in between. Other sections of the book contain similarly complete, detailed stories of our health, our education, our religion and ethics, our business lives, our love lives, our children, how and where we live, what we own, what we do for fun, and even what we eat and drink.

The value of these portraits goes far beyond satisfying our natural curiosity about how our lives compare to those of other people. The value lies in the difference between information and understanding. We live in an increasingly complex society buffeted by very rapid change. Since technology has made this the "information age," this complexity and change are well-documented in mountains of computer print-outs and tons of statistical books.

The volume of information, however, often makes it more difficult, not easier, to make important business, political, social, and personal decisions. The greater the number of statistics, the harder it is to sort out the most important facts and relate them to each other. In the absence of understanding, it's easy to make bad decisions on the basis of incomplete or isolated bits of information that prove disastrous in the long run.

In writing *THE ALMANAC OF THE AMERICAN PEOPLE*, however, we've taken great care to not only select the most important facts about everyday life in today's U.S.A., but also to tie these statistics together in a comprehensible narrative. For example, this book not only tells you how many more women are working and why, but also explains the effects their entrance into the work force is having on leisure time, marriage, children, spending patterns, housing trends, and a wide variety of other issues.

As a result, *THE ALMANAC OF THE AMERICAN PEOPLE* is an important addition to the reference library of every business person, social scientist, politician, and anyone fascinated by life in the United States.

SOURCES

The two important questions always asked about statistics are how accurate and how current they are. We'll discuss both subjects briefly, so you can evaluate the sources of the statistics we use in this book.

The Federal Government is by far the largest source of statistics about life in the United States, and thus is the source of the majority of facts in this book. Government agencies collect information in basically two ways: counting and surveys. By way of example, we'll use the National Center for Health Statistics (NCHS). One responsibility of the NCHS is keeping track of the nation's "vital statistics," that is, births, marriages, divorces, and deaths. To find out how many people have married, the agency records information from every single marriage certificate filed in every year. The result is an actual count of every marriage and, assuming the information on the certificates is accurate, a very detailed look at who's getting married.

This counting method is very reliable, but also very laborious and time consuming—so much so that detailed 1983 statistics became available only in late 1987 and early 1988. That's why the NCHS, like other federal agencies, surveys a large, scientifically selected sample of the U.S. population to obtain information on issues relating to the health of Americans. For example, rather than take on the awesome task of contacting every single hospital in the United States to obtain records of every patient admitted or treated, the agency conducts an annual Hospital Discharge Survey to discover such information as how many Americans were hospitalized, the reasons for the hospitalization, the length of stay, etc. These surveys are quite accurate and, since the number of people surveyed are in the tens of thousands rather than the millions, the results are available in two to three years, rather than in four or five years.

The U.S. Census Bureau uses similar methods. As everyone knows, every ten years the Bureau takes on the massive and difficult task of obtaining information from every resident of the United States. Because of the enormity of this task, the results of the census are made available to the public over a period of several years. That's why the Census Bureau tracks important changes in the population during the decade betwen censuses through its Current Population Surveys. Every month, Census Bureau interviewers contact a representative sample of 65,000 Americans to ask them a list of selected questions. Since such information as age, sex, and place of residence is always asked, the Census Bureau, in the publication series entitled "Current Population Reports," annually issues its estimates of the population of the U.S. by age, sex, state, and household status. Other information, such as the number of Americans who have recently moved or the number of Americans collecting government benefits, is obtained at intervals that range from every two years to every ten years.

All of the federal statistics in this book are the most up to date available. The year of reference, however, depends on the manner in which the statistics are compiled and, in some cases, the efficiency of the agency that collects them. For example, our statistics on the number of Americans enrolled in college are taken from the Census Bureau's Current Population Surveys. Therefore, they are available sooner than statistics on the actual numbers of people who graduate from colleges, which are counted by the U.S. Department of Education.

Obviously, the Federal Government is far from the only source of statistics about American life. Corporations, non-profit organizations, industry groups, and academic researchers are also keenly interested in what Americans do, what they drink, how they spend their money, and what they do with their time. The vast majority of the statistics they collect are based on surveys, and many of the results are released to the general public.

The reliability of the results, however, varies widely. Many well-publicized statistics, including those in some best-selling books, have been either fabricated or based on studies of groups that are not representative of the population of the United States. For this book, we have made an exhaustive effort to locate the most recent and most reliable studies available. Taken as a whole, in connection with Federal statistics, we believe they provide as accurate look as possible at everyday life in the United States.

CHAPTER
ONE

ALL ABOUT YOU

WHO ARE YOU?

You're one of approximately 115 billion human beings who have lived in the last 2.5 million years. You're also one of 8 billion of these people (about 6% of all people who have ever lived) whose names will have survived in books, on monuments or in public records. This proportion will reach 10% in the next 100 years.

YOUR RACE
AND ETHNIC ORIGINS

The population of the United States in 1987 was approximately 85% white, 12% black, 1.6% Asian, .6% American Indian, and .8% "other." [1] Approximately 7.1% of the population was of "Spanish-origin," and these Americans could be either black or white. [2]

Below is a look at some social and economic characteristics of the white, black, and Spanish-origin population in 1987: [3]

	White	Black	Spanish-origin
Age			
Under 5 years	7.3%	9.4%	10.6%
65 and over	13.1%	8.2%	4.8%

	White	Black	Spanish-origin
Years of school			
0–8	12.0%	18.4%	35.2%
9–11	11.0%	18.2%	13.9%
12 (H.S. graduate)	39.2%	37.1%	29.0%
Some college	17.2%	15.7%	13.3%
College graduate	20.5%	10.7%	8.6%
Employment			
Employed	65.8%	55.6%	60.5%
Unemployed	3.5%	8.3%	5.8%
Not in labor force	34.2%	36.2%	33.6%
Type of family			
Married couples	83.4%	52.7%	74.8%
with children	39.1%	28.5%	46.2%
Female head	13.0%	41.8%	23.4%
with children	7.4%	28.5%	16.6%
Male head	3.7%	5.4%	5.7%
with children	1.4%	1.9%	2.2%
Family income			
Less than $9,999	10.2%	30.1%	23.3%
$10,000–$14,999	9.1%	13.8%	15.2%
$15,000–$24,999	19.5%	20.2%	22.4%
$25,000–$49,999	39.2%	27.1%	29.0%
$50,000+	22.0%	8.8%	10.2%
Housing			
Own home	66.8%	45.4%	40.6%
Rent	33.1%	54.6%	59.5%

The most recent Census Bureau projections were that the population of the United States would reach 267,000,000 by the year 2000. At that time, about one-quarter of the American people is expected to be black, Hispanic, or Asian. [4]

AMERICA, THE MELTING POT

Except for the 6,716,000 American Indians, the rest of you trace your origins to points all over the globe. You may be surprised to find out that the influx of immigrants between 1971 and 1980 was greater than for any ten year period in American history, with the exception of the two decades between 1901 and 1920. In 1980, 14,080,000 Americans, about 6% of the population, had been born in a foreign country. About half of these foreign born Americans were naturalized citizens. [5]

According to the 1980 Census, 60% of Americans identified themselves as having English, German, or Irish ethnic origins. By country, the ethnic origins of Americans were: [6]

Ancestry group	Number of Americans
English	49,584,000
German	49,224,000
Irish	40,166,000
Afro-American	20,965,000
French	12,892,000
Italian	12,184,000
Scottish	10,049,000
Polish	8,228,000
Mexican	7,693,000
Dutch	6,304,000
Swedish	4,345,000
Norwegian	3,454,000
Russian	2,781,000
Spanish	2,687,000
Czech	1,892,000
Hungarian	1,777,000
Welsh	1,685,000
Danish	1,518,000
Puerto Rican	1,444,000
Portuguese	1,024,000
Chinese	894,000
Filipino	795,000
Japanese	791,000
French-Canadian	780,000
Cuban	580,000
Canadian	456,000
Korean	377,000
Asian Indian	312,000
Lebanese	295,000
Vietnamese	215,000
Armenian	213,000

Between 1981 and 1985, nearly half the immigrants admitted legally into this country came from Asia. In order, the top areas of origin of immigrants during this period were the Caribbean, Mexico, Vietnam, the Philippines, and Korea.

Immigrants accounted for about 25% of the population increase in the United States between 1981 and 1985. By continent, those immigrants came from: [7]

Continent	Percent of immigrants
Europe	11%
Asia	48%
North America	31%
South America	6%
Africa	3%
Other	1%

ILLEGAL ALIENS

Although accurate figures are impossible to come by, experts estimate the number of illegal aliens in this country could be as high as 20 million people. In 1987, the U.S. Immigration and Naturalization Service captured 1,158,000 illegal aliens, three times the number of legal immigrants admitted. The Service estimated, however, that 4,000,000 other illegal aliens slipped through their nets. 97% of the aliens captured were from Mexico. [8]

A language other than English was spoken in 11% of American homes at the time of the 1980 Census. About 20% of those speaking another language at home were unable to communicate in English.

Half of all Americans speaking another language at home spoke Spanish. The next most common languages were Italian, German, and French. [9]

U.S. POPULATION BY AGE

The population of the United States by age in 1987 was: [10]

Age	Males	Females	Males/1000 females
Under 5	9,341,000	8,910,000	1048
5–9	9,037,000	8,625,000	1048
10–14	8,450,000	8,035,000	1052
15–19	9,412,000	9,047,000	1040

Age	Males	Females	Males/1000 females
20–24	9,915,000	9,878,000	1004
25–29	11,009,000	10,971,000	1003
30–34	10,661,000	10,674,000	999
35–39	9,273,000	9,465,000	980
40–44	7,639,000	7,928,000	964
45–49	6,025,000	6,326,000	952
50–54	5,285,000	5,641,000	937
55–59	5,298,000	5,823,000	910
60–64	5,068,000	5,831,000	869
65–74	7,824,000	9,844,000	795
75+	4,295,000	7,873,000	546

The median age of the United States reached 32.1 years in 1987, the highest in history. Median age for white Americans was 32.7, median age for black Americans was 26.9. To show how far we've come in longevity, the median age in the year 1800 was 16.0 and in 1900 had climbed to only 22.9 years.

Average median age for all countries in the world in 1986 was 23.5 years. West Germany had the highest median age (37.6), largely because only 15% of the population was 14 or under (compared with 23% for the U.S.). Lowest median ages were in Third World countries such as Kenya, where half the population was under age 14. [11]

YOUR LIFE EXPECTANCY

The biggest demographic surprise of the last two decades has been a very large decrease in the death rate, which means life expectancy has soared. Between 1970 and 1986, according to the National Center for Health Statistics, the average life expectancy for a male rose 4.3 years and the average life expectancy for a female increased 3.7 years. [12]

Although men closed the gap a little, women could still expect to live 7 years longer. The only advantage for men has been that they have tended to be healthier in their later years. In 1986, men age 65 or older could expect to live 71% of their remaining years in good health, while women 65 or older could expect to live only 54% of their remaining years in good health.

In the table below, you can find out how many years, on the average, you have left to live: [13]

	EXPECTED YEARS TO LIVE			
Your present age	White male	White female	Black male	Black female
0	71.8	78.7	65.4	73.6
18	55.0	61.7	49.5	57.3
21	52.2	58.8	46.7	54.4
25	48.5	54.9	43.1	50.6
30	43.9	50.1	38.7	45.9
35	39.2	45.2	34.4	41.2
40	34.6	40.4	30.2	36.7
45	30.0	35.7	26.2	32.2
50	25.7	31.2	22.5	28.1
55	21.6	26.8	19.1	24.1
60	17.9	22.6	16.0	20.5
65	14.5	18.7	13.4	17.3
70	11.5	15.1	10.9	14.1
75	9.0	11.8	9.0	11.5
80	6.9	8.8	7.1	9.0
85	5.2	6.5	6.0	7.4

Another way to look at life expectancy is to look at the percentage of all men and women born who have survived to a specific age: [14]

Age	% men surviving	% women surviving
1	98.7%	98.9%
20	97.5	98.3
30	95.8	97.7
40	93.9	96.8
50	89.8	94.5
60	80.1	88.9
65	72.0	84.1
70	61.1	77.3
75	47.9	67.9
80	33.4	55.3
85	19.5	39.3

According to a Gallup Poll, the average age Americans thought was middle-aged was 46; the average age they thought was "older" was 68; and the average American believed he or she would live to age 78.

In 1985, the 28,530,000 Americans age 65 and over constituted 11.8% of the population. That was a 130% increase since 1950, when only 8% of the population was 65 or older. People age 65 and over will make up 15% of the population in the year 2000, 24% of the population in 2030, and an enormous 30% of the population in the year 2080.

Of these older Americans, 16,995,000 were age 65–74, 8,835,000 were age 75–84, and 2,700,000 were age 85 and over. The percentage of elderly Americans who are age 75 and older will increase from 39% in 1980 to 50% in the year 2000.

The percentage of these Americans who were women increased dramatically with age: [15]

Age 65–74, there were 78 men for every 100 women

Age 75–84, there were 57 men for every 100 women

Age 85+, there were 44 men for every 100 women

The fastest growing of all population group has been the "oldest old," Americans 85 and over. The number of people in this age group soared 141% between 1960 and 1980, to 2,240,067 people. The Census Bureau estimated a 123% increase between 1980 and 2000. The number of Americans in this group should reach 3.3 million by 1990, 4.9 million by 2000, and 13 million by 2040. [16]

The 1980 Census found 14,170 Americans age 100 or older, 3,323 men and 10,347 women. Of these centenarians, 12,838 were between age 100 and 104, while 1,332 were 105 or older. These Americans survived odds of 400 to 1 to live to age 100.

The Census Bureau estimated, however, that the number of centenarians nearly doubled to 25,000 by 1986. With advances in medical care, an estimated 100,000 Americans will be 100 years old or older in the year 2000. The Census Bureau estimated that for babies born in 1980, the odds of living to age 100 would be 87–1, the odds of living to 105 would be 559 to 1, and the odds of living to age 110 would be 4,762 to 1. [17]

YOUR ODDS
OF DYING THIS YEAR

Men have been far more accident-prone than women, and that's why the odds of men under 35 dying during the course of a year have been three times as great as those of women under 35. Still, you should find the table below very reassuring. [18]

	YOUR ODDS OF DYING THIS YEAR			
Your age	White male	White female	Black male	Black female
25	561 to 1	1754 to 1	311 to 1	943 to 1
35	552 to 1	1136 to 1	200 to 1	483 to 1
45	242 to 1	438 to 1	101 to 1	209 to 1
55	89 to 1	172 to 1	48 to 1	91 to 1
65	37 to 1	73 to 1	25 to 1	46 to 1
75	16 to 1	30 to 1	15 to 1	24 to 1

LEADING CAUSES OF DEATH

According to the most recent statistics, the leading causes of death in America were: [19]

Cause	Percent of all deaths
Heart disease	38.2%
Cancers	21.9%
Strokes	7.7%
Accidents	4.6%
Respiratory disease	3.3%
Pneumonia and influenza	2.8%
Diabetes	1.8%
Suicide	1.4%
Liver disease	1.4%
Atherosclerosis	1.3%
Homicide	1.0%
All other	14.6%

While nearly 4 out of every 10 Americans died of heart disease, the death rate for these conditions dropped 30% since 1972. This sharp decline—and a 70% drop in deaths from strokes—was the primary reason life expectancy climbed so steeply in recent years.

The most significant difference between causes of death for men and women has been that three times as many men have died of accidents, three times as many have committed suicide, and four times as many men have been murdered. Men have been twice as prone to fatal liver disease and 33% more likely to have had cancer.

Looking to add a few years? Try a move to Hawaii, whose residents lived 3.14 years longer than the U.S. average. Other states with high life expectancy were Minnesota, Utah, Iowa, and North Dakota. States with the lowest average life expectancies were South Carolina, Georgia, Mississippi, Louisiana, and Alaska. [20]

One reason for the low ranking of these states was that cancer rates have been 10% higher in the Southeast, especially Alabama, South Carolina, Kentucky, Maryland, Louisiana, and Delaware. On the other hand, the cancer rate in Utah was half the national average. Similarly low cancer rates have been found in other Mountain states: Montana, Idaho, Wyoming, Colorado, New Mexico, and Arizona. [21]

YOU AND YOUR HEART

63 million Americans—1 in 4—suffered from some form of heart disease in 1984, according to the American Heart Association. 1.5 million have heart attacks during the average year. 45% of these victims are under 65, and 5% are under 40.

About a third of those that have suffered heart attacks died immediately. Part of the reason has been that the average victim waited three hours before seeking help.

Heart attack risk doubled for smokers and those with high cholesterol, and it quadrupled for those who had high blood pressure in addition to the above conditions.

Recently, researchers have also discovered a link between heart attack risk and income. Men earning under $13,000 a year had a 40% greater risk of fatal heart attacks then men earning over $28,000 per year. Lowest income women had a 27% greater risk than highest income women. [22]

YOU AND CANCER

The bad news is that of today's total U.S. population, 30% (74 million people) will eventually come down with some form of cancer. The good news is that medical science has made major strides in treating malignancy. In the 1930's, only 1 in 5 cancer patients survived for five years; by the 1960's that figure was 1 in 3, and in 1985 the survival rate neared 1 in 2.

965,000 Americans were diagnosed with cancer in 1987. Of these, about 385,000 should be alive in 1992. Subtracting unrelated causes of death for the remaining 580,000 people—heart attacks, accidents, etc.—the survival rate for 5 years or more was 49%. That's 50,000 more survivors a year than were saved a decade ago. Experts estimate another 170,000 people per year—35% of cancer deaths—could be saved with earlier detection and treatment. [23]

The types of cancer most commonly suffered by men and women in 1986 were: [24]

Men Type of cancer	% of total cases
Prostate	20%
Lung	20%
Colon and rectum	14%
Urinary	10%
Leukemia and lymphomas	8%
Oral	4%
Skin	3%
Pancreas	3%
Other	18%

Women Type of cancer	% of total cases
Breast	27%
Colon and rectum	16%
Lung	11%
Uterus	10%
Leukemia and lymphomas	7%
Ovary	4%
Urinary	4%
Skin	3%
Pancreas	3%
Oral	2%
Other	13%

The percentage of cancer sufferers who survived for at least five years after their diagnosis, by type of cancer, were: [25]

Type of cancer	Survival rate
Testes	89%
Uterine Corpus	83%
Melanoma of skin	80%
Bladder	75%
Breast	74%
Hodgkin's disease	74%
Prostate	70%
Larynx	67%
Uterine cervix	66%
Colon	52%
Oral	51%
Kidney	50%
Rectum	49%
Non-Hodgkin's lymphoma	48%
Ovary	38%
Leukemia	33%
Brain	22%
Stomach	15%
Lung	13%
Esophagus	6%
Pancreas	3%

YOU AND HIGH BLOOD PRESSURE

The American Heart Association estimated that 57,710,000 Americans had high blood pressure (hypertension). The group defined high blood pressure as readings over 140 over 90. People who had such readings were, in the words of the Heart Association, "at increased risk of disease or premature death."

The percentage of people with high blood pressure increased with age: [26]

Age	% of men	% of women
18–24	15%	4%
25–34	21%	7%
35–44	28%	19%
45–54	44%	39%
55–64	53%	53%
65+	60%	68%

Parents should particularly concerned with high blood pressure in their children. A recent study by the Yale Medical School showed that 80% of children with high blood pressure still had high blood pressure 30 years later, putting them at greater risk of early death.

SUICIDE

Almost 30,000 Americans have taken their own lives every year during the 1980's, a 70% increase over the average yearly deaths by suicide in the 1960's. 58% of suicide victims used firearms, 20% poisoned themselves, 15% hanged themselves, and the rest used other methods.

Below are the current suicide rates by sex and age: [27]

| Age | SUICIDES PER 100,000 PEOPLE | |
	Males	Females
10-14	2.4	.7
15-19	18.2	4.1
20-24	28.4	5.3
25-34	26.4	6.2
35-44	23.9	8.3
45-54	26.3	9.6
55-64	28.7	9.0
65+	45.6	7.5

A large percentage of the increase in suicides since 1960 resulted from a 73% rise in the suicide rate for 15-19 year olds. An estimated 1,000 teen-agers attempted suicide every day—that's over 1% of all teen-agers who tried to kill themselves. 6,000 teen-agers succeeded.

YOUR ACCIDENTS

In 1986, 95,277 Americans died in accidents, 69% of them men. Below were the deaths in various types of accidents: [28]

Type of accident	Deaths
Motor vehicle accidents	47,865
Boating accidents	1,102
Airplane accidents	1,148

Type of accident	Deaths
Railway accidents	556
Accidental falls	11,444
Accidental drowning	4,777
Accidents caused by	
Fires and flames	4,835
Firearms	1,452
Electric current	854
Accidental poisonings	
Drugs and medicines	4,187
Other solids and liquids	544
Gases and vapors	1,009
Complications of medical treatment	3,069
Inhalation and ingestion of objects	3,692

62,565,000 Americans suffered accidental injuries in 1985 that led to restricted activity or medical attention—29.8% of all males and 23.7% of all females. 8 million of the accidents occurred at work, 22 million at home, 7 million in motor vehicles, and 25 million in other locations. [29]

The leading cause of non-fatal accidents (except for motor vehicle accidents and work-related accidents) was stairs, ramps, and landings, which injured 1,390,085 Americans in 1985. Next in cause of injuries were: [30]

> Bicycle riding
> Playing basketball
> Playing baseball
> Playing football
> Knives and scissors
> Furniture
> Non-glass doors

When frequency of accidents and severity of injuries were considered, the most dangerous products were: [31]

> Cigarette lighters
> Gasoline
> Batteries
> Drain and oven cleaners
> Heating equipment
> Stoves and ovens
> Swimming pools
> Power mowers

What about catastrophic accidents? In 1985, there were 69 accidents that killed 5 or more people. By type, they were: [32]

Type of accident	Number of catastrophes
Fires/explosions	22
Airplane crashes	16
Motor vehicle	10
Tornadoes	6
Floods	4
Blizzards	3
Other	8

A study of weather-related deaths over the 25 year period 1962–1986, the average annual deaths from various kinds of weather were: [33]

Heat	200
Floods	151
Lightning	94
Tornadoes	87
Hurricanes	31

The National Safety Council estimated that the total cost of all accidents in 1986 was $118 billion. [34]

HOW'S YOUR HEALTH?

When asked by interviewers for the National Center for Health Statistics, over all, two-thirds of you classified your health as "excellent" or "very good," with only 1 in 10 replying "fair" or "poor." As you'd expect, the percentage of people in poor health increased over age 50, with a third of those over 65 reporting chronic health problems.

Money may not buy happiness, but it may buy good health. 4.6% of those making over $35,000 had "fair" or "poor" health, compared with 21% of those earning less than $10,000 per year. [35]

On a scale of 1 to 10, how do you feel today? If you're average, you replied 7 or 8—pretty good. Even if you're young, however, minor complaints may bother you a third of the time. People who kept a daily diary of how they felt for 6 weeks had the following percentage of days on which they had at least one symptom of discomfort, such as a headache: [36]

Age	% days men felt discomfort	% days women felt discomfort
18–44	30%	43%
45–64	26%	44%
65+	57%	57%

For adults 18 to 44, the leading causes of discomfort, in order of frequency, were: [37]

	Men	Women
1.	Headache	Headache
2.	Nasal congestion	Tiredness
3.	Tiredness	Nasal congestion
4.	Sore throat	Sinus problems
5.	Sinus problems	Tension/nervousness
6.	Back trouble	Back troubles
7.	Leg trouble	Cough
8.	Tension/nervousness	Sore throat
9.	Cough	Upset stomach
10.	Neck trouble	Menstrual pain

The leading causes of discomfort for adults age 45 to 64 were: [38]

	Men	Women
1.	Headache	Headache
2.	Nasal congestion	Back trouble
3.	Leg trouble	Knee trouble
4.	Tiredness	Tension/nervouness
5.	Knee trouble	Joint pain, several joints
6.	Cough	Sinus problems
7.	Neck trouble	Leg trouble
8.	Back trouble	Tiredness
9.	Sore throat	Nasal congestion
10.	General pain	Neck trouble

The leading causes of discomfort for adults age 65 and over were: [39]

Men	Women
1. Leg trouble	Knee trouble
2. Skin irritation	Leg trouble
3. Hand/finger trouble	Tiredness
4. General pain	Back trouble
5. Back trouble	Tension/nervousness
6. Foot/toe trouble	Nasal congestion
7. Shoulder trouble	Circulation problems
8. Knee trouble	Headache
9. Chest pain	Shoulder trouble
10. Hip trouble	Eye problems

HOW OFTEN YOU'RE SICK

There are two ways the National Center for Health Statistics looks at illness. The first is what they call "restricted activity" days—days when you have to cut down on your usual activities because you're not feeling up to par. The second is "bed-disability" days—days when you're so ill you have to spend all or most of the day in bed. Below were the figures by age, sex, and other selected characteristics: [40]

Restricted activity days	Yearly days per person
Male	12.3
Female	16.5
Under 65 years old	12.2
65 and older	32.1
Income under $5,000	24.7
Income $5,000–$9,999	23.7
Income $10,000–$14,999	17.5
Income $15,000–$24,999	12.3
Income $25,000+	10.0
Bed disability days	
Male	5.7
Female	7.6
Under 65 years old	5.4
65 and older	16.7

Work loss days	Yearly days per person
Male	3.7
Female	4.9
School loss days	
Male	4.7
Female	5.4

The striking statistics above are those that reflect illness and income. Studies have shown that people's health improved dramatically with income, both for serious and routine illnesses. The reasons were that wealthier Americans ate healthier foods, exercised more, and could afford higher quality medical care. [41]

The leading cause of illness for all of you was respiratory congestion caused by colds or the flu, which afflicted 44% of Americans. 20% of you came down with bacterial or parasitic infections, and 8% of you succumbed to digestive problems. [42]

According to the National Center for Health Statistics, the percentage of you who caught colds dropped with age: [43]

Age	% who had colds in a year
Under 6	93%
6–16	63%
17–44	35%
45–64	23%
65+	18%

YOUR CHRONIC MEDICAL PROBLEMS

High blood pressure, which afflicted 58 million Americans, has been by far the most common chronic condition. Below is a table showing the number of Americans who suffered from other chronic medical problems: [44]

Chronic condition	Persons with condition
Chronic sinusitis	30,767,000
Arthritis	30,115,000
Deformities or orthopedic impairments	22,152,000

Chronic condition	Persons with condition
Hearing impairments	20,698,000
Hay fever	19,771,000
Heart conditions	18,978,000
Hemorrhoids	10,928,000
Chronic bronchitis	10,864,000
Eczema or dermatitis	9,108,000
Asthma	8,787,000
Visual impairments	8,081,000
Migraine headaches	7,258,000
Diseases of urinary system	7,061,000
Varicose veins	6,838,000
Acne	6,192,000
Diabetes	5,613,000

37 million Americans (19.8% of those age 15 and over) had chronic conditions that limited their activity during the course of the year. 13.5 million (7.1%) had severe limitations.

Following is a look at the numbers of Americans who had trouble doing some of the things most of you take for granted: [45]

	Age 15–64	Age 65+
1. Had trouble seeing ordinary newsprint, even with glasses.		
Had limitation	7,061,000	5,742,000
Had severe limitation	491,000	1,196,000
2. Had difficulty hearing normal conversation.		
Had limitation	3,677,000	4,017,000
Had severe limitation	297,000	184,000
3. Had problems having speech understood.		
Had limitation	1,586,000	923,000
4. Had difficulty lifting or carrying a bag of groceries.		
Had limitation	9,286,000	8,922,000
Had severe limitation	3,383,000	4,460,000
5. Had difficulty walking one–quarter mile.		
Had limitation	9,272,000	8,922,000
Had severe limitation	3,072,000	4,877,000
6. Had difficulty walking up flight of stairs without resting.		
Had limitation	8,833,000	9,230,000
Had severe limitation	1,814,000	3,376,000

	Age 15–64	Age 65+
7. Had trouble getting around outside the house.		
Had limitation	2,038,000	3,960,000
Had severe limitation	1,091,000	2,510,000
8. Had trouble getting around inside the house.		
Had limitation	867,000	1,661,000
Had severe limitation	413,000	816,000
9. Had difficulty getting in and out of bed.		
Had limitation	735,000	1,322,000
Had severe limitation	509,000	699,000

Of the people who had difficulty with everyday activities, 17% were limited by heart conditions, 19% by arthritis or rheumatism, 10% by back problems, 9% by deformity or paralysis of the lower body, and 12% by severe high blood pressure. [46]

YOU AND YOUR DOCTOR

76% of Americans visited the doctor at least once in 1987. People age 65 and older averaged the most visits (8.9), followed by children under age 5 (6.7 visits). The average adult man saw the doctor 4.6 times and the average adult woman, 5.0 times.

Nearly 7 out of 10 contacts with the doctor were in his or her office or clinic, 14% in hospital emergency rooms, and 17% over the phone. The house call has practically become extinct, accounting for only .7% of all visits. [47]

The National Ambulatory Medical Care Survey conducted by the National Center for Health Statistics showed that 36% of your visits were caused by new symptoms or a new medical problem, 28% were for examination of a routine chronic health problem, 9% were caused by a flare-up of chronic problems, 9% resulted from injuries or recent surgery, and the remaining 18% were routine physical check ups.

About 80% of you were asked about your medical history when you went to the doctor. A third of you had your blood pressure checked, 21% of you had to undergo a blood or urine test, and 7% of you had x-rays taken. Nearly two-thirds of all patients walked out of doctors' offices with prescriptions. The most commonly prescribed drug categories were central nervous system drugs (painkillers, sedatives, anti-depressants, etc.), anti-infective medications (antibiotics, etc.), and cardiovascular drugs.

Exactly two-thirds of all patients were asked to make a specific appointment for a follow-up visit. 2.6% were referred to a specialist and 2.5% were sent to the hospital.

45% of the time, the visit lasted less than 10 minutes. That's why the average doctor saw 123 patients per week. 75% of the time, the diagnosis was an illness or injury that wasn't serious. The average charge for the visit was $25. **[48]**

In 1985, of the 492,000 U.S. physicians, 85.2% were male, 14.8% were female, and 3.2% were black. If you had checked the diplomas on the wall, you would have found 20% were graduates of foreign medical schools. **[49]** If you had checked very closely, you would have found that 1 in 200 people claiming to be M.D.'s had fraudulent diplomas, according to a study by Congressman Claude Pepper.

80% of all physicians were office-based, with the rest affiliated full time with hospitals or research facilities. Below is a chart of the percentage of physicians in each major medical speciality in 1985: **[50]**

Specialty	Percent of physicians
General practice	12.5%
Medical	27.2%
Internal	15.5%
Pediatrics	6.1%
Surgical	23.4%
General surgery	7.1%
Obstetrics, gynecology	5.6%
Orthopedic	3.0%
Ophthalmology	2.7%
Other	25.6%
Psychiatry	5.9%
Anesthesiology	3.5%
Pathology	2.9%
Radiology	2.2%

In two out of three families, women chose the physician who treated a family member. Three-quarters of all people chose their doctors upon the recommendations of friends or family, about 20%

depended on professional referrals, and only 2% found a doctor in the yellow pages. [51]

WHO HAS ALLERGIES?

An estimated 58 million Americans, including 22% of men and 18% of women, have allergies. Most common sources are pollen (16%), house dusts (6%) and animals (4%). [52]

YOUR HEALTH COMPLAINTS

What bothers you physically during the course of a year? The number one complaint you all had was pain. During the course of a year, you suffered from the following: [53]

Complaint	% of Americans who had that complaint
Headaches	73%
6 or more per year	43%
Backaches	56%
Muscle pains	53%
Joint pains	51%
Stomach pains	46%
Menstrual pains	40%

What else sent you to the pharmacy or the physician during the course of a year? [54]

Complaint	% of Americans who had that complaint
Congested nose	77%
Coughing, sore throat	60%
Flu, lung infection	51%
Indigestion or stomach problems	42%
Insomnia	34%
Menstrual or premenstrual problems	31%
Constipation	30%
Allergies	23%
Hemorrhoids	19%
Athletes foot	17%
Warts	9%

You spent billions of dollars on non-prescription drugs to relieve your symptoms. That included $1.9 billion on pain relievers, $1.6 billion on cold remedies, $1.3 billion on digestive aids, $912 million on first aid supplies, and $238 million on foot care. [55]

Below is a table of the percentage of you who said you used: [56]

Product	Percent of users
Pain relievers	94%
Decongestants	64%
Lozenges	51%
Cough syrup	39%
Cough drops	30%
Laxatives	27%
Diarrhea remedies	26%
Sunburn remedies	25%
Nasal spray	25%
Athletes foot remedies	17%
Non-prescription sleeping pills	5%

Nearly 1 in 5 Americans has taken a non-prescription pain reliever in the last 24 hours. The pain reliever market in 1986 was divided as follows: [57]

Aspirin	46%
Anacin	8%
Bayer	7%
Excedrin	7%
Bufferin	6%
Acetaminophen	45%
Tylenol	35%
Ibuprofen	9%

WOMEN AND THE PREMENSTRUAL SYNDROME

About 70% of women noticed at least one emotional, physical or behavioral change in the week or so before menstruation. About 3 in 10 women experienced a dozen or more negative changes. About 12% of women, on the other hand, had positive changes. [58]

YOUR HOSPITAL STAY

In 1984, 37 million people (excluding newborn babies) were hospitalized in the United States. About 8 million more women than men were hospitalized, about half of them because of childbirth. But men stayed longer in the hospital—7.0 days, compared with 6.3 days for women. [59]

Below is a table of the most common reasons for hospitalization by sex and age, with the average stay for that condition: [60]

Male	Average stay in days
Under 15 years old	
Pneumonia	4.6
Acute respiratory infection	3.2
Bronchitis, emphysema	3.4
Tonsils, adenoids	1.6
Congenital anomalies	5.6
15–44 years	7.1
Fracture	6.2
Diseases of the heart	10.4
Alcohol dependence	14.2
Psychosis	4.3
Lacerations	
45–64 years	7.1
Diseases of heart	9.7
Malignancies	4.1
Hernia	9.6
Cerebrovascular disease	9.5
Alcohol dependence	
65 years and over	8.1
Diseases of heart	10.7
Malignancies	9.9
Cerebrovascular diseases	7.8
Prostrate problems	9.4
Pneumonia	
Female	
Under 15 years	1.7
Tonsils, adenoids	3.3
Acute respiratory infection	3.6
Colitis	5.2
Pneumonia	3.7
Bronchitis, emphysema	

Female	Average stay in days
15–44 years	3.4
Delivery of baby	2.3
Abortion	4.9
Disease of female pelvic organs	5.0
Benign tumors	3.4
Disorders of menstruation	
45–64 years	7.2
Diseases of heart	8.7
Malignancies	6.7
Benign tumors	8.0
Diabetes	6.5
Bronchitis, emphysema	
Over 65 years	8.6
Diseases of heart	10.8
Malignancies	10.7
Cerebrovascular diseases	2.7
Eye diseases	13.1
Fractures	

About 8% of men and 11% of women had operations. Below is a table of the most common operations by sex and age: [61]

Male	Female
Under 15 years	
Tonsillectomy	Tonsillectomy
Relieving pressure on ear	Relieving pressure on ear
Repair hernia	Appendectomy
Repair of fracture	Dilation of urethra
Appendectomy	Repair of fracture
15–44 years	
Repair of hernia	Dilation and curettage of uterus
Knee operation	Hysterectomy
Appendectomy	Caesarean section
Suture of skin	Ligation of fallopian tubes
Biopsy	Biopsy
45–64 years	
Repair of hernia	Biopsy
Biopsy	Dilation and curettage of uterus
Cardiac catheterization	Hysterectomy
Prostate operation	Removal of ovary
Removal of skin growth	Gall bladder removal

Male	Female
65 years and older	
Prostate operation	Biopsy
Biopsy	Extraction of lens
Repair of hernia	Repair of fracture
Extraction of lens	Gall bladder removal
Bladder operation	Removal of skin growth

The average daily cost of a hospital room was $225 in 1986. The average total cost per day was $411, and the average cost for a stay, $2,995. [62]

YOUR PLASTIC SURGERY

In 1986, plastic surgeons performed approximately 1,850,000 procedures. About 60% were reconstructive surgery to correct birth defects or repair damage caused by accidents or disease.

The most rapid growth in plastic surgery, however, has been in aesthetic plastic surgery, or surgery to improve appearance. The number of aesthetic plastic surgery procedures jumped 24% between 1984 and 1986.

The most popular operation was lipectomy, or the suctioning of fat from the body. Use of that technique increased from 55,900 cases in 1984 to 99,300 cases in 1986. The most popular procedures in 1986, with average costs, were: [63]

Procedure	Number performed	Average cost
Lipectomy (fat suctioning)	99,300	$ 500-$ 4000
Breast augmentation	94,000	$1800-$ 4000
Blepharoplasty (tightening skin around the eyes)	84,670	$1000-$ 4000
Rhinoplasty (reshaping of nose)	82,230	$1500-$ 6000
Rhytidectomy (face-lift)	66,900	$2000-$10000

Men were the patients in 12% of all plastic surgery procedures, including 25% of all operations to reshape the nose.

YOUR DENTAL VISITS

According to the National Center for Health Statistics, most of you have been surprisingly good at getting your twice yearly checkups—the average yearly dental visits for everyone in the country was 1.8. About a quarter of you, however, hadn't seen a dentist in more than two years, and 13% hadn't seen a dentist for 5 years or more. [64]

About two-thirds of you, however, found a reason to delay going in to get your teeth checked. The main reason—71% of you disliked going or were just plain afraid.

Most of you, however, do need dental care at any given time: 1 in 5 of you need your teeth cleaned; 2 in 5 of you need a filling; and 1 in 20 of you need a tooth pulled. The average person has lost 2 teeth by age 30, 7 teeth by age 50, and 10 teeth by age 70. Only 2% of Americans age 65 and older had not lost a single tooth. The percentage of people who had lost all of their teeth in 1985 was 9% of those age 45–54, 14.6% of those 55–64, and 37.5% of those 65–74. [65]

Visiting the dentist can cut down on tooth loss. People with incomes over $25,000 visited the dentist twice as often as people earning half that much. The result was that 29% of people with incomes under $10,000 had to wear full dentures, while only 7% of those earning over $25,000 had lost all of their teeth. [66]

YOUR VISION AND HEARING

Over half of you wear glasses or contact lens, with the percentage needing vision correction increasing dramatically with age. 36.5% of people 17–24 needed correction, 45.9% of people 25–44, and 89.9% of people age 45 and older. One out of ten adults with a vision problem wore contact lenses. [67]

About 500,000 Americans were legally blind in 1985, and about 47,000 people become blind every year. Diabetes has been the leading cause of blindness in Americans under 75 years of age. 10% of Americans age 65–74 had trouble seeing, as did 27% of Americans age 85 and over. [68]

About 20 million Americans suffered from serious hearing impairments in 1985, including 21% of people age 65–74 and 48% of Americans 85 and over. [69]

AMERICA'S MENTAL HEALTH

A survey of 17,000 adults conducted by the National Institute of Mental Health revealed that 29% to 38% of all Americans have or once had at some time in their lives some form of recognized psychiatric disorder. About 20% reported having some mental problem in the six months prior to the survey, and 6% had consulted a doctor or mental health specialist about that mental problem. However, in about one-third of those doctor visits, the professional failed to diagnose any specific mental disorder. The end result was that only 1 in 5 adults suffering from a mental problem obtained professional help.

People with schizophrenia were most likely to get care (50%). One-third of people suffering from depression received treatment, as did 23% of those suffering from anxiety or panic disorders. Least likely to get treatment were alcoholics and drug users. In all categories, women were twice as likely to seek treatment as men.

Who suffers from serious problems during their lifetimes? **[70]**

13% of Americans will suffer from alcohol abuse

11% will experience some phobia, such as fear of heights

6% will experience a major depression

6% will become dependent on drugs.

3% will suffer from an antisocial or obsessive-compulsive disorder

2% will suffer from a panic disorder or mental impairment

.2% (1 in 500) will suffer from schizophrenia, severe sleep problems, or anorexia nervosa

At any given time, about 2% of women and about 9% of men have drinking problems.

A poll of mental health professionals conducted by *USA TODAY* revealed the reasons most Americans sought help, in order of frequency, were problems with:

1. Marriage or intimate relationships

2. Depression

3. Relationships with parents, children, co-workers

4. Lack of self-esteem, excessive insecurity

5. Anxiety
6. Alcohol or drug dependence
7. Personality or character disorders
8. Sex

THERAPIST-CLIENT SEX

Studies have shown that between 5% and 13% of physicians and psychologists have had some kind of erotic contact with their patients, and about 5% have had actual intercourse. [71]

WHO WORRIES?

About 15% of you are chronic worriers, fretting away at least 8 hours a day, according to a study by psychologist William Carter of Penn State University. On the other hand, 30% of you are non-worriers, spending less than 1.5 hours a day on your problems. The rest of you fall somewhere in between.

According to a survey by medical researchers, the situations that cause you the most anxiety are: [72]

Situation	% of people anxious
Party with strangers	74%
Giving a speech	70%
Asked personal questions in public	65%
Meeting a date's parents	59%
First day on a new job	59%
Victim of a practical joke	56%
Talking with someone in authority	53%
Job interview	46%
Formal dinner party	44%
Blind date	42%

WHEN YOU'RE HAPPY AND WHEN YOU'RE DEPRESSED

No doubt you've read countless stories every Christmas about the "holiday blues" suffered by so many Americans. These "blues", however, are really a Christmas fable. A survey by R.H. Bruskin

Associates showed that Americans listed December as the happiest month of the year (July is next happiest, February is the least happy). The suicide rate in December has been the lowest of any month in the year (April was highest). The rate of mental hospital admissions has been highest in the summer, and studies of mental hospital patients have shown depression peaked in fall. [73]

Another myth is "Monday morning blues." A study by the Long Island Research Institute and the State University of New York at Stony Brook has shown that people were no more likely to be depressed on Monday morning than on any other weekday. It was true, however, that most of you were happier on weekends.

What's your happiest time of day? Morning, reported 56% of you—but a third of you reported morning as the worst time of day in a poll conducted by the Roper Organization. Similar responses marked your view of the evenings—20% said it was your best time of day, 26% listed it as your worst.

The happiest years of your life may depend on your personality, according to psychologist Jane Berry of Washington University in St. Louis. Her survey of adults found that hard-driving "Type A" people were happiest between ages 35 and 54, while more laid-back "Type B" personalities became happier the older they got, with happiness peaking after age 65.

When adult Americans were asked to keep track of their hassles and pleasures over a one year period, the top ten hassles they listed were: [74]

1. Concern about weight

2. Health of a family member

3. Rising prices

4. Home maintenance

5. Too many things to do

6. Misplacing or losing things

7. Yard work or exterior home maintenance

8. Investments or taxes

9. Crime

10. Physical appearance

Their top ten uplifting experiences were:

1. Relating well with spouse or lover

2. Relating well with friends

3. Completing a task

4. Feeling healthy

5. Getting enough sleep

6. Eating out

7. Meeting responsibilities

8. Visiting, phoning or writing someone

9. Spending time with family

10. Taking pride in home

What makes Americans angry or impatient? A survey showed the percentage who blew their stacks over the following situations were: [75]

Situation	Percentage who got angry
Waiting for late people	65%
Being caught in traffic	63%
Waiting in line	61%
Waiting in doctor's office	59%
Slow restaurant service	51%
Waiting for government to act	48%
Waiting for a repair person	44%
Looking for a parking space	42%
Waiting for an airplane to take off	26%
Waiting for a bus	19%

WHAT YOU SHOULD WEIGH

Americans are obsessed with weight, and there's a great deal of medical evidence that suggests they should be. The National Institutes of Health has issued a warning of health risk for people more than 20% over their "standard" weight.

The big question is, what is that "standard" weight? Below are two answers. The first is the widely used tables compiled by the Metropolitan Life Insurance Company, based on data from 4.2

million life insurance policy holders. This table gives ideal weight ranges based on body type for men and women aged 25–59.

The second—and more recent table—is based on research by the Gerontology Research Center of the National Institute on Aging. In contrast to the Metropolitan standards, this table recommends the same weight goals for men and women and recommends moderate weight gain in middle age.

What's the best weight for you? Take your pick.

METROPOLITAN LIFE

Men

Height	Small frame	Medium frame	Large frame
5'2"	128–138	131–141	138–150
5'3"	130–136	133–143	140–153
5'4"	132–138	135–145	142–156
5'5"	134–140	137–148	144–160
5'6"	136–142	139–151	146–164
5'7"	138–145	142–154	149–168
5'8"	140–148	145–157	152–172
5'9"	142–151	148–160	155–176
5'10"	144–154	151–163	158–180
5'11"	146–157	154–166	161–184
6'0"	149–160	157–170	164–188
6'1"	152–164	160–174	168–192
6'2"	155–168	164–178	172–197
6'3"	158–172	167–182	176–202
6'4"	162–176	171–187	181–207

Women

Height	Small frame	Medium frame	Large frame
4'10"	102–111	109–121	118–130
4'11"	103–113	111–123	120–134
5'0"	104–115	113–126	122–137
5'1"	106–118	115–129	125–140
5'2"	108–121	118–132	128–143
5'3"	111–124	121–135	121–147
5'4"	114–127	124–138	134–151
5'5"	117–130	127–141	137–155
5'6"	120–133	130–144	140–159
5'7"	123–136	133–147	143–163
5'8"	126–139	136–150	146–167
5'9"	129–142	139–153	149–170
5'10"	132–145	142–156	152–173
5'11"	135–148	145–159	155–176
6'0"	139–151	148–162	158–179

GERONTOLOGY RESEARCH CENTER TABLE				
		AGE RANGE		
	20–29	30–39	40–49	50–59	60–69
4'10"	84–111	92–119	99–127	107–135	115–142
4'11"	87–115	95–123	103–131	111–139	119–147
5'0"	90–119	98–127	106–135	114–143	123–152
5'1"	93–123	101–131	110–140	118–148	127–157
5'2"	96–127	105–136	113–144	122–153	131–163
5'3"	99–131	108–140	117–149	126–158	135–168
5'4"	102–135	112–145	121–154	130–163	140–173
5'5"	106–140	115–149	125–159	134–168	144–179
5'6"	109–144	119–154	129–164	138–174	148–184
5'7"	112–148	122–159	133–169	143–179	153–190
5'8"	116–153	126–163	137–174	147–184	158–196
5'9"	119–157	130–168	141–179	151–190	162–201
5'10"	122–162	134–173	145–184	156–195	167–207
5'11"	126–167	137–178	149–190	160–201	172–213
6'0"	129–171	141–183	153–195	165–207	177–219
6'1"	133–176	145–188	157–200	169–213	182–225
6'2"	137–181	149–194	162–206	174–219	187–232
6'3"	141–186	153–199	166–212	179–225	192–238
6'4"	144–191	157–205	171–218	184–231	197–244

Depressed by the tables above? Cheer up. Below is a table, based on National Center for Health Statistics research, that shows the *actual average* weight of Americans. This study showed that the average 35 year old American man was a little over 5'9" tall and weighed 173 pounds. The average woman was a little over 5'4" tall and weighed 143 pounds. [76]

AVERAGE WEIGHT BY HEIGHT, AGE, AND SEX				
		AGE RANGE		
Men	25–34	35–44	45–54	55–64	65–74
5'2"	139	146	148	147	143
5'3"	145	149	154	151	148
5'4"	151	155	158	156	152
5'5"	155	159	163	160	156
5'6"	159	164	167	165	161
5'7"	164	169	171	170	165
5'8"	168	174	176	174	169
5'9"	173	178	180	178	174
5'10"	177	183	185	173	178
5'11"	182	188	190	187	182
6'0"	186	192	194	192	187
6'1"	191	197	198	197	192
6'2"	196	212	204	201	195

Women	AGE RANGE				
	25-34	35-44	45-54	55-64	65-74
4'10"	123	133	132	135	135
4'11"	126	136	136	138	133
5'0"	130	139	139	142	142
5'1"	133	141	143	145	145
5'2"	136	144	146	148	148
5'3"	139	146	150	151	151
5'4"	142	149	153	154	154
5'5"	146	151	157	157	157
5'6"	149	154	160	161	169
5'7"	152	156	164	164	163
5'8"	155	159	168	167	166

WHO DIETS?

According to a survey by the National Center for Health Statistics, nearly 9 of 10 Americans thought they needed to lose weight. About a third of them wanted to drop less than 10 pounds, 27% said they had 10 to 20 pounds to shed, and another 27% had a whopping 30+ pounds to take off.

When it came to actually starting a diet, however, women had a lot more get up and go. In any one year, 65% of women and 25% of men began at least one diet. The average length of the diet was a little under two weeks and the average weight loss was a little under 10 pounds.

Unfortunately, only 10% of dieters managed to keep the weight off for as long as a year. [77]

The most recent National Health and Nutrition Examination Survey found 26% of women and 23% of men were 10% to 20% overweight. Another 26% of women and 12% of men were "obese": that is, more than 20% overweight.

Most overweight were black women, a third of whom could be classified obese. Curiously, only 1 in 20 black males was obese, making them the leanest demographic group. [78]

A study by the U.S. Department of Agriculture revealed that the average American consumed 4% more calories than he or she burned each day. That doesn't sound like much—a mere 64 extra calories for the average women (who consumes 1600 per day) and 96 calories for the average man (who consumes 2400 per day). But over the course of a year, those calories would add up to a 6.7

pound weight gain for the average woman and a 10 pound weight gain for the average man—if they didn't diet or increase their physical activity.

These "average" Americans could easily avoid this weight gain if they looked to just three foods in their diet. White bread accounts for a rather amazing 9.6% of our daily calories, pastries for 5.7%, and alcoholic beverages for 5.5%. **[79]**

WHO SHOULDN'T DIET?

The old saw that "you can't be too thin" has been taken far too seriously by far too many young women ages 12 to 25. For example, a University of Alabama study of college age women and college graduate women age 35–44 revealed that:

- 19% of today's students took diet pills "frequently" and 16% named vomiting as their preferred dieting method. Only 6% of the older women took diet pills and less than 1% vomited.

- 47% of college women fasted, compared with 18% of older women.

- 31% of the younger women were truly underweight, compared with just 13% of the older women.

Overindulgence in extreme forms of dieting has led to what experts call a "true epidemic" of eating disorders in young women. An estimated 15% of women ages 12–25 suffered from mild to severe forms of anorexia (compulsive dieting to the point of self-starvation) or bulimia (binge-eating followed by self-induced vomiting).

YOUR SLEEP

According to a study reported in the June, 1986 issue of *Psychology Today*, two-thirds of adult Americans averaged between 7 and 8 hours of sleep per night. About 20% got by on six hours or less, while 10% slept more than 9 hours. After age 50, however, average sleep time began to drop to about 6.5 hours per night.

A 1986 study by R.H. Bruskin Associates showed that about 4 out of 5 of you used alarm clocks to wake up at the same time every morning. That time was:

Before 6 a.m.	25%
6:00 a.m. to 6:59 a.m.	32%
7:00 a.m. to 7:59 a.m.	14%
8:00 a.m. to 8:59 a.m.	5%
After 9:00 a.m.	5%

About one-third of you have occasional problems sleeping, and 15% to 20% of you have chronic insomnia. To help themselves sleep, Americans received about 24 million prescriptions for sleeping pills annually, enough pills to put all 230 million Americans to sleep for 200 hours. Sleeping pills are dangerous, however—the death rate for those taking pills is 50% higher than for those of you who don't take pills. **[152]**

Does your spouse snore? You better get used to it, because snoring becomes a lot more prevalent with age. Of people age 30–35, about 20% of men and 5% of women snore; of people age 60 and over, 60% of men and 40% of women snore. Scientists have discovered that obese people are three times more likely sound like lawn mowers during the night, but they have no idea why more men than women snore. **[150]**

The average snorer emits a combination of loud grunts, rumbles, rasps and whistles. The *Guinness Book of World Records* lists the loudest snore at 87.5 decibels. In a medical setting, researchers have recorded snores of 80 decibels, as loud as the sound of a diesel engine or a pneumatic drill breaking up concrete. **[151]**

YOUR DREAMS

According to a survey by R.H. Bruskin Associates, 71% of women and 65% of men said they dream while asleep. Of these people, only 12% say they have had bad or scary dreams.

A 1986 Roper Poll revealed the percentages of American men and women who daydreamed about the following:

	% of men	% of women
Traveling abroad	56%	58%
Being rich	58%	49%
Being smarter	38%	46%
The future	34%	40%
Having a better job	39%	29%
The past	33%	31%

YOUR HEIGHT

In 1984, the average American man was 5'9" tall, and the average woman was 5'4". The percent distribution of American men by height was: [80]

Under 5'6"	14%
5'6" to 5'8"	36%
5'9" to 6'1"	47%
6'2" and over	3%

WHAT COLOR IS YOUR HAIR?

Of all American men and women, according to Clairol, Inc.,

69% have brown hair

15% have blonde hair

10% have black hair

6% have red hair

Whatever the color, in about 65% of men and women that hair is straight, in about 25% it's wavy, and in about 10% it's curly. [81]

WHO'S BALD?

Below is a chart of the number of men and the percentage of men in each age group who have experienced significant hair loss:

Age	Number of men	% of men that age
20–29	4.1 million	20%
30–39	4.7 million	30%
40–49	4.4 million	40%
50–59	5.6 million	50%
60–69	5.6 million	65%
70–79	2.1 million	75%

In addition, about 25% of women age 25–54 experienced some overall thinning of hair.

YOUR HAIR TREATMENTS

In 1985, about 35% of American women colored their hair. Of these women: [82]

10% colored their hair red

40% colored their hair blonde

50% colored their hair black

57% of American women permed their hair, including 65% of those who colored their hair. Women annually spend about $550 million on hair color, $800 million on hair conditioners and rinses, and $500 million on hair spray. [83]

YOUR EDUCATION

In 1940, the average American had only a grade school education. Only 1 out of 4 had a high school diploma, and only 1 out of 20 had a college degree. In 1987, the average American had 1 year of college. Of all Americans age 25 and over, nearly 3 out of 4 had a high school diploma, and 1 in 5 had a 4-year college degree. Of Americans age 25-34, 87% were high school graduates and 26% had college degrees. [84]

Below is a table of educational achievement by age in 1987: [85]

Educational level	Age 25–29	Age 30–34	Age 35–44	Age 45–54	Age 55+
Less than 8 years	5.3%	5.5%	7.2%	12.1%	27.9%
1–3 years high school	10.9%	9.6%	9.5%	13.4%	18.2%
H.S. graduate	42.2%	40.0%	39.1%	40.9%	32.2%
1–3 years college	21.6%	21.0%	19.8%	15.4%	10.7%
4 or more years college	19.9%	23.9%	24.3%	18.2%	10.9%

What about education by region? [86]

	Percent high school graduates	Percent college graduates
Northeast	67.1%	17.2%
Midwest	68.0%	14.7%
South	60.2%	15.0%
West	74.5%	19.3%

Alaska topped the list of states with the highest percentage of adults having graduated from high school (82.5%). Next were Utah, Colorado, Washington, and Oregon. The worst state was Kentucky (only 53.1% of adults with high school degrees), followed by South Carolina, Mississippi, North Carolina, and Arkansas. [87]

Heading the list with the highest percentage of college graduates was the District of Columbia (27%), followed by Colorado, Alaska, Connecticut, and Maryland. Lowest percentage of college graduates was in West Virginia (10%), followed by Arkansas, Kentucky, Alabama, and Mississippi. [88]

Given the above, it isn't surprising that 5 of the 10 counties with the highest educational attainment were suburbs of Washington, D.C. Three were ski areas in Colorado, one was a suburb of San Francisco, and the last was the home of the Los Alamos National Laboratory in New Mexico. [89]

COLLEGE ENROLLMENT

In 1986, according to the National Center for Education Statistics, America had 12,501,000 college students attending 3,406 institutions of higher learning. 7,117,000 were attending school full time, 5,384,000 were attending part time. 7,826,000 were going to 4-year schools, 4,675,000 were going to 2-year schools. 78% of students attended public colleges and universities, 22% attended private institutions. [90]

The most remarkable demographic change in college enrollment has been the huge increase in the number of women. In the last 20 years, the percentage of undergraduates who were female has soared from 40% to 54%. A large percentage of this increase was women over age 25 who were returning to school. Four out of 10 women students were over 25, and 53% attended school part time. [91]

Who went to college? In 1986, 36% of males and 37% of females enrolled went straight on to college after high school graduation, and 54.8% of high school graduates ages 18-24 were attending an institution of higher earning or had completed at least 1 year of college. Below was the percent of high school graduates who went on to college by family income: [92]

Family income	% attending college
Under $10,000	15.4%
$10,000–$19,999	24.8%
$20,000–$29,999	33.4%

Family income	% attending college
$30,000–$39,999	44.2%
$40,000–$49,999	49.7%
Over $50,000	53.8%

Below were the average charges for tuition, room, and board at public and private institutions in 1986: **[93]**

	Tuition	Board	Dormitory
Public			
2 year	$ 620	$1,370	$1,010
4 year	$1,510	$1,310	$1,336
Private			
2 year	$3,620	$1,310	$1,480
4 year	$7,440	$1,720	$1,940

College tuition has risen at an average rate of 10.5% per year during the 1980's. This rise in tuition, however, exactly matched the rate of the costs of providing the college education. Tuition payments made up 20% of college revenues in 1970 and 21% of college revenues in 1984. **[94]**

To meet these costs, 51% of college students received some sort of financial aid. The most common assistance was the federal Guaranteed Student Loan program. 4,804,000 students received such loans in 1986, and the average loan was $2,381. The program is being jeopardized, however, by a loan default rate that reached 9.9% in 1986. **[95]**

Who got financial aid? 71% of students with an A average in high school, compared with 33% of students with a C average or lower. 69% of black students and 48% of white students received aid. 63% of students with a family income of under $12,000 received aid, but only 35% with a family income of over $48,000. 63% of graduate students received aid, 58% of candidates for bachelor's degrees, and 43% of students at 2 year institutions. **[96]**

Three-quarters of college freshman also worked to pay part of their college costs. More than half of those who worked spent more than 16 hours per week on the job. **[97]**

WHAT DO STUDENTS STUDY?

Nearly one out of every four students was a business major, a 71% increase since 1966. Students seeking a degree in education, on the other hand, decreased from 18.6% to just 6.7%. The number of engineering students increased 26% and the number of students in the social sciences decreased 35%. **[98]**

Below is a table of the percentage of students in each major field of study: **[99]**

Field of study	Percent of students
Agriculture, forestry	2.4
Biological sciences	2.9
Health, medical professions	12.0
Business, commerce	23.7
Education	6.7
Engineering	11.3
English, journalism	2.8
Liberal arts, humanities	7.8
Law	2.3
Mathematics, statistics	1.7
Physical sciences	2.4
Social sciences	7.0
Vocational, technical	3.8

COLLEGE DEGREES

Two year institutions awarded 604,634 degrees in 1986. According to the National Center for Education Statistics, those degrees by field of subject were: **[100]**

	Number of degrees	% female
Liberal studies	109,529	56.4%
Visual/performing arts	24,015	32.9%
Health services	104,051	86.4%
Mechanical and engineering	97,609	8.1%
Home economics	14,760	72.6%
Data processing	13,307	49.5%
Business management	168,168	70.3%
Public service (police, fire, etc.)	15,592	25.2%

Four-year colleges awarded 987,823 bachelor's degrees, in the following fields:

	Number of degrees
Agriculture	16,823
Architecture	9,119
Business/management	238,160

	Number of degrees
Communications	43,091
Computer sciences	41,889
Education	87,221
Engineering	95,953
Foreign languages	10,102
Health professions	64,535
Home economics	15,288
Letters	35,434
Liberal/general studies	19,248
Life sciences	38,524
Mathematics	16,306
Multi/interdisciplinary	15,700
Philosophy/religion	11,841
Physical sciences	21,731
Psychology	40,521
Protective services	12,704
Public affairs	13,786
Social sciences	93,703
Visual/performing arts	36,949

According to the National Center for Education Statistics, only 49% of students who received bachelor degrees completed their course of study in 4 years. 27% took 5 years, 9% took six years, 5% took 7 years, and 10% took over ten years to complete requirements for their degrees. [101]

Students earned 288,567 master's degrees and 33,653 doctorates. 26% of master's degrees were awarded in education, followed by 23% in in business administration. [102]

In terms of professional degrees, the big story was the huge increase in the percentage of women earning those diplomas. Women garnered 30.8% of M.D.'s in 1986, up from 5.5% in 1960; 22.6% of dental degrees, up from .8% in 1960; and 39.0% of law degrees, up from 2.5% in 1960. [103]

VOCATIONAL SCHOOLS

1,687,100 students attended 9,208 vocational schools. The most popular programs were: [104]

Type of school	Number of students
Cosmetology	153,400
Secretarial	106,500
Real estate	100,700
Welding	46,800

Type of school	Number of students
Clothes designing	45,800
Accounting	40,700
Practical nursing	36,200
Entertainment services	35,100
Computer programmer	34,800
Truck driver	34,800

ADULT EDUCATION

According to the National Center for Education Statistics, one out of every eight adult Americans—23,303,000 people—were enrolled in some form of adult education. 65% of these people were enrolled to get a new job or advance in their present job, 5% were seeking a high school equivalency degree, and 30% were taking courses for pleasure. [105]

The percentage of people taking classes increased dramatically with education and income. 11% of high school graduates took adult education classes, compared with 20% of college graduates and 30% of people with graduate degrees. One in ten people earning $10,000–$15,000 took classes, compared with one in five people earning $50,000 or over. [106]

WHO NEEDS EDUCATION

According to a study by the Ford Foundation, over one in five Americans—22% of all adults—were functionally illiterate. That means they couldn't read and write well enough to write a check, read a sign in a store, or fill out a job application. The majority of these illiterates were high school graduates. The U.S. government estimated the cost of this illiteracy in welfare payments, incompetence on the job, etc. has been $225 billion a year. The United States recently ranked only 49th of 158 United Nations countries in percentage of literate adults.

Reading and writing aren't the only tasks a lot of Americans couldn't handle. A study by the University of Texas revealed that:

33%   of adults couldn't do simple arithmetic computations.

29%   couldn't manage a family budget.

28% couldn't solve problems.

23% didn't know how to use community resources.

YOUR CHURCH ATTENDANCE

According to the 1986 Gallup Poll, "Religion in America," the number of Americans who had attended a church or synagogue in the last seven days dropped from 49% in 1958 to 40% in 1986. Nearly half of all people over 50 years old had gone to church in the last week (48%), compared with 39% of those ages 30–49 and just 33% of those under age 30. 46% of women attended church, compared with 33% of men. Attendance rates were 49% for Catholics, 41% for Protestants, and 20% for Jews. [107]

95% of Americans reported being born into a religion: 65% born Protestant, 28% Catholic, and 2% Jewish. 93% of Americans age 15 and over identified themselves as "affiliated" with an organized religion. [108] However, only 60% of all Americans—143, 926, 363—identified themselves as members of one of this country's 341,111 churches in 1985. By major religious bodies, membership was: [109]

Protestant	78,702,000	55%
Roman Catholic	52,286,000	37%
Jewish	5,817,000	4%
Eastern churches	4,053,000	3%
Other	1,723,000	1%

These members were served by 329,802 pastors. Average membership in Protestant churches was 247; average membership of Roman Catholic churches was 2,163.

A little over one-third of all Protestants (34) were Baptists. 20% were Methodists, 13% were Lutherans, 7.5% were Presbyterians, 4.3% were Episcopalians, and 21% were members of many dozens of smaller denominations and many hundreds of sects.

Contributions to these churches exceeded $10 billion, with the average church member placing $240 in the collection plate. The generosity of church members ranged from tithing groups like the Seventh-Day Adventists and the Mormons, who gave 10% of their income or more, to Roman Catholics, whose contribution was betwen 1% and 2% of their income. Of reporting denominations, Seventh-Day Adventists had by far the highest household contribution ($2,400). Household contributions for other denominations were: **[110]**

Presbyterians	$ 690
United Church of Christ	$ 510
Lutherans	$ 480
Methodists	$ 435
Baptists	$ 395
Episcopalians	$ 295
Roman Catholics	$ 275

YOUR RELIGIOUS BELIEFS

Although only 40% of Americans had attended church in the last 7 days, a 1987 survey revealed that 61% said that religion was "very important" in their lives. Another 26% considered religion "fairly important," and only 12% considered religion "not very important." **[111]**

Americans with other religious beliefs were: **[112]**

	Percent of Americans
Believe in God	94%
Pray to God	89%
Believe Jesus Christ is divine	83%
Believe in life after death	
Yes	69%
No	20%
Uncertain	11%
Believe Scripture is word of God	67%
Urge others to be religious	57%
Believe Scripture is literally true	42%
Had a "born-again" experience	34%
Read Bible weekly or more often	30%

Of the people who believed in a life after death, two-thirds rated their chances of going to heaven as excellent or good. By far the most smug were college graduates, a whopping 77% who believed that they had earned a trip through the Pearly Gates. In contrast, only 61% of high school graduates were confident of their eternal reward. **[113]**

In another survey, nearly 1 in 4 Americans named Hitler as the person "most likely to be found in Hell." 15% named Stalin, 5% tabbed *Playboy* founder Hugh Hefner, and 2% listed Richard Nixon. **[114]**

SINS

Sometimes, after reading the papers for a few days, it's hard to believe that Americans consider *anything* a sin these days. While that certainly isn't true, it is a fact that your actions speak louder than words—that is, there's a big difference between what you consider to be "sinful" or "immoral" and what you actually do.

First, what do you consider sinful? When asked to rate 61 activities on a "sin" scale from 1 (least sinful) to 10 (most sinful), Americans ranked the activities: **[115]**

Activity	Rating
Murder	9.94
Sexually abusing children	9.92
Rape	9.70
Lying about a sexual disease	9.68
Spouse beating	9.31
Spying for a foreign country	9.22
Driving while intoxicated	9.04
Bank robbery	8.84
Racial harassment	8.67
Hitting children	8.66
Cheating a customer	8.41
Sexual harassment	8.27
Lying about birth control	8.24
Selling cocaine	7.80
Shoplifting	7.43
Lying to your spouse	7.08
Lying to your children	7.04
Parking in a handicapped zone	6.71
Lying to Congress	6.48
Suicide	6.37
Serving alcohol to minors	6.25
Adultery	6.21
Using cocaine	6.11
Selling marijuana	6.07
Cheating on an expense account	5.81
Buying a stolen television	5.80
White collar crime	5.67
Industrial spying	5.61
Spouse swapping	5.49
Lying to your boss	5.23

Activity	Rating
Leaving scene of a minor accident	5.17
Smoking marijuana	5.08
Cheating on taxes	4.92
Smoking	4.84
Homosexuality	4.79
Producing x-rated video tapes	4.64
Killing to protect your home	4.22
Abortion	4.21
Lying on a resume	4.17
Cutting into lines	4.13
Taking home office supplies	3.88
Owning an illegal firearm	3.88
Premarital sex	3.67
Calling in sick when healthy	3.63
Having AIDS	3.60
Mercy killing	3.57
Watching x-rated video tapes	3.51
Giving condoms to teen-agers	3.44
Swearing	3.41
Gambling	3.36
Living together without marriage	3.33
Not believing in God	3.21
Divorce	3.12
Surrogate motherhood	3.10
Artificial insemination	3.01
Sex education	2.97
Nudity in the movies	2.91
Drinking alcohol	2.90
Nude sunbathing	2.87
Masturbation	2.22

How well do you live up to your moral standards? It depends on how likely you think it is that you'll get caught. For example, almost 5 times as many of you will drive faster than the speed limit (where you have a small chance to get caught) than will cut into a line (where someone will surely yell at you). Below is a poll showing what percentage of Americans admitted to the following "unethical" behavior in a *Psychology Today* survey:

Driving faster than the speed limit	93%
Telling white lies	88%
Taking home office supplies	68%
Cheating on examinations	67%
Parking illegally	60%
Calling in sick when you're healthy	47%
Driving while drunk	41%

Cheating on tax returns	38%
Making personal long distance calls at work	37%
Deceiving your best friend	33%
Cheating on your expense account	28%
Cutting into line	19%

YOUR POLITICAL AFFILIATION

There have been two recent trends in the political affiliations of Americans. First, the number of people who classified themselves as "independent" increased from 23% in 1952 to 32% in 1985. Secondly, an almost 2–1 margin Democrats enjoyed in 1952 narrowed dramatically, to the point where the party preference of American men was virtually even.

Below was the party identifications of Americans in 1985: **[116]**

	Democratic	Republican	Independent
By sex			
Male	34%	34%	32%
Female	40%	34%	26%
By race			
Black	73%	10%	17%
By region			
Northeast	38%	32%	30%
Midwest	32%	34	34%
South	42%	34%	24%
West	36%	37%	27%

Who were Democrats and who were Republicans? Below is a demographic look at Americans who identified themselves with one of these two parties: **[117]**

	Democrats	Republicans
Liberal	25%	12%
Middle-of-the-road	45%	44%
Conservative	24%	40%
Male	43%	50%
Female	57%	50%

	Democrats	Republicans
Income		
Under $12,500	22%	11%
$12,500–$24,999	35%	34%
$25,000–$34,999	24%	25%
$35,000–$50,000	14%	18%
Over $50,000	5%	11%
Education		
High school or less	72%	60%
Some college	16%	19%
College grad or more	12%	21%
Protestant	60%	70%
Catholic	35%	24%
Jewish	3%	1%
Black	21%	2%
White	79%	98%
18–29 years old	26%	32%
30–44	26%	26/
45–64	31%	24%
65+	17%	18%

While political affiliation has been changing, the ideological lean-ings of the country have remained amazingly stable. Below is a comparison of the average responses of Americans over the last 20 years with the results of a poll taken in 1985: [118]

Ideology	Average	1985
Conservative	34%	36%
Middle-of-the-road	40%	40%
Liberal	17%	18%

YOUR VOTING

The number of Americans voting in Presidential elections has re-mained remarkably constant since 1976. 59.2% of the population voted in 1976 and 1980, and 59.9% voted in 1984. Below is a demographic look at who voted in 1984: [119]

	Percent voting
Total	59.9%
Male	59.0%
Female	60.8%
White	61.4%
Black	55.8%
18–20 years old	36.7%
21–24	43.5%
25–34	54.5%
35–44	63.5%
45–64	69.8%
65+	67.7%
Less than high school education	42.9%
High school graduates	58.7%
College graduates or more	79.1%
Employed	61.6%
Unemployed	44.0%
Not in labor force	58.9%

The percentage of Americans who voted was even more dismal for elections of congressmen and senators in non-Presidential election years—48.5% in 1982 and 46.0% in 1986. But that low turnout may be a blessing when you take into account a 1986 Roper poll that reveled only 1 out of 3 Americans could name both their U.S. Senators, and 37% couldn't name one.

WHO SMOKES CIGARETTES?

Have all the warnings about the dangers of cigarette smoking worked? The statistics show that a lot of American men have listened. The percentage of men who smoke plummeted from 53% in 1964 to 29.5% in 1985. 60% of all men smoked at one time, but half of them have quit. [120]

The percentage of all women who smoke has also dropped, although not quite as dramatically as the percentage of men. In 1964, the year the Surgeon-General of the United States issued the first dramatic health warning about the relationship between smoking and cancer, heart disease, and other health problems, 32% of American women smoked. That rate stayed relatively constant until 1982, when 30% of women still smoked. However, since 1982, the percentage of women who smoke has plummeted from 30% to 23.8%. Perhaps the reason has been a dramatic rise in the number of women who suffered from lung cancer. In 1975, only 1 out of every 9 lung cancer patients was a woman; in 1985, 2 out of every 5 were women. Lung cancer has replaced breast cancer as the leading cause of cancer death in women. [121]

Despite the drop in the number of smokers, smoking was a direct cause of an estimated 350,000 deaths in 1985–8 times a many deaths as those caused by motor vehicle accidents and more than all the deaths caused by drugs and alcohol combined. The health cost of disease attributed to smoking was $53 billion in 1985. [122]

By age, the highest percentage of smokers were men age 35–44 (37% smokers). Lowest rate was for women age 65 and older (12% smokers). About two-thirds of smokers consumed less than 25 cigarettes a day, while about 15% puffed away two packs or more. All smokers, however, find the habit very difficult to quit. The average person who tried to quit smoking cigarettes had a relapse in just 17 days, compared with 30 days for alcoholics and 32 days for drug addicts. [123]

5.4% of Americans smoked cigars, 4.5% smoked pipes and 3.2% chewed tobacco. [124]

WHO SMOKES MARIJUANA?

Marijuana smoking has declined from the peak years of 1978–1979. But an estimated 20 million American users consumed enough of the drug to make marijuana the nation's number one cash crop in 1985. In that year, American growers illegally harvested an estimated $18.6 billion in marijuana, compared with $18.58 billion in corn legally grown. Oregon, California, and Hawaii each produced over $1 billion in marijuana, which was the number one crop in an estimated 18 states. [125]

According to the National Institute on Drug Abuse figures, the percentage of Americans who had ever tried marijuana and who currently smoked it were: [126]

Age	Ever tried	Current users
12–17	27%	12%
18–25	64%	27%
26 and older	23%	7%

The percentage of people using marijuana peaked in 1979, when 17% of those age 12–17 and 35% of those 18–25 regularly smoked.

Although the percentage of people using the drug had fallen, problems relating from use increased. The reason was that the average potency of marijuana jumped from an average of .5% THC (the active chemical in the drug) in 1970 to 4% THC today. In 1985, 70,000 young people sought treatment related to their marijuana use.

WHO DRINKS ALCOHOL?

The percentage of Americans who drank alcohol also declined from its peak in the late 1970's, but the large majority of you still enjoyed a nip now and then. Over 9 out of 10 adults have tried drinking, and 70% of you drank at least once in a year. By sex, age, and income, Americans' drinking habits were: **[127]**

	Didn't drink	Less than 1 drink/week	1 or 2 drinks per week	3+ drinks per week
Male	24%	27%	17%	32%
Female	36%	39%	12%	13%
Age				
20–34	22%	36%	18%	24%
35–54	28%	35%	14%	23%
55+	45%	26%	9%	18%
Income				
Under $6,000	46%	29%	13%	13%
$6–$15,000	38%	32%	14%	16%
$15–$30,000	27%	38%	13%	21%
$30,000+	19%	32%	17%	32%

As you can see, men drank more than women, and high-income people were more likely to drink than those with low incomes. Men and high-income earners were also more likely to drink heavily. About 30% of all men drinkers occasionally consumed 5 or more drinks at a sitting, compared with 20% of women drinkers. Nearly half of all drinkers who earned more than $15,000 per year occasionally downed 5 or more drinks at a sitting, compared with less than 20% of low income drinkers.

In terms of regions of the country, far fewer people in the South drank (only 60%), compared with the West (73% drank), the Northeast (72%), and the Midwest (70%). **[128]**

As many as 9% of adult Americans are either alcoholics or are problem drinkers at any one time. **[129]** The number of deaths in which alcohol was a major contributing factor has been estimated at 100,000 per year. However, a 1987 study by the Centers for Disease Control found that six times more deaths were alcohol—related than were listed on death certificates. Among the major reasons were death certificates filled out before blood-alcohol test results were received and doctors' reluctance to embarrass the families of deceased victims.

WHO ABUSES DRUGS

With all the publicity about the problems of illegal drugs in America, you may be surprised to know that abuse of prescription drugs—especially sedatives and tranquilizers—accounted for 60% of hospital emergency room admissions for drug overdose and 70% of all drug-related deaths in 1984. **[130]** A group of experts interviewed for a report in USA Today commented that "illegal drug use is a serious and growing problem in society, but legal drug use is far and away the most serious problem in the workplace."

The National Institute on Drug Abuse estimated that by age, the percentage of Americans who have ever used and currently used both legal and illegal drugs was: **[131]**

| Type of drug | Age 12–17 | | Age 18–25 | | Age 25+ | |
	Ever used	Current user	Ever used	Current user	Ever used	Current user
Hallucinogens	5.2%	1.4%	21.1%	1.7%	6.4%	.5%
Cocaine	6.5%	1.6%	28.3%	6.8%	8.5%	1.2%
Heroin	1.0%	.5%	1.2%	.5%	1.1%	.5%
Analgesics	4.2%	.7%	12.1%	1.0%	3.2%	.5%
Stimulants	6.7%	2.6%	18.0%	4.7%	6.2%	.6%
Sedatives	5.8%	1.3%	18.7%	2.6%	4.8%	.5%
Tranquilizers	4.9%	1.0%	15.1%	1.6%	3.6%	.5%

YOU AND CRIME

The Federal Bureau of Investigation listed 13,509,000 "serious" crimes that were reported to the police in 1987: **[132]**

Violent crime	1,484,000
Murder	20,100
Forcible rape	91,100
Robbery	518,000
Aggravated assault	855,000
Property crime	12,025,000
Burglary	3,236,000
Larceny-theft	7,500,000
Motor vehicle theft	1,289,000

A survey by the U.S. Bureau of Justice Statistics, however, found that only 35% of all crimes were reported—including only 48% of violent crimes. The most common reason people gave for not reporting a crime was their belief that nothing could be done anyway. The most important reason why people did report crimes was proof for insurance purposes—that's why motor vehicle theft was the most commonly reported crime. In 2 of 5 crimes, it was a bystander, relative, or friend of the victim who made the report. The results of the survey: **[133]**

Crime	Percentage reported
Violent crime	
Aggravated assault	58%
Robbery	52%
Rape	47%
Simple assault	41%
Theft	
Purse snatching	51%
Pocket picking	29%
Larceny	26%
Household crime	
Motor vehicle theft	69%
Burglary	49%
Household larceny	25%

What are your chances of being a victim of crime? About 1 in 4 households (24%) were touched by crime in the course of 1987.

Crime touched about 29% of urban households, 24% of suburban households, and only 19% of rural households. 5.8% of black households had members who were victims of violent crime, compared with 4.4% of white households. 7.9% of black households and 4.8% of white households were burglarized. 25% of households with annual incomes of over $25,000 had thefts, compared with 16% of households with incomes under $7,500. [134]

According to a study by the U.S. Bureau of Justice Statistics, 99% of Americans will be a crime victim in their lifetimes and 4 out of 5 will be the victim of attempted or completed violent crime. The study showed that: [135]

99% of all men and women will be the victims of personal theft.

82% of men/62% of women will be the victims of attempted or completed assault.

37% of men/22% of women will be robbed.

8% of women will be raped.

The study also found that 7 out of 8 Americans will be the victims of theft at least three times in their lifetimes. Over a 20 year period, 7 out of 10 homes will be burglarized at least once.

One third of American households had taken some preventative steps against crime. One quarter of American families had engraved valuables with an identification number, 7% had burglar alarms, and 7% participated in neighborhood watch programs. [136]

MURDER

What are your chances of being a murder victim? It depends very much on your race and sex: [137]

Black male	1 in 21 chance of being murdered
Black female	1 in 104 chance of being murdered
White male	1 in 131 chance of being murdered
White female	1 in 369 chance of being murdered

How did most murders take place? [138]

Felony or suspected felony	20%
Argument	37%

Revenge, jealousy, etc.	17%
Motive unknown	25%

How were most victims dispatched? For every 100 corpses: **[139]**

59 were shot,

    44 with handguns

20 were cut or stabbed

9 were beaten or strangled

6 were clubbed with a blunt instrument

1 was burned

5 were poisoned, drowned, or other method

Nine out of every 100,000 Americans have been murdered every year. Your odds of being a victim doubled if you live in a city of more than 250,000 people. Safest locations have been the suburbs and cities of under 10,000 people. 60% more murders took place in the South than in the Midwest or Northeast. Residents of Texas and Louisiana have been 7 times more likely to be murder victims than residents of New Hampshire or Vermont. **[140]**

DOES CRIME DAY?

Below is a table showing the average "take" for crimes in 1987: **[141]**

Crime	Average value lost
Robbery	
Street	$ 492
Business	$ 1,017
Gas station	$ 321
Convenience store	$ 292
Residence	$ 796
Bank	$ 3,013
Burglary	
Residence	$ 1,004
Non-residence	$ 914

Crime	Average value lost
Larceny	
Pocket picking	$ 286
Purse snatching	$ 238
Shoplifting	$ 96
From motor vehicles	$ 434
Motor vehicle accessories	$ 288
Bicycles	$ 172
Coin operated machines	$ 128

What about "organized" crime? The President's Commission on Organized Crime estimates that crime syndicates raked in $106.2 billion in 1986 from the following activities:

Cocaine	$ 24.6 billion
Heroin	$ 17.5 billion
Marijuana	$ 16.5 billion
Loan sharking	$ 13.4 billion
Prostitution	$ 6.7 billion
Employee theft	$ 6.0 billion
Illegal gambling	$ 2.3 billion
Theft	$ 1.9 billion
Other (smuggling, counterfeiting, arson, etc.)	$ 2.0 billion

GUNS AND CRIME

In 1986, firearms were used in 59% of murders, 34% of robberies, and 21% of aggravated assaults. 43% of convicted criminals bought their weapons in a store or on the black market; 32% stole the weapons; and the rest either borrowed the guns or got them as a gift. [142]

WHO GETS CAUGHT

The F.B.I reported that 10,796,000 people were arrested in 1987, 2,266,000 of them for serious crimes. 82% of those arrested were men, 18% were women. 21.7% of those arrested were under 18 years old, 31.1% were 18-24, and 44.7% were 25-44.

By far the most common of the "non-serious" arrests was driving while intoxicated (1.4 million). Next came drug abuse violations

(811,000), drunkenness (701,000), disorderly conduct (600,000), fraud (281,000), vandalism (230,000), and prostitution (101,000).

Young people made up a much higher percentage of arrests for serious crimes: 30.0% of those arrested were under 18 and 29.8% were 18-24. People under age 25 made up 88% of arson arrests, 83% of motor vehicle theft arrests, 73% of burglary arrests, 66% of robbery arrests, and 72% of larceny arrests. The only serious crime for which Americans 25 and older made up more than half of all arrests was murder. [143]

WHITE COLLAR CRIME

In 1985, 10,733 people were convicted of "white collar" crimes, an 18% increase since 1980. Their crimes were: [144]

Fraud, including tax fraud	55%
Forgery	19%
Embezzlement	16%
Counterfeiting	5%

140 cases involved thefts of $1 million or more, and 64 cases involved $10 million or more. Courts continued to be lenient with white collar criminals, however, despite the massive dollar amounts involved. Only 40% of convicted white collar criminals received prison sentences, compared with 59% of all convicted felons. The average sentence was 29 months, compared with 50 months for all convicted felons. [145]

WHO SERVES TIME?

According to the U.S. Bureau of Justice Statistics, the population of Federal and state prisons at the end of 1987 was 557,256 people, 95% of them male. Approximately 274,000 other people were serving time in local jails. About 2,093,000 people were on probation at the same time, and 327,000 were on parole. The total of 3,230,000 Americans under the supervision of the criminal justice system was 30.2% higher than in 1983. [146]

The average sentence received by prisoners was 36 months and the average time served was just 16 months, an all-time low. The average term served for major crimes was: **[147]**

Crime	Average time served
Murder	5 years 9 months
Rape	3 years
Manslaughter	2 years, 4 months
Robbery	2 years, 1 month
Assault	1 year, 3 months
Burglary	1 year, 2 months

WHO'S IN JAIL?

A U.S. Bureau of Justice Statistics study of jail inmates found that: **[148]**

56% were white, 41% were black

61% had not completed high school

43% were unemployed when arrested

Their average yearly income before arrest was $3,714

According to a poll by the Roper Organization, 20% of all men and 3% of all women have spent a night in jail. The U.S. Bureau of Justice Statistics estimated that about 4% of males and 1% of females have served sentences in federal or state prisons.

DEATH ROW

93 convicted criminals were executed in the United States between 1977 and October, 1987. 70 of those executions took place in just 4 states, Texas, Florida, Louisiana, and Georgia. Another 1,911 inmates were awaiting execution on death row, 56% of them white, 44% black. Approximately 250 convicted murderers have been sentenced to death each year in the 37 states which have the death penalty. **[149]**

CHAPTER ONE NOTES

1. U.S. Bureau of the Census, Current Population Reports
2. U.S. Bureau of the Census, Current Population Reports
3. U.S. Bureau of the Census, Current Population Reports
4. U.S. Bureau of the Census, Current Population Reports
5. U.S. Bureau of the Census, Current Population Reports
6. U.S. Bureau of the Census, 1980 Census of the Population
7. U.S. Immigration and Naturalization Service, Statistical Yearbook
8. U.S. Immigration and Naturalization Service, Statistical Yearbook
9. U.S. Bureau of the Census, 1980 Census of the Population
10. U.S. Bureau of the Census, Current Population Reports
11. U.S. Bureau of the Census, World Population Profile
12. National Center for Health Statistics, Vital Statistics of the United States
13. National Center for Health Statistics, Vital Statistics of the United States
14. National Center for Health Statistics, Vital Statistics of the United States
15. U.S. Bureau of the Census, Current Population Reports
16. U.S. Bureau of the Census, Current Population Reports
17. U.S. Bureau of the Census, Current Population Reports
18. Compiled by authors, from the National Center for Health Statistics, Vital Statistics of the United States
19. National Center for Health Statistics, Vital Statistics of the United States
20. U.S. Public Health Service, Public Health Reports
21. National Center for Health Statistics, Vital Statistics of the United States
22. American Heart Association, 1987 Heart Facts
23. American Cancer Society, Cancer Facts and Figures-1987
24. American Cancer Society, Cancer Facts and Figures-1987
25. American Cancer Society, Cancer Facts and Figures-1987
26. American Heart Association, 1987 Heart Facts
27. National Center for Health Statistics, Vital Statistics of the United States
28. National Center for Health Statistics, National Safety Council
29. National Center for Health Statistics, Vital and Health Statistics
30. Consumer Product Safety Commission
31. Consumer Product Safety Commission
32. Metropolitan Life Insurance Co., Statistical Bulletin
33. National Weather Service
34. National Safety Council, Accident Facts—1987
35. National Center For Health Statistics, Americans Assess Their Health
36. Social Science and Medicine, 1986, "From Sneezes to Adieux: Stages of Health for U.S. Men and Women"
37. Social Science and Medicine, 1986, "From Sneezes to Adieux: Stages of Health for U.S. Men and Women"
38. Social Science and Medicine, 1986, "From Sneezes to Adieux: Stages of Health for U.S. Men and Women"
39. Social Science and Medicine, 1986, "From Sneezes to Adieux: Stages of Health for U.S. Men and Women"
40. National Center for Health Statistics, Vital and Health Statistics
41. National Center for Health Statistics, Provisional Data from the Health Promotion and Disease Prevention Supplement to the National Health Interview Survey
42. National Center for Health Statistics, Vital and Health Statistics

43. National Center for Health Statistics, Vital and Health Statistics
44. National Center for Health Statistics, Vital and Health Statistics
45. U.S. Bureau of the Census, Disability, Functional Limitation, and Health Insurance Coverage
46. National Center for Health Statistics, Vital and Health Statistics
47. National Center for Health Statistics, Health United States, 1986
48. National Center for Health Statistics, National Ambulatory Medical Care Survey
49. U.S. Bureau of Labor Statistics, Employment and Earnings.
50. American Medical Association, Physician Characteristics and Distribution in the United States
51. American Medical Association
52. The Asthma and Allergy Foundation of America
53. Bristol-Myers Co., The Nuprin Pain Report
54. Compiled by authors from several sources
55. Medical Economics Co., Drug Topics
56. Progressive Grocer
57. Paine-Webber, Inc.
58. Psychology Today, August, 1984
59. National Center for Health Statistics, National Hospital Discharge Survey
60. National Center for Health Statistics, Health United States, 1986
61. National Center for Health Statistics, Health United States, 1986
62. Health Insurance Association of America
63. American Society of Plastic and Reconstructive Surgeons
64. American Dental Association, 1987 Dental Statistics Handbook
65. American Dental Association, 1987 Dental Statistics Handbook
66. National Institute of Dental Research
67. National Center for Health Statistics, Vital and Health Statistics
68. National Center for Health Statistics, Vital and Health Statistics
69. National Center for Health Statistics, Vital and Health Statistics
70. National Institute of Mental Health
71. Jerry Edelwich and Archie Brodsky, Sexual Dilemmas for the Helping Professional
72. Warren Jones, University of Toledo and Dan Russell, University of Ohio College of Medicine
73. National Center for Health Statistics, Vital and Health Statistics
74. Psychology Today, July, 1981
75. U.S.A. Today
76. National Center for Health Statistics, Vital and Health Statistics
77. National Center for Health Statistics, National Health and Nutrition Examination Survey
78. National Center for Health Statistics, National Health and Nutrition Examination Survey
79. U.S. Department of Agriculture, Food Commonly Eaten by Individuals and National Center for Health Statistics, Vital and Health Statistics
80. Metropolitan Life Insurance Company
81. U.S. Department of Commerce
82. Clairol, Inc.
83. Clairol, Inc.
84. U.S. Bureau of the Census, Current Population Reports
85. U.S. Bureau of the Census, Current Population Reports

86. National Center for Education Statistics, Digest of Education Statistics
87. National Center for Education Statistics, Digest of Education Statistics
88. The Congressional Quarterly, September, 1983
89. Donnelly Marketing Information Services
90. National Center for Education Statistics, Digest of Education Statistics
91. National Center for Education Statistics, Condition of Education
92. U.S. Bureau of the Census, Current Population Reports
93. National Center for Education Statistics, Digest of Education Statistics
94. National Center for Education Statistics, Financial Statistics of Institutions of Higher Education
95. U.S. Department of Education, Office of Student Financial Assistance
96. U.S. Department of Education, Office of Student Financial Assistance
97. The American Freshman—National Norms for Fall 1986
98. National Center for Education Statistics, Digest of Education Statistics
99. National Center for Education Statistics, Digest of Education Statistics
100. National Center for Education Statistics, Associate Degrees and Other Formal Awards Below the Baccalaureate
101. National Center for Education Statistics, Digest of Education Statistics
102. National Center for Education Statistics, Digest of Education Statistics
103. National Center for Education Statistics, Digest of Education Statistics
104. National Center for Education Statistics, Digest of Education Statistics
105. National Center for Education Statistics, Survey of Adult Education
106. National Center for Education Statistics, Survey of Adult Education
107. Gallup Poll, "Religion in America"
108. Gallup Poll, "Religion in America"
109. National Council of Churches, Yearbook of American and Canadian Churches
110. Money Magazine, August, 1982
111. U.S.A. Today
112. Gallup Poll, "Religion in America"
113. Gallup Poll, "Religion in America"
114. U.S. Catholic Magazine
115. The Paragon Project, Scandal Annual—1988
116. New York Times/CBS News polls
117. New York Times/CBS News polls
118. Louis Harris survey
119. U.S. Bureau of the Census, Current Population Reports
120. Centers for Disease Control, Adult Use of Tobacco Survey
121. Centers for Disease Control, Adult Use of Tobacco Survey
122. National Center for Health Statistics, Advanced Report of Final Yearly Mortality Statistics
123. Centers for Disease Control, Adult Use of Tobacco Survey
124. National Center for Health Statistics, Vital and Health Statistics
125. National Organization for the Reform of Marijuana Laws
126. National Institute on Drug Abuse, National Survey on Drug Abuse
127. Medical Research Institute of San Francisco
128. Medical Research Group of San Francisco
129. National Institute of Mental Health
130. Bureau of National Affairs
131. National Institute on Drug Abuse, National Survey on Drug Abuse
132. Federal Bureau of Investigation, Crime in the United States
133. U.S. Bureau of Justice Statistics, National Crime Survey

134. U.S. Bureau of Justice Statistics, Criminal Victimization in the United States
135. U.S. Bureau of Justice Statistics, Criminal Victimization in the United States
136. U.S. Department of Justice survey
137. U.S. Bureau of Justice Statistics, Special Report
138. Federal Bureau of Investigation, Crime in the United States
139. Federal Bureau of Investigation, Crime in the United States
140. U.S. Bureau of Justice Statistics, Criminal Victimization in the United States
141. Federal Bureau of Investigation, Crime in the United States
142. The National Institute of Justice
143. Federal Bureau of Investigations, Crime in the United States
144. U.S. Bureau of Justice Statistics, White Collar Crime
145. U.S. Bureau of Justice Statistics, White Collar Crime
146. U.S. Bureau of Justice Statistics, Prisoners in State and Federal Institutions, The Jail Census, and Probation and Parole
147. U.S. Bureau of Prisons, Statistical Report
148. U.S. Bureau of Justice Statistics, Jail Inmates
149. U.S. Bureau of Justice Statistics, Capital Punishment
150. Dr. David N.F. Fairbanks, George Washington Medical School, Washington, D.C.
151. National Center for Health Statistics, Vital and Health Statistics
152. Psychology Today, June, 1986

CHAPTER
TWO

WHERE YOU LIVE

YOUR WORLD

At the end of 1986, 4,942,000,000 people were living in your world. That was 62% more people than were alive in 1960. By the year 2000, the population of our planet should grow another 25%, to 6.2 billion people. The world's birth rate, however, has dropped 25% since 1985.

58% of the world's population lived in Asia. 12% lived in Africa, 10% in Europe, 8% in Central and South America, 6% in the Soviet Union, 5% in North America, and 1% on islands in the Pacific. Three-quarters of the world's people lived in "under-developed" nations. There were 94 people alive for every square mile of our planet. [1]

YOUR COUNTRY

The population of the United States was 244,425,000 on October 1, 1987, 67 people for every square mile in the country. We were the fourth largest country in the world, after China (1,045,537,00 people), India (783,940,000), and the Soviet Union (279,904,000). [2]

YOUR STATE

Does it seem that New York and California dominate the news? Well, in 1987, one out of every five Americans lived in those two states. Half of you lived in the eleven largest states, two-thirds in the 16 largest states.

The most populous region of the country in 1987, however, was the South, home to 83,900,000 Americans, 34% of the U.S. population. Fastest growing region was the West, where the 1987 population of 49,700,000 people was 15.1% higher than the population in 1980. Population of the Midwest in 1987 was 59,500,000 people and the Northeast was home to 50,300,000 Americans.

Fastest growing state in the last half century has been the Sunshine State. Florida has leaped from 27th in 1940 to 4th in 1987. By the year 2000, Florida will be the third largest state, behind California and Texas. In terms of percentage of growth since 1980, Alaska topped the list, followed by Arizona, Nevada, Florida, Texas, Utah, and California. The only state that has lost population since 1970 is New York, down over one-half million people.

Below is a table of the population of each state in order, from largest to smallest, according to 1987 Census Bureau estimates: [3]

Rank	State	Population
1	California	27,660,000
2	New York	17,830,000
3	Texas	16,790,000
4	Florida	12,020,000
5	Pennsylvania	11,940,000
6	Illinois	11,580,000
7	Ohio	10,780,000
8	Michigan	9,200,000
9	New Jersey	7,670,000
10	North Carolina	6,410,000
11	Georgia	6,220,000
12	Virginia	5,900,000
13	Massachusetts	5,860,000
14	Indiana	5,530,000
15	Missouri	5,100,000
16	Tennessee	4,860,000
17	Wisconsin	4,810,000
18	Washington	4,541,000
19	Maryland	4,540,000
20	Louisiana	4,460,000
21	Minnesota	4,250,000
22	Alabama	4,080,000
23	Kentucky	3,730,000

Rank	State	Population
24	South Carolina	3,430,000
25	Arizona	3,390,000
26	Colorado	3,330,000
27	Oklahoma	3,270,000
28	Connecticut	3,210,000
29	Iowa	2,830,000
30	Oregon	2,720,000
31	Mississippi	2,630,000
32	Kansas	2,480,000
33	Arkansas	2,390,000
34	West Virginia	1,900,000
35	Utah	1,680,000
36	Nebraska	1,590,000
37	New Mexico	1,500,000
38	Maine	1,190,000
39	Hawaii	1,080,000
40	New Hampshire	1,060,000
41	Nevada	1,010,000
42	Idaho	1,000,000
43	Rhode Island	990,000
44	Montana	810,000
45	South Dakota	710,000
46	North Dakota	670,000
47	Delaware	640,000
	District of Columbia	620,000
48	Vermont	550,000
49	Alaska	530,000
50	Wyoming	490,000

It's not surprising that Americans love water sports, because an amazing 52% of you lived within 50 miles of the coastline of our country in 1985. 22% of Americans lived within 50 miles of the Atlantic Ocean, 12% near the Pacific, 12% near the Great Lakes, and 6% had an easy drive to the Gulf of Mexico. [4]

In 1986, according to the Western Interstate Commission on Higher Education, 50% of you lived in the Eastern Time Zone, 30% in the Central Time Zone, 15% in the Pacific Time Zone, and just 5% in the Mountain Time Zone. [5]

URBAN AND RURAL POPULATION

In 1985, 77% of Americans lived in metropolitan areas, 32% in central cities, 45% in suburbs. The remaining 23% lived in rural America.

About half of all Americans lived in the 37 metropolitan areas that had a population of over 1,000,000 people in 1986. These areas were: [6]

Metropolitan area	Population
New York	17,678,100
Los Angeles	13,074,800
Chicago	8,116,100
San Francisco	5,877,800
Philadelphia	5,832,600
Detroit	4,600,700
Boston	4,055,700
Dallas	3,655,300
Houston	3,634,300
Washington	3,563,000
Miami	2,912,000
Cleveland	2,765,600
Atlanta	2,560,000
St. Louis	2,438,000
Pittsburgh	2,316,100
Minneapolis	2,295,200
Seattle	2,284,500
Baltimore	2,280,000
San Diego	2,201,300
Tampa	1,914,300
Phoenix	1,900,200
Denver	1,847,400
Cincinnati	1,690,100
Milwaukee	1,552,000
Kansas City	1,517,800
Portland, OR	1,364,100
New Orleans	1,334,400
Norfolk, VA	1,390,500
Columbus, OH	1,299,400
Sacramento	1,291,400
San Antonio	1,276,400
Indianapolis	1,212,600
Buffalo	1,181,600
Providence	1,108,500
Charlotte	1,065,400
Hartford	1,043,500
Salt Lake City	1,041,400

By the year 2000, the number of metropolitan areas with populations over a million will climb to 55. Los Angeles will leap past New York into the number one spot on the list.

Phoenix, Arizona (853,266 population) was the nation's largest capital city in 1986, followed by Honolulu (805,266), Indianapolis (710,280), and Boston (570,719). Smallest capital city was Montpelier, Vermont, with just 8,167 residents.

YOUR COUNTY

In 1986, Americans lived in one of 3,096 counties. According to NPA Data Services, Inc., over one-third of all population growth between 1986 and the year 2000 will occur in just 38 of those counties. Six of the 10 fastest growing counties are in California, with the rest in Arizona, Texas, and Florida. [7] In 1987, the five largest U.S. counties were: [8] Los Angeles, CA (8,300,000), Cook, IL (5,300,000), Harris, TX (2,800,000), Brooklyn, NY (2,292,200), and San Diego, CA (2,200,000).

U.S. TERRITORIES AND POSSESSIONS

In 1986, the population of the Pacific and Caribbean possessions of the United States was: [9]

Puerto Rico	3,274,000
Guam	126,800
Virgin Islands	109,000
American Samoa	37,300
Northern Mariana Islands	19,700

At the time of the 1980 Census, the Trust Territory of Pacific Islands, which consists of 96 populated islands, was 116,000.

AMERICANS LIVING ABROAD

On May 6, 1986, 4,235,500 Americans, excluding military personnel, were out of the country. These included 1,852,500 U.S. citizens who were residents of other countries; 1,632,000 government employees, their dependents, and military civilian dependents; and

751,000 tourists. The 10 countries with the largest population of permanent U.S. residents were: **[10]**

Country	American residents
Mexico	333,700
Canada	309,700
United Kingdom	100,700
Germany	100,200
Italy	82,900
Australia	61,800
Israel	55,700
Greece	54,200
Saudi Arabia	42,800
Brazil	40,300

Every year, about 100,000 Americans leave the U.S. to permanently live in another country. **[11]**

YOUR CLIMATE

Arguments about who has the best climate are a lot like arguments about who has the prettiest wife—there's no final answer because "best" depends on individual preferences. Fanatic skiers prefer greatly different climates from fanatic surfers. Below, however, are some facts about the climates in major U.S. cities. **[12]**

Sunshine

The National Oceanic and Atmospheric Administration has been keeping records of the annual percentage of daylight hours the sun shines in major U.S. cities over the last several decades. The U.S. cities with the most sunshine have been:

City	% of possible sunshine
Phoenix	85%
El Paso	83%
Reno	79%
Sacramento	77%
Albuquerque	76%

City	% of possible sunshine
Los Angeles	73%
Miami	72%
Denver	70%
Honolulu	67%
Oklahoma City	67%
Salt Lake City	67%

Cities with the least annual sunshine have been:

City	% of annual sunshine
Juneau, Alaska	32%
Seattle	46%
Pittsburgh	47%
Portland, Oregon	47%
Buffalo, NY	49%
Cleveland	49%
Burlington, VT	49%
Duluth, MN	52%
Milwaukee	54%
Detroit	54%

Precipitation

The National Oceanic and Atmospheric Administration has also been keeping records of the annual number of days on which precipitation falls. The wettest U.S. cities have been:

City	Number of days with precipitation
Juneau, Alaska	220
Buffalo, NY	169
Seattle	158
Cleveland	156
Portland, OR	154
Pittsburgh	154
Burlington, VT	153
Charleston, WV	151
Duluth, MN	135
Detroit	133

The driest U.S. cities have been:

City	Number of days with precipitation
Phoenix	36
Los Angeles	36
El Paso	47
Reno	51
Sacramento	58
Albuquerque	59
San Francisco	63
Dallas	78
Oklahoma City	82
Wichita	85

Snow

The U.S. cities with most annual inches of snow fall have been:

City	Annual inches of snow
Juneau, Alaska	103
Buffalo, NY	92
Burlington, VT	78
Duluth	77
Portland, ME	72
Denver	60
Salt Lake City	59
Cleveland	54
Spokane	51
Hartford	50

Cold Weather

The U.S. cities with the most days on which the temperature has reached 32 degrees Fahrenheit or below have been:

City	Annual number of days below freezing
Bismark, ND	186
Duluth, MN	184
Reno	182

City	Annual number of days below freezing
Denver	159
Portland, Maine	158
Burlington, VT	157
Minneapolis-St. Paul	156
Juneau, Alaska	146
Milwaukee	143
Omaha	140

The cities with the fewest days on which the temperature dips below freezing have been:

City	Annual number of days below freezing
Honolulu	0
Los Angeles	0
Miami	0
San Francisco	2
Phoenix	9
New Orleans	13
Sacramento	16
Mobile	22
Houston	23
Seattle	30

WHO LIVES IN YOUR HOUSEHOLD

By type, the number of American households in 1988 were: [13]

	Number	Per cent of households
All households	91,061,000	100%
Family households	65,133,000	72%
Married couples	51,809,000	57%
No children under 18	27,072,000	30%
Children under 18	24,737,000	27%
Female head of household	10,608,000	12%
Male head of household	2,715,000	3%
Non-family households	25,929,000	28%
People living alone	21,884,000	24%
Unrelated people	4,045,000	4%

Between 1950 and 1987, the percentage of American households headed by married couples plummeted from 78% to 58%, and the percentage of households containing people living alone soared from 9% to 24%. In 1987, however, because the baby boomers are now marrying, the number of family households increased more than the number of non-family households for the first time in over 20 years.

The fastest growth rate in new households in the last five years has been family households headed by a single woman or man. This rate growth slowed dramatically in 1987. The high marriage rate among "baby boomers" means that the fastest growth rate by 1990 will be in family households with children under 18.

WHO LIVES ALONE?

The number of people living alone doubled between 1970 and 1985. The increase has been often attributed to young people delaying marriage and more couples getting divorced. That explanation, however, is only partially correct.

Statistics do show that half the increase in the number of single person households was due to more people under 45 living alone. But people under 45 living alone were still a very small minority of all people under 45 years old in 1985: [14]

Age	Live alone	With spouse	With relatives	With non-relatives
Men				
20–24	6.8%	21.2%	57.6%	14.4%
25–44	10.5%	66.3%	14.5%	8.7%
45–64	8.7%	80.4%	7.4%	3.5%
65+	14.7%	75.0%	7.5%	2.9%
Women				
20–24	4.9%	34.9%	49.0%	11.2%
25–44	6.9%	67.5%	21.3%	4.3%
45–65	13.3%	69.6%	15.1%	2.0%
65+	41.1%	38.3%	18.4%	2.2%

The reason the figures were not higher was that that the number of young people living at home has also increased dramatically in the last 15 years—to the point where 1 in 5 women under age 45 still hadn't left the nest.

The number of divorced people living alone hadn't risen as

dramatically in the last 15 years—to the point where 1 in 5 women under age 45 still hadn't left the nest.

The number of divorced people living alone hadn't risen as dramatically as the divorce rate. The reason was that the majority of divorced men and women have remarried quickly. Due to remarriage, the percentage of people age 45-64 living alone actually declined in the last 15 years.

WHO COHABITS?

The number of unmarried couples living together quadrupled between 1970 and 1984. After a slight decline in 1985, the number of cohabiting couples topped 2.3 million in 1987.

Nearly two-thirds of the men and women who lived together were between 25 and 44 years of age. About 56% had never been married, 32% had been divorced, 5% had been widowed, and 7% were separated. A third of these couples had one or more children living with them. [15]

HOW MANY PEOPLE LIVE IN YOUR HOUSEHOLD?

From 1960 to 1987, the size of the average household dropped from 3.5 people to 2.64 people. As the table below shows, over half of you lived either alone or with just one other person in 1987: [16]

Number of people	% of households
1	24.0%
2	32.2%
3	17.8%
4	15.5%
5	6.7%
6	2.4%
7+	1.4%

YOUR HOME OWNERSHIP

In 1987, 63.9% of you owned your residence, and 36.1% of you paid rent. The rate of home ownership for married couples was 78%, and it reached 95% for married couples who both worked. Only 46% of unmarried people owned their residences. [17]

THE BUILDING
WHERE YOU LIVE

In 1985, the Census Bureau found that two-thirds of you lived in single family homes, as the table below shows: [18]

	% of housing
Single family home	67.0%
2–4 units	11.4%
5 or more units	16.4%
Mobile home	5.2%

Over half of you lived in buildings that were over 25 years old, and 29% of you lived in buildings built before 1940.

The average number of rooms in your dwelling was 5, although one-third of owner-occupied homes had 7 or more rooms. Your living space averaged 1700 square feet.

WHERE OLDER
AMERICANS LIVE

In 1985, 53% of Americans age 65 and older lived with a spouse, 30% lived alone, 13% lived with relatives, and 4% lived in nursing homes or other institutions. Because women outlive men, four times as many women as men 65 and over lived alone. [19]

72% of the elderly owned their own homes, with 40% of those living in homes built before 1940. 80% of people age 65–74 and 95% of people age 75 and older had paid off mortgages; their annual housing costs were 37% lower than for people age 45–54. [20]

Those Americans living in nursing homes in 1985 consisted of 1.5% of those age 65–74, 6.8% of those age 75–84, and 21.6% of those age 85 and over.

Contrary to popular belief, three out of every four nursing home residents have left the home alive. The median stay for those who were discharged was 60 days, but that increased dramatically with age: average stays were 263 days for those 85–89, 302 days for those 90–94, and 791 days for those 95 and over. The average cost of nursing home care was $67 a day. [21]

HOW LONG YOU'VE LIVED IN YOUR HOME

Americans are a mobile people, and less than 1 in 5 of you have lived in the same residence for more than 15 years. By region, the length of time you had lived in your present home in 1985 was: [22]

Region	% in homes 5 years or less	% in homes 15 years or more
Northeast	33.1%	24.1%
North Central	39.1%	21.1%
South	44.0%	14.8%
West	51.4%	12.9%

61% of you lived in the same states in which you were born. But very few of you had lived in the same home all of your lives. In only 4 states had 9% of the residents never moved—New Mexico, Mississippi, Louisiana, and North Dakota. In 7 states, 8% of the residents had lived in the same house since birth—South Carolina, Maine, West Virginia, South Dakota, Pennsylvania, and Vermont. [23]

46,470,000 of you moved in 1986, 20.2% of all Americans. As you'd expect, people in their 20's moved most often (1 in 3 move every year) and people over 45 moved least frequently (less than 1 in 10 change addresses yearly). The Census Bureau projects the average American moves at least 11 times in his or her lifetime.

Of those of you who moved, 65% moved to another house in the same county, 17% stayed in the same state, 15% moved to a different state, and 3% moved abroad. [24]

Most settled of all Americans were New Yorkers, 96% of whom had lived in the Empire State for the last 5 years. At the opposite end of the spectrum was Alaska, where 41% of the population had arrived in the last 5 years. [25]

A 1983 Gallup Survey found people moved for these reasons:

Job change	23%
Job transfer	20%
Larger residence	13%
Better location	11%
Rental to owned home	10%
Closer to relatives	5%
Retirement	3%
Health	2%
Other	12%

A 1983 study by the University of Maryland's Transportation Studies Group showed that 55% of movers used their own or borrowed trucks, 21% rented trucks, and 21% hired moving companies.

HOW YOU HEAT AND COOL YOUR HOUSE

In 1984, you heated your homes as follows: [26]

Type of fuel	% of homes
Utility gas	55%
Fuel oil/kerosene	15%
Electricity	19%
Bottled gas	5%
Wood	5%
None	1%

Fuel you used for cooking: [27]

Electricity	52%
Gas	48%

Nationally, 31% of your homes were cooled by room air conditioners and 27% of you had central air conditioning. Regionally, the percentage of air conditioned homes varied from a low of 34% in the West to a high of 75% in the South. [28]

In 1985, the average household spent $1,123 to heat and cool the home. By region of the country, average expenditures varied from $1,443 in the Northeast to $853 in Western states. **[29]**

WHAT YOU SPEND ON ELECTRICITY

In 1985, the average U.S. residential electric bill for 750 kilowatt hours of service was $54.76. **[30]**

HOW MUCH WATER YOU USE

In 1980, the average person used 38 gallons of water per day at home.**[31]**

YOUR NEW HOUSE

Of all new houses built in 1985:

57% had 3 bedrooms

18% had 4 or more bedrooms

77% had 2 or more bathrooms

35% had a full or partial basement

70% were centrally air conditioned

70% had a garage

The average sale price for these new houses was $84,300, and 24% sold for more than $120,000. **[32]**

According to a 1987 survey of 2,706 people shopping for new homes, the features they were looking for most in a new house, in order of popularity, were:

1. Dishwasher

2. Dead-bolt locks

3. Walk-in closets

4. Disposal

5. Fireplace

6. Bay windows

7. Upgraded carpeting

8. Microwave oven

9. Walk-in pantry

10. Ceramic tiles in tub

Among new home owners, contemporary and colonial style homes were by far the most popular. Shoppers preferred two story homes to one story homes by a 2 to 1 margin. 48% wanted 4 bedrooms, while 42% were looking for two bedroom houses.

78% of those surveyed already owned homes. They were in the market for homes about 25% more expensive and about 13% larger than their present residences.

WHAT YOUR HOUSE IS WORTH

The average value of homes across the country in 1985 was $59,700. If you owned your home, the average equity you had in that home was a tidy $36,400, which made up about three-quarters of your financial net worth. [33]

If you lived in a major metropolitan area, your house was worth considerably more. The average resale price for a home in 53 largest metropolitan areas in 1987 was $85,400. Below is a list of the average resale prices in those areas: [34]

Akron, OH	$ 57,800
Albany, NY	88,600
Albuquerque, NM	84,400
Baltimore	81,900
Baton Rouge	69,200
Boston	181,600
Buffalo	55,900
Chicago	91,200
Cincinnati	68,800
Cleveland	69,000
Columbus, OH	72,700
Dallas-Fort Worth	89,300
Denver	91,000
Des Moines	56,200
Detroit	65,900
El Paso	62,600
Fort Lauderdale, FL	80,800
Grand Rapids, MI	54,000

Hartford	165,400
Houston	67,300
Indianapolis	62,800
Jacksonville, FL	66,300
Kansas City	69,200
Las Vegas	76,700
Los Angeles	145,400
Louisville	53,300
Memphis	75,200
Miami	83,500
Milwaukee	70,900
Minneapolis	80,900
Nashville, TN	75,500
New York	183,000
Oklahoma City	61,400
Omaha	59,700
Orange Co., CA	167,700
Orlando	72,900
Philadelphia	84,400
Phoenix	82,700
Portland, OR	64,000
Providence, RI	126,600
Rochester, NY	74,100
St. Louis	75,700
Salt Lake City	71,100
San Antonio	72,100
San Diego	131,700
San Francisco	175,900
Syracuse, NY	71,300
Tampa	65,000
Toledo, OH	56,900
Tulsa, OK	66,700
Washington, DC	108,400
W. Palm Beach, FL	99,000

According to the Mortgage Bankers Association, the average monthly house expense in 1985—for mortgage, real estate taxes, utilities, and insurance—was $770. Most expensive region of the country was the West, where the average payment was $1,020; least expensive—$666 paid by the average Midwesterner.

WHO'S BUYING HOMES AND WHAT DO THEY PAY?

According to the Chicago Title Insurance Company, in 1985, over 3,000,000 million housing units changed hands. 76% were existing housing, 24% were new. 87% were single family homes.

63% of the buyers were repeat home buyers. They paid an

average of $106,200, put an average of 33% down on the price of the house, and paid a monthly mortgage of $868, which represented 28% of their monthly gross income. The median household income of these buyers was $42,200.

37% were first time home buyers. Before they made their purchase, they looked at an average of 13 houses over a 4 month period. The house they bought averaged $75,100. First time buyers put an average of 11% down, 80% of which came from their savings. Their mortgage payment averaged $810 a month, 33.7% of their monthly income. 76% of first time buyers were married couples, and 85% of these couples were both working. Their median household income was $35,070. [35]

IF YOU'RE SELLING YOUR HOME . . .

In 1986, the average home sold after being on the market for 86 days. In relation to asking prices, the selling prices were: [36]

% below asking price	% of homes
1–2%	5%
3–4%	16%
5–6%	28%
7–8%	10%
9–10%	16%
11%+	8%

WHO'S GETTING IN TROUBLE?

As of August, 1987, 5.8% of homeowners were late on their mortgage payments, 2% were more than 60 days late, and foreclosure proceedings had been started about 1/4 of 1%. [37]

IF MONEY'S NO OBJECT

According to the RELO Broker Network, a real estate reference service, the most expensive communities in the United States in 1987 were: [38]

Community	Average home price
Greenwich, CT	$1,200,000
Mill Neck, NY	$1,200,000
Alpine, NJ	$1,180,000
Saddle River, NJ	$1,150,000
Atherton, CA	$ 910,000
Laurel Hollow, NY	$ 900,000
Hillsborough, CA	$ 850,000
New Canaan, CT	$ 800,000
Darien, CT	$ 800,000
Muttontown, NJ	$ 770,000

WHAT CAN YOU AFFORD TO PAY FOR A HOUSE?

With the rise in mortgage defaults, most banks today have placed a limit of 28% of gross income on a combination of monthly mortgage payment, insurance, and taxes. Assuming a fixed rate mortgage of 10%, a 30 year term, and a 20% down payment, below is a table of the maximum monthly payment, maximum mortgage, and maximum value of the house for a range of gross incomes: [39]

Gross income	Maximum monthly payment	Maximum mortgage	Value of home
$ 20,000	$ 466.66	$ 47,859	$ 59,824
$ 30,000	$ 700.00	$ 71,789	$ 89,736
$ 40,000	$ 933.33	$ 95,718	$119,647
$ 50,000	$1166.66	$119,648	$149,560
$ 60,000	$1400.00	$143,578	$179,473
$ 70,000	$1633.33	$167,508	$209,385
$ 80,000	$1866.66	$191,437	$239,296
$ 90,000	$2100.00	$215,367	$269,209
$100,000	$2333.33	$239,297	$299,121

WHO DOESN'T NEED A MORTGAGE?

According to the Chicago Title Insurance Company, 6.5% of 1985 repeat homeowners plunked down the entire purchase price of their new house, compared with just .5% of first time home buyers. A little under 10% of buyers put up more than 50% of the purchase price as a down payment.

WHAT YOU SPEND ON YOUR NEW HOUSE

A 1986 survey conducted by New Home magazine found that the average new homeowner spent $3,600 on new furnishings in the first six months after moving in, and another $2,900 in the following six months. 40% of the new homeowners did some remodeling in the first six months, half did some inside painting, and 20% painted the exterior of the house.

WHAT'S WRONG WITH YOUR HOUSE?

The most common problems with your houses were: **[40]**

Problem	% of houses
Leaky basement	27%
Mice in house	11%
Leaky roof	8%
Cracks/holes ceiling	7%
Broken plaster	4%
Broken electrical outlets	3%
Exposed wiring	3%
Holes in floors	2%

WHO DOES THE HOUSEWORK?

Despite increasingly widespread acceptance of "shared responsibility" in marriage, the most recent studies still have shown that women do the overwhelming majority of work around the house. The massive time-use study conducted by the Institute for Social Research of the University of Michigan revealed that the average woman spent three times as many hours per week as men on work around the house. Tulane University sociologist Shelley Coverman discovered that young, educated professional men who claimed to be for sexual equality were no more likely to do the dishes or clean the refrigerator than were blue-collar men.

Husbands of working wives have spent more time helping around the house, but that increased time averaged 5 minutes a week for every hour the wife worked—or an average of 3.5 hours per week for the husband of a woman employed full time.

How much time do women spend on housework? You may be very surprised to discover that despite the introduction of so many "labor-saving devices" in this century (e.g., the washing machine, dryer, refrigerator, vacuum cleaner, microwave oven, dishwasher, etc.), the amount of hours the typical housewife spent on housework remained virtually unchanged from 1900 to 1977. The reason, according to sociologist Joann Vanek and economist Kathryn Walker, who did the research, are that new household technologies, while eliminating some tasks, have created new standards of cleanliness and have greatly expanded the time spent on other activities. An example of the new standards of cleanliness is the washing of clothing. The washing machine saved a lot of labor, but it has also meant that clothing is now washed much more frequently—after one wearing today, as opposed to after several wearings a century ago. An example of the expansion of some jobs is cooking. Before the advances in food storage and food preparation techniques and equipment, women served simple one–dish meals. Today, women spend almost triple the time in shopping for and cooking multi-dish meals.

The end result has been that Vanek and Walker found that women who don't work outside the house spent an average of 50 hours per week on household work and child care, while women who worked full time spent an average of 25 hours a week on those tasks. The Institute for Social Research found that men who worked full time averaged 12.7 hours per week in work around the house, including time spent on lawn maintenance and home repair.

What kinds of housework do husbands do today? Mostly "light" housework tasks such as shopping and preparing meals, according to a study done by the advertising firm of Cunningham & Walsh. The percentage of husbands who at least occasionally did the following tasks were:

Take out the garbage	80%
Major grocery shopping	56%
Vacuuming	47%
Cook complete meals	44%
Wash dishes	41%
Make the bed	37%

Do laundry	33%
Clean the bathroom	27%
Dust	23%
Dry the dishes	23%
Clean refrigerator	16%
Clean oven	14%

Among two-income couples, 30% of husbands prepared at least one meal per week and 10% prepared three or more meals per week. Husbands averaged 4 trips to the grocery store per month, compared with an average 7 trips per month for women. In terms of laundry, on the other hand, men averaged doing 1 load every 2 months, compared with an average for woman of 2 loads per week for every person in the household.

What's the bottom line in housework? When housework and outside employment (including commuting time) were combined, all wives averaged 71 hours a week of work, compared with 55 hours per week for all men. **[41]**

THE REPAIRS YOU DO YOURSELF

Below is a list of the percentage of homeowners who do the following repairs themselves: **[42]**

Inside painting	85%
Outside painting	73%
Wallpapering	82%
Plumbing	52%
Electrical work	59%
Carpentry	69%
Masonry	59%

The average male homeowner spent 7 hours per week on clean up and repairs inside and outside the house. Average cost per year of home maintenance and repair was about 3% of gross income. **[43]**

HOW YOU LIKE
YOUR NEIGHBORHOOD

When both home owners and renters were asked to evaluate their neighborhoods, they responded as follows: **[44]**

Rating	% of owners	% of renters
Excellent	41.7%	23.3%
Good	44.8%	47.6%
Fair	11.3%	22.8%
Poor	2.1%	6.3%

People's specific complaints about their neighborhoods were:

Too much street noise	18%
Heavy traffic	15%
Crime	14%
Streets need repair	14%
Odors, smoke or gas	13%
Trash, junk and litter	11%
Noise from airplanes	8%
Poor street lighting	8%
Other houses in poor condition	7%

A 1983 study by the U.S. Bureau of Justice Statistics found that 26% of men and 62% of women were afraid to walk at night within a mile of their residence.

YOUR SECOND HOME
OR PROPERTY

11% of you owned a second home or real estate other than your primary residence in 1987. **[45]**

WHAT YOU PAY IN RENT

Census Bureau reports for 1984 revealed that you were most likely to rent if you were young (81% of people under 25 and 53% of people under 35 rented), or if you lived in a big city (77% of New Yorkers and 73% of people living in Boston rented). **[46]**

If you did rent, you noticed your payments soaring in the last 10 years. It cost over twice as much to rent a newly built apartment in 1987 as it did in 1975—$515 compared with $211. Only 7% of new apartments rented in 1987 cost less than $350 per month. 54% rented for $500 or more, and 43% went for more than $550. **[47]**

The average rental price of previously occupied apartments was

$332 per month in 1987. The percentage of apartments by rental price was: **[48]**

Rental price per month	% of available apartments
Less than $100	4%
$100–$149	4%
$150–$199	17%
$200–$249	14%
$250–$299	27%
$300–$399	15%
$400–$499	12%
$500 or more	6%

Your rent was likely to eat up a large portion of your income, as the table below shows: **[49]**

% of income used to pay rent	% of people paying that rent
Under 14%	16.8%
15% to 19%	16.4%
20% to 24%	15.3%
25% to 34%	19.8%
Over 35%	31.7%

WHO LIVES IN MOBILE HOMES OR TRAILERS?

In 1985, 4,537,000 housing units were mobile homes or trailers, 5.2% of all housing units. The average sale price for a brand new mobile home was $21,800. **[50]**

WHO USES OUTHOUSES?

In 1985, 2.4% of all housing units didn't have indoor plumbing and .8% had no heat. **[51]**

WHO LIVES
IN GROUP QUARTERS?

At the time of the last census in 1980, about 2.5% of the population were living in some sort of group quarters. Of these people, 43% were inmates of institutions.

The total number of people living in group quarters remained virtually the same since 1970, but there was a major change in the type of quarters. About 500,000 more people lived in homes for the aged, and about 500,000 less lived in military quarters. The number of students living in college dormitories doubled, while the number of people in mental institutions and in rooming houses was cut in half. Below is a table showing the population in institutions and other group quarters in 1980: [52]

Institutional inmates	2,492,000
Homes for aged	1,426,000
Mental hospitals	255,000
Prisons	466,000
Tuberculosis hospitals	8,000
Other chronic disease hospitals	61,000
Homes for mentally handicapped	149,000
Homes for physically handicapped	27,000
Homes for neglected children	38,000
Homes for unwed mothers	2,000
Schools for juvenile delinquents	42,000
Detention homes	17,000
Non-Institutional residents	3,246,000
College dormitories	1,994,000
Military quarters	671,000
Rooming and boarding houses	176,000

WHO'S HOMELESS?

The actual number of homeless Americans has been the subject of a great deal of dispute, for a number of reasons. First, because they don't have a permanent place to live, they're almost impossible to count in the way most of us are counted by the Census Bureau. Secondly, there's no agreement on a definition of homeless—for example, is a family living in a welfare hotel "homeless?" And thirdly, estimates are routinely inflated or deflated by social service agencies and politicians who are either seeking to exaggerate or minimize the problem. The result is that estimates of the number of homeless people across the country range from 1,000,000 to 3,000,000.

CHAPTER TWO NOTES

1. U.S. Bureau of the Census, World Population Profile-1986
2. U.S. Bureau of the Census, World Population Profile-1986
3. U.S. Bureau of the Census, Current Population Reports
4. U.S. Bureau of the Census, unpublished data
5. Western Interstate Commission on Higher Education
6. U.S. Bureau of the Census, General Population Characteristics
7. NPA Data Services, Inc., Key Indicators of County Growth
8. U.S. Bureau of the Census, Current Population Reports
9. U.S. Bureau of the Census, Current Population Reports
10. U.S. Department of State
11. U.S. Department of State
12. National Oceanic and Atmospheric Administration, Comparative Climatic Data
13. U.S. Bureau of the Census, 1987 Current Population Survey
14. U.S. Bureau of the Census, Current Population Reports
15. U.S. Bureau of the Census, Current Population Reports
16. U.S. Bureau of the Census, Current Population Reports
17. U.S. Bureau of the Census, Current Housing Reports
18. U.S. Bureau of the Census, Current Housing Reports
19. U.S. Bureau of the Census, Current Population Reports
20. Monthly Labor Review, October, 1986
21. The National Center for Health Statistics, National Nursing Home Survey
22. U.S. Bureau of the Census, Current Population Reports
23. U.S. Bureau of the Census, Current Population Reports
24. U.S. Bureau of the Census, Current Population Reports
25. U.S. Bureau of the Census, Current Population Reports
26. U.S. Energy Information Administration, Residential Energy Consumption Survey
27. U.S. Bureau of the Census, Current Housing Reports
28. U.S. Energy Information Administration, Residential Energy Consumption Survey
29. U.S. Energy Information Administration, Residential Energy Consumption Survey
30. U.S. Energy Information Administration, Residential Energy Consumption Survey
31. U.S. Geological Survey, Estimated Use of Water in the United States in 1980
32. U.S. Bureau of the Census and U.S. Department of Housing and Urban Development, Characteristics of New Housing
33. Mortgage Bankers Association
34. National Association of Realtors
35. Chicago Title Insurance Company, The Guarantor

36. Opinion Research of St. Louis
37. Mortgage Bankers Association, National Delinquency Survey
38. RELO Broker Network
39. Computed by author
40. U.S. Bureau of the Census, Current Housing Reports
41. Institute for Social Research, Time, Goods, and Well-Being
42. Institute for Social Research, Time, Goods, and Well-Being
43. Institute for Social Research, Time, Goods, and Well-Being
44. U.S. Bureau of the Census, Current Housing Reports
45. Money Magazine, Americans and Their Money, 1987
46. U.S. Bureau of the Census, Current Housing Reports
47. U.S. Bureau of the Census, Current Housing Reports
48. U.S. Bureau of the Census, Current Housing Reports
49. U.S. Bureau of the Census, Current Housing Reports
50. U.S. Bureau of the Census, Current Housing Reports
51. U.S. Bureau of the Census, Current Housing Reports
52. U.S. Bureau of the Census, 1980 Census of the Population

CHAPTER
THREE

YOUR MONEY

YOUR INCOME

Money may not buy happiness, but it does buy housing, food, transportation, clothing, and all the other things that make life more comfortable. That's why almost all of you are very curious about what other people make, spend, and what they have left over.

What you make is called "income." While most of us think of income as what we're paid at work, the Census Bureau discovered that wages and salaries made up, on the average, only 78% of our total income in 1985. [1] The rest came from interest, dividends, capital gains, pensions, Social Security, and other sources.

One of the most interesting ways to look at what people make is to look at family income—that is, all the money received by members of the same family who live together. With so many husbands and wives working today, it's the family income that determines the kind of lifestyle most Americans lead.

YOUR FAMILY INCOME

The median income of the American family in 1987 was $30,853 dollars, as compared with $9,867 in 1970. In terms of what those dollars bought, however, the average family was little better off in 1987. When inflation was taken into account, the "real" increase over 17 years was just 6.8%. or $1,973. Without so many women having gone to work, the income of the average family would have dramatically dropped. [2]

When you examine the distribution of income rather than the average income, you find that since 1970, the rich have been getting richer and the poor have been getting poorer. Using constant dollars adjusted for inflation, in 1987 49% more families earned over $50,000 per year, and 5% more families earned under $10,000 per year. [3]

How did your family income rate? Below is a table of the percent distribution by income level in 1987: [4]

Family income	% of families at that level	% of families that level or below
Under $5,000	4.4%	4.4%
$ 5,000–$ 9,999	7.3%	11.7%
$10,000–$14,999	9.1%	20.8%
$15,000–$19,999	9.5%	30.3%
$20,000–$24,999	9.2%	39.5%
$25,000–$34,999	17.5%	57.0%
$35,000–$49,999	20.2%	77.2%
$50,000+	22.9%	100.0%

How was income distributed in 1987? The poorest Americans, the lowest 20% of families, received just 4.6% of all income. The richest Americans, the highest 20%, received 43.7% of all income. These wealthiest families were those who received more than $44,280 in income annually. A family income of $86,300 placed a family in the highest 5%. [5]

If we take a look at marital status and family income, it's no surprise that families headed by married couples had the highest family income ($34,700). And it's also no surprise that the median income of families headed by men, with no wife present, was $24,800, while the median income of families headed by women, with no husband present, was only $14,620. [6]

One of the reasons families headed by married couples had higher incomes was that a majority of married women worked. In 1985, the average family income when married women were employed was $40,422, compared with an average income of $26,652 for families in which the wife didn't work. 69% of wives worked in families who had an income of $35,000 or more, compared to just 32% of wives in families with a income of less than $20,000. [7]

A final way to look at family income is by race. The median family income of white families in 1987 was $32,274, of Spanish-origin families was $20,509, and of black families was $18,098. While the inflation-adjusted income of white families rose just 7% since 1970, the adjusted median income of black families fell 2%. The adjusted median income of Hispanic families rose 1%. [8]

WHERE YOUR MONEY COMES FROM

A few decades ago, Americans earned virtually all of their income by the sweat of their brows. Today, working is still our chief source of income, but the percentage contributed by earnings has shrunk to 78%. An increasing number of Americans receive significant money every year from sources that didn't exist a quarter-century ago—such as money market funds, certificates of deposit, interest-bearing checking accounts, food stamps, and many other government benefit programs.

In 1985, according to the Census Bureau, 116,985,000 Americans received money from wages or salaries. 100,240,000 earned interest from savings, although the money received averaged less than 4% of their incomes.

Nearly half of all American households (47%) contained at least one person who received some sort of government benefit. By far the largest number of recipients of any program were the over 33,000,000 Americans getting Social Security checks. Social Security accounted for nearly 7% of our national income.

Below is a table of the major sources of income and the number of Americans who received money from those sources in 1985: [9]

Income source	# of Americans
Wages and salaries	116,983,000
Interest	100,240,000
Social Security	33,006,000
Dividends	18,073,000
Self-employment	12,636,000
Rents	8,773,000
Private pensions	8,116,000
Unemployment compensation	7,046,000
Welfare payments	4,751,000
Supplemental security income	3,561,000
Child support and alimony	3,446,000
Mortgage interest	3,414,000
Royalties and other investments	2,900,000

Income source	# of Americans
Veterans' pensions	2,807,000
State employee pensions	2,377,000
Federal employee pensions	1,433,000
Relatives or friends	1,106,000
U.S. military pensions	936,000
Paid up life insurance/annuities	729,000
Workers' compensation	666,000

The most enlightening way to look at sources of income is to separate Americans by their total annual income. About 80% of households earning less than $7200 a year received government benefits, and those benefits averaged nearly 70% of their total incomes. At the other end of the scale, only 22% of households earning over $60,000 a year received any government money, and those funds accounted for less than 3% of total income.

Below is a table of the sources of income by total annual household income in 1984: [10]

	INCOME						
	Below $7200	$7200– $14,000	$14,000– $24,000	$24,000– $36,000	$36,000– $48,000	$48,000– $60,000	Over $60,000
Wages	20.4%	48.8%	70.8%	82.8%	86.8%	87.1%	80.0%
Interest, dividends, etc.	7.7%	12.1%	10.1%	7.2%	6.8%	7.5%	15.6%
Government sources	68.2%	35.3%	16.7%	8.5%	5.3%	4.3%	2.5%

YOUR PERSONAL INCOME

The average personal income for American men was $22,684 in 1987; the average personal income for American women that same year was $11,435. When we look at median income, half of all men with income earned under $17,114 and half of all women earned under $8,101. [11]

As you'd expect, those of you with full-time, year-around jobs had higher median incomes. Men working full time all year had a median income of $26,760 in 1985, while women working the same schedule had a median income of $17,504. [12]

THE INCOME OF
OLDER AMERICANS

Census Bureau figures show a very dramatic change in the income of older Americans in the last thirty years. In 1959, more than one-third of people age 65 or older were at the poverty level or below; in 1969, one in four older Americans were living in poverty; in 1987, the percentage had fallen to just 12.2%, below the poverty level of 13.5% for the population as a whole. [13]

When we take a look at those Americans living in extreme poverty over a 5 year period, the percentage of those 65 and over has dropped from 9% in 1968 to just 3.7% in 1985. The number of affluent older Americans, those with a five year income of more than 5 times the poverty level, have doubled from 7.1% in 1968 to 14.2% in 1985. [14]

A final measure of the rising fortunes of older Americans is that their average after-tax personal income in 1987 was $9,574 compared with a average of $8,894 for all Americans. [15]

The older Americans most likely to be having financial problems were those who were unmarried. 25.3% of unmarried people age 65 and older were below the poverty line in 1987, compared with just 6.2% of senior citizen married couples. The average income of married couples 65 and over was $20,740 in 1985, compared with an income of $7,833 for unmarried female senior citizens. [16]

Social Security benefits are by far the biggest reason that older Americans are better off financially. A study conducted by the Social Security Administration of people who retired in 1980 and 1981 showed that 98.3% of those who were married and 97.1% of those who were unmarried received social security payments. Other sources of income were:

Source	Married couples	Unmarried people
Pensions	55.7%	42.4%
Income from assets	83.8%	69.1%
Earnings from work	43.7%	27.1%
Other	16.5%	15.2%

Median monthly income for married couples was $1,511 and $775 for unmarried people. The median monthly amount of income from various sources (among people receiving income from those sources) was:

Source	Married couples	Unmarried people
Social security	$671	$421
Earnings	$617	$392
Pensions	$490	$291
Asset income	$180	$ 99

The least well off senior citizens by age were those 85 and older. They were relatively poor for two major reasons. First and foremost, many of them worked most or all of their lives outside the social security system, and thus only 34.4% received any social security payments. Secondly, only 20.7% were currently married, and married older couples were far better off than unmarried senior citizens.

Despite their lower incomes, however, only 16.2% of Americans 85 and over were below the poverty level in 1984. Their average income of $5,540, however, was 26% below the average income of all people 65 and over.

WHAT YOU EARN

In the way it tends to dominate our thoughts and our conversation, the subject of salaries and wages is a lot like sex. We're intensely curious about what other people earn (do in bed), we spend large amounts of time daydreaming and scheming to make more (do it more), and we regularly lie about how much we really take in (how often we do it).

People don't make as much as you think they do. In 1988, less than one-quarter of all American workers earned more than $30,000 a year, and only 5% earned more than $50,000 a year. Half of all full-time, year-around workers earned less than $392 per week ($20,384 per year). Half the men working full time earned under $458 per week, and half the women working full time earned under $320 per week. [17]

While these overall figures may make you feel a little better, you're probably a lot more interested in earnings figures from your occupation and those of your friends and relatives. In this section, you'll find wage and salary information on a wide variety of occupations that has been compiled by the U.S. Government and many private trade groups and research organizations. When you're looking over these statistics, you should remember that:

1. Average wages in metropolitan areas have been 25% higher than in non-metropolitan areas.

2. In terms of regions of the country, wages have been highest in the West, second highest in the Northeast, and lowest in the Midwest and South.

3. Wages paid by large corporations (employing 2500 people or more) have been about 5% higher than those paid by small businesses.

4. The figures provided don't include fringe benefits, which make comparing the actual value of different jobs very difficult.

AN OVERALL LOOK AT A WIDE RANGE OF OCCUPATIONS

The Bureau of Labor Statistics presented the median weekly earnings of salaried workers in a variety of selected occupations in 1985: [18]

Occupation	Weekly earnings
Over $700 per week	
Airplane pilot	$738
Chemical engineer	$723
Lawyer	$719
Over $600 per week	
Aerospace engineer	$691
Purchasing manager	$676
Mechanical engineer	$665
Electrical engineer	$664
Civil engineer	$620
Advertising, PR manager	$627
Economist	$624
Physician	$604
Computer systems analyst	$602

Occupation	Weekly earnings
Over $500 per week	
Rail transportation occupations	$599
Industrial engineer	$598
Securities sales reps.	$593
Chemist	$588
Management analyst	$583
College/university teacher	$582
Financial manager	$581
Pharmacist	$566
Education administrator	$561
Personnel manager	$540
Police supervisor	$534
Telephone installer/repairer	$530
Mechanic supervisor	$520
Data processing equip. repair	$510
Public administration official	$510
Biological scientist	$506
Computer programmer	$502
Over $400 per week	
Millwright	$497
Stationary engineer	$495
Tool and die maker	$491
Aircraft engine mechanic	$491
Medicine/health manager	$490
Educ./vocational counselor	$488
Psychologist	$472
Underwriter	$468
Mail carrier	$466
Public relations specialist	$460
Inspector/compliance officer	$459
Accountant/auditor	$458
Postal clerk	$457
Electrician	$456
Personnel training specialist	$454
Policeman/detective	$452
High school teacher	$439
Crane/tower operator	$438
Firefighter	$436
Registered nurse	$434
Plumber/pipefitter	$431
Editor/reporter	$430
Electrical/electronic technician	$426
Advertising sales rep.	$422
Administrative support super.	$420
Financial records supervisor	$419
Buyer	$416
Insurance sales rep.	$415

Occupation	Weekly earnings
Sheetmetal worker	$415
Elementary teacher	$412
Machinist	$409
Real estate sales rep.	$406
Therapist	$406
Industrial machinery repair	$404
Mechanic/repairer	$400

Over $300 per week

Drafting	$399
Driver-sales worker	$399
Office supervisor	$399
Motor vehicle sales	$393
Science technician	$393
Transportation ticket sales	$392
Librarian	$391
Bus/truck mechanic	$384
Social worker	$376
Welder/cutter	$371
Heavy truck driver	$363
Corrections officer	$352
Brickmason/stonemason	$349
Legal assistant	$347
Photographer	$346
Bus driver	$344
Printing machine operator	$339
Carpenter	$337
Dietitian	$336
Metal/plastic machine operator	$336
Personnel clerk	$323
Production inspector	$321
Dispatcher	$321
Health technician	$319
Radio/TV/appliance sales	$315
Computer operator	$311
Automobile body repairer	$310
Automobile mechanic	$309
Insurance adjuster	$309
Farm manager	$303
Payroll clerk	$302
Telephone operator	$302

Under $300 per week

Stock clerk	$299
Assembler	$298
Butcher	$297
Practical nurse	$294
Shipping/receiving clerk	$287

Occupation	Weekly earnings
Secretary	$279
Data entry keyers	$277
Construction laborer	$276
Other laborer	$273
Light truckdriver	$273
Bookkeeping/accounting clerk	$272
Baker	$267
General office clerk	$267
Billing clerk	$264
Typist	$259
Stock/freight handler	$254
Guards	$248
Janitor	$235
Receptionist	$225
Dental assistant	$224
Bank teller	$219
Retail sales worker	$210
Nursing aide/orderly	$202
Teacher's aide	$196
Cooks	$186
Sewing machine operator	$176

YOUR AVERAGE HOURLY AND WEEKLY WAGE

In 1985, 59% of American workers were paid by the hour. The median hourly wage for men was $7.45, while the median hourly wage for women was $5.26. [19]

The average weekly wage by industry in June, 1985, was: [20]

Industry	Average weekly wage
Manufacturing	$386
Mining	$520
Construction	$464
Transportation	$450
Wholesale trade	$352
Retail trade	$175
Finance/insurance/real estate	$289
Services	$256

YOUR EARNINGS BY OCCUPATIONAL GROUP

The highest paid American men have been those in executive, administrative, and managerial jobs. Perhaps because women continued to encounter some barriers to advancement in corporations, the highest paid women have been those in the professions. On the lowest end of the scale have been men who eked out a living in farming, forestry and fishing and women who did domestic work.

By occupational group, the median 1988 earnings for full-time workers were: [21]

Occupational group	Men's average annual earnings	Women's average annual earnings
Executive, administrative managerial	$35,672	$22,984
Professional specialties	$34,372	$25,636
Technical, sales, administrative support	$25,012	$16,120
Service occupations	$15,496	$10,972
Private household	—	$ 7,956
Farming, forestry, fishing	$12,740	$10,608
Precision production, crafts, repairs	$23,556	$14,404
Machine operators, assemblers, inspectors	$18,616	$12,584
Transportation, material moving	$20,748	$15,236
Handlers, cleaners, helpers, laborers	$15,444	$12,688

WHAT GOVERNMENTS PAY

About 18 million Americans worked for some level of government in 1984, and they made up 20% of the total workforce in the United States, according to the Census Bureau.

Of these 18 million, 2.9 million were federal civilian employees. The average salary for white collar federal workers was $26,186, and the average blue collar salary was $22,054. The following table below shows the average salaries for white and blue collar federal positions employing more than 10,000 people in 1984: [22]

Occupation	Average salary
White collar jobs	
Air traffic controller	$34,000
Clerk-typist	$12,150
Computer operator	$19,444
Computer specialist	$32,183
Computer program analyst	$35,683
Criminal investigator	$35,393
General engineer	$42,482
Civil engineer	$35,479
Mechanical engineer	$34,018
Engineering technician	$24,144
Internal revenue agent	$31,985
Lawyer	$43,995
Nurse	$24,613
Nurses' assistant	$14,521
Secretary	$16,515
Social security claims exam.	$22,918
Blue collar jobs	
Aircraft mechanic	$24,389
Custodian	$15,786
Electrician	$23,562
Electronics mechanic	$24,258
Heavy equipment mechanic	$23,451
Food service worker	$15,629
Janitor	$14,579
Laborer	$15,761
Machinist	$23,908
Maintenance mechanic	$22,558
Motor vehicle operator	$20,189
Pipefitter	$24,657
Sheetmetal mechanic	$23,204
Warehouse worker	$19,321

THE POSTAL SERVICE

The Postal Service reported 744,000 employees in 1985, 586,000 of them full time and 158,000 part time. Average annual compensation, including employee benefits, was $32,727. **[23]**

THE MILITARY

Between 1980 and 1986, according to the Defense Department, the average total compensation for officers rose from $25,000 to $51,500, and the average total compensation for enlisted men jumped from $11,200 to $22,800. Total compensation for members of the armed services included free on-base housing or off-base housing allowances ranging from about $2800 for privates to about $8000 a year for generals. It also included meal allowances of about $100 per month for both officers and enlisted men. [24]

Below is a list of base salaries by rank for the Army and Navy, based on average time in rank, as of October, 1986: [25]

Pay grade	Army rank	Navy rank	Annual base pay
O–10	General	Admiral	$ 68,700
O–9	Lieut. General	Vice-Admiral	$ 68,700
O–8	Major General	Rear Admiral	$ 68,700
O–7	Brig. General	Commodore	$ 60,900
O–6	Colonel	Captain	$ 53,520
O–5	Lieut. Colonel	Commander	$ 42,192
O–4	Major	Lieut. Commander	$ 34,020
O–3	Captain	Lieutenant	$ 26,892
O–2	First Lieutenant	Lieutenant (J.G.)	$ 18,480
O–1	Second Lieutenant	Ensign	$ 14,688
W–4	Chief Warrant	Comm. Warrant	$ 33,786
W–1	Warrant Officer	Warrant Officer	$ 18,480
E–9	Sergeant Major	Master C.P.O.	$ 26,988
E–8	Master Sergeant	Senior C.P.O.	$ 22,476
E–7	Sgt. First Class	Chief Petty Off.	$ 19,572
E–6	Staff Sergeant	Petty Off., 1st	$ 16,068
E–5	Sergeant	Petty Off., 2nd	$ 12,108
E–4	Corporal	Petty Off., 3rd	$ 10,020
E–3	P.F.C.	Seaman	$ 8,940
E–2	Private	Seaman Apprentice	$ 8,592
E–1	Private	Seaman Recruit	$ 7,632

STATE AND LOCAL GOVERNMENT

In 1985, the Census Bureau reported that 13 million people were employed by state and local governments. Nation wide, state government employees earned an average of $23,220 and local government employees received an average annual wage of $22,280.

The range of average pay between states, however, was very great--$18,936 between the highest pay on the state level (Alaska, $36,048) and lowest (Mississippi and Nebraska, $17,112) and $23,700 between the highest pay on the local level (Alaska, $38,532) and the lowest (Mississippi, $14,832). **[26]**

TEACHERS

According to the National Education Association, America's 15,746 public school districts employed over 2,176,000 teachers in 1986. Average salary for teachers across the country was $25,257 a year. While that was close to the national average salary for all workers, it was 20% lower than the average salary for the average college graduate. Compounding the problem of recruiting capable new teachers was the fact that starting salaries for teachers nationwide were 17% lower than the starting salaries of liberal arts graduates in private business and 43% lower than starting salaries of engineering graduates. **[27]**

COLLEGE AND UNIVERSITY PROFESSORS

358,602 people taught in 3,331 accredited colleges and universities in 1985. **[28]** Average pay for full professors was $42,300 at public institutions and $47,000 in private institutions. Fringe benefits added an average $7,000 to $8,000 to the average professor's compensation. **[29]**

WHAT ARE THE BEST PAYING OCCUPATIONS?

Only one-half of one percent of the U.S. population earned more than $280,000 a year in 1984. Their occupations were: **[30]**

Bankers, insurance, real estate	31%
Lawyers, accountants	12%
Doctors, health professionals	2%
Executives, other professionals	43%
Live on investments	11%

In her book *90 Highest Paying Careers for the '80's,* Anita Gates took data from the Bureau of Labor Statistics and professional organizations to compile the following list of the top 10 occupations:

Investment banker	$ 100,000+
Physician	$ 100,000
Osteopathic physician	$ 100,000
Securities trader	$ 60,000–$ 100,000
Securities salesperson	$ 60,000–$ 90,000
Airline pilot	$ 75,000
Dentist	$ 65,900
Financial planner	$ 50,000–$ 55,000
Lawyer	$ 52,000
Optometrist	$ 50,000

WHAT PROFESSIONALS MAKE

Doctors

In 1985, the average physician netted a little more than $100,000 per year, after payment of all expenses. A better look at doctors' incomes, however, is obtained by breaking physicians down into specialities. Even within specialties, doctors who formed personal corporations tended to have higher incomes than physicians who weren't incorporated, as the table below shows: [31]

Specialty	Net income, incorporated	Net income, unincorporated
Neurosurgeons	$ 204,810	N/A
Orthopedic surgeons	$ 173,430	N/A
Plastic surgeons	$ 164,420	$ 125,000
Obstetricians/ gynecologists	$ 132,500	$ 92,140
General surgeons	$ 130,000	$ 89,380
Internists	$ 105,290	$ 76,000
Psychiatrists	$ 90,530	$ 72,500
Pediatricians	$ 86,250	$ 72,500
Family practitioners	$ 83,940	$ 68,280
General practitioners	$ 78,920	$ 63,790

Lawyers

There's a glut of lawyers in the United States, with 682,000 practicing in 1986 and nearly 40,000 new attorneys graduating from law schools each year. A growing number of these graduates are having trouble finding jobs. Many are being forced to take positions with legal clinics that pay beginning lawyers $17,000 to $19,000 a year. [32]

The most prestigious positions for new attorneys are positions with Wall Street law firms, which are paying first year associates as much as $65,000 a year. Partners in these powerful firms earn between $200,000 and $800,000 per year.

Nationwide, in 1985, the American Bar Association reported that first year associates with law firms began at $26,000 a year, and the income of partners averaged $110,000. Lawyers in practice for themselves averaged $61,000.

The salary range for lawyers working for corporations ranged from an average of $29,000 for the first three years, to an average of $91,000 for top level corporate counsels. [33]

Dentists

The average net income for that nation's 126,000 dentists was about $65,460 per year in 1984, according to the American Dental Association. Dental specialists averaged $94,050 in annual net income. [34]

Accountants

The U.S. labor force included over 1 million accountants in 1984, according to the Census Bureau, and job openings in the field are expected to increase 30% by 1995. Financial training has been very important for success in business, and 30% of the chief executives of the nation's major corporations had an accounting background.

About 60% of accountants worked for corporations, and the Bureau of Labor Statistics reported that their average incomes ranged from $20,460 for entry level positions to $58,677 for senior accountants. C.P.A.'s usually commanded 10% more money than accountants who hadn't been certified.

The nation's public accountants averaged slightly higher incomes than than those of corporate accountants.

WHAT TOP EXECUTIVES MAKE

According to a survey by the firm of Towers, Perrin, Forster, and Crosby, the top executives of America's top 100 industrial corporations earned the following in average salary and bonus in 1985:

Chief executive	$869,000
2nd officer	$588,800
3rd highest	$466,400
4th highest	$413,300

Bonuses made up a larger percentage of the compensation of top executives at large corporations. Below is the percentage of base salary paid in bonus to the top five executives of 1,000 large corporations in 1983, as compiled by the Conference Board:

Industry	% of salary
Manufacturing	48%
Retailing	44%
Construction	38%
Insurance	29%
Banking	25%
Utilities	24%

The vast majority of executives worked for smaller corporations—only 1 in 60 corporations in the U.S. had annual revenues of more than $10 million, according to the Commerce Department. Below is the average annual compensation for top executives in smaller corporations, as reported in Inc. Magazine in September, 1986:

Corporate revenue	Chief executive officer	Chief operating officer	Chief financial officer	Chief marketing officer
$10,000,000+	$120,920	$ 76,049	$61,645	$64,082
$5,000,000– $9,900,000	$164,472	$102,124	$72,339	$78,143
$2,500,000– $4,900,000	$104,735	$ 72,538	$53,532	$57,865
$1,000,000– $2,490,000	$ 74,572	$ 54,512	$33,582	$43,920
$500,000– $990,000	$ 45,434	$ 31,706	$25,796	$26,600

The average compensation you'd have received if you sat on the board of directors of a corporation in 1985 was $19,544. One-quarter of board members received over $25,000 per year. [35]

WHAT NEW COLLEGE GRADUATES EARN

A college degree is required for almost all of the top paying occupations listed in this chapter. One way to judge the value of a college degree is to take a look at the list of average starting salaries offered to new graduates in June of 1986. The starting annual salary for graduates in *every single curriculum* was higher than the average salary earned by the average American worker in 1985. [36]

Curriculum	Average offer
Business	
Accounting	$21,216
Management	$19,656
Management information	$22,836
Marketing/distribution	$19,272
Humanities/social sciences	
Humanities	$19,296
Economics	$22,404
Social sciences	$19,980
Engineering	
Aerospace	$27,780
Chemical	$29,256
Civil	$24,012
Electrical	$28,368
Geological	$22,596
Industrial	$27,408
Mechanical	$27,864
Metallurgical	$27,864
Mining	$25,956
Nuclear	$27,696
Petroleum	$33,000
Engineering technology	$26,196
Sciences	
Agricultural sciences	$19,164
Health professions	$20,424
Biological sciences	$19,068
Chemistry	$23,376
Computer science	$26,592
Mathematics	$24,444
Other physical/earth science	$25,200

Every year, the nation's 450 business schools graduate over 60,000 students receiving Masters in Business Administration degrees. In 1984, the average starting salary for these new M.B.A.'s was $28,561. Graduates of the top business schools (Harvard, Wharton, Stanford, etc.) averaged close to $50,000 per year. Starting salaries were also much higher in large cities, with the top of the heap being M.B.A.'s working in New York City (average starting salary $42,032).

DOES EDUCATION PAY?

There's no question that education has been a terrific investment, in a number of ways. First of all, the more education you had, the less likely you were to be unemployed, as demonstrated by these 1986 figures: [37]

Educational attainment	Unemployment rate
Elementary	
Under 5 years	16.8%
5–8 years	17.1%
8 years	15.3%
High school	
1–3 years	20.6%
High school graduate	11.7%
College	
1–3 years	8.1%
4 or more years	3.8%

Education drastically affected how much you earned. Following is a table showing the average yearly income by educational attainment in 1985: [38]

Educational attainment	Average income
No high school diploma	$ 8,316
High school diploma	$12,540
Vocational training	$14,628
Associate degree	$16,152
Bachelor's degree	$22,092
Master's degree	$27,456
Professional degree	$46,452
Doctorate	$39,180

To look at the effect of education another way, below is a table showing the percentage of households with incomes of $35,000 or more and $50,000 or more in 1985, by educational attainment of the head of the household: [39]

Educational attainment	% with income $35,000+	% with income $50,000+
8 years elementary school	8.6%	2.6%
1–3 years high school	14.7%	5.0%
High school graduate	26.7%	10.0%
1–3 years college	35.3%	15.8%
4 years college or more	57.2%	35.9%

WOMEN'S INCOME

The Census Bureau reported that the percentage of American women with some income—from jobs, interest, investments, etc.— soared from 56% in 1960 to 89% in 1985. The major reason was women flooding the employment market—in the same time period, the number of women working full time jumped 64% and the number working part time climbed 87%. In 1987, 56% of all women were in the work force, and they were taking 80% of all new jobs. By 1995, an estimated 80% of all women will be working. [40]

Women have left home to join men at work, but what they've been taking home from those jobs and what they've earned from other sources fell far short of the average income of men. The median income for women in 1987 was $7,612, compared with $17,114 for men. A comparison of income brackets for men and women: [41]

Income	Percent of women	Percent of men
Less than $2,000	17.5%	7.2%
$2,000—$3,999	12.2%	5.4%
$4,000—$5,999	12.3%	6.0%
$6,000—$9,999	16.6%	11.6%
$10,000—$14,999	15.1%	14.0%
$15,000—$24,999	17.0%	22.1%
Over $25,000	9.4%	33.0%

Below is a table of the percentage of women age 15 and over who had the following types of income in 1985: [42]

Type of income	Percent of women
Wages	55.3%
Self-employment	3.8%
Interest	53.5%
Dividends	9.2%
Social Security	19.9%
Public assistance	3.9%
Unemployment or workman's comp	3.7%
Pensions	5.3%
Alimony and child support	3.4%

WHAT WOMEN EARN WORKING

The average income of women with full-time, year-around jobs was 63% of men's income in 1985, compared with 65% of men's in 1955. The median income of full–time women workers was $16,252 compared with a median income of $24,999 for male full time workers. [43]

There were four main reasons for this disparity between men's and women's income. They were:

1. *Women work in lower paying fields.* 15% of men were managers and administrators, compared with 7% of women; 20% of men worked at skilled trades, compared with just 2% of women. On the other hand, 35% of women were clerical workers, compared with 6% of men. [44]

The effects of working in lower paying fields is vividly shown in the table below that compares the average salary of women's top 5 occupations with the average salary of men's top 5 occupations, according to the Bureau of Labor Statistics:

Top 5 women's occupations	Average women's salary	Average men's salary	Top 5 men's occupations
Secretary	$10,622	$29,666	Manager/ Administ.
Bookkeeper	$10,420	$21,290	Manuf. sup.
Manager/ administrator	$13,592	$17,419	Truck driv.

Top 5 women's occupations	Average women's salary	Average men's salary	Top 5 men's occupations
Office clerk	$10,160	$21,135	Wholesale/retail owner
Registered nurse	$14,834	$23,634	Sales/manufact.

2. *Women earned less than men for the same jobs.* After decades of lobbying for equal pay for equal work, women earned 70 cents for every dollar earned by men working in the same field of endeavor in 1986. Female lawyers earned $.63 for every dollar earned by male lawyers, female computer operators earned $.73 for every dollar earned by male computer analysts, and women accountants earned only $.72 for every dollar earned by male accountants. Although federal white collar jobs were split equally between men and women, the average male salary was $30,229 and the average female salary was $18,864. Women fell behind even in female-dominated professions—female secretaries earned 33% less than male secretaries and female teachers earned 18% less than male teachers. [45]

3. *Women moved in and out of the work force much more frequently than men.* In 1986, the starting salary for women in entry-level jobs was 82% of the average starting salary for men. However, 65% of women have had to leave the work force for more than a year because of family responsibilities, compared with just 2% of men. Also, 50% more men than women had been in their jobs more than 10 years. Leaving the work force for long periods of time hampers women's career progress and prevents building seniority. [46]

4. *The female work force was younger than the male work force.* Peak earning years for all workers are between ages 35–54, and nearly 30% more men than women in this age group were employed in 1984. The surge of young women into the work force, however, means that difference will be cut by more than 50% by the year 2000.

Progress in narrowing the long-standing gap between men's and women's income is projected to be very slow. Although education has been touted as the answer, the male-female wage gap has narrowed only slightly with education—grade school graduate women earned 59% of the income of grade school graduate men, while college graduate women earned 67% of the income of college graduate men. The major inroads made by women have been in the professions and in self-employment. But the bottom line is that the most optimistic projection, that of the Rand Corporation, is that by the year 2000, the average woman's income will be 74% of the average man's income.

WOMEN WHO EARN MORE THAN THEIR HUSBANDS

In 1986, the Census Bureau found 50,933,000 married couples in the United States. Both husband and wife worked in 25,428,000 marriages, and of these couples, the wife earned more than her husband in 18%, or 4,577,000. Another 8% of wives earned at least 80% of their husbands' income. [47]

Most of the wives who earned more than their husbands were young—34% were aged 25–34 and 25% were age 35–44. Over half of the women had no children, 43% had attended college, and the overwhelming majority worked as professionals or managers.

Couples in which both husband and wife worked full-time had much higher family incomes, regardless of which spouse earned the most. The median family income of all married couples in 1985 was $31,100 but the median family income of couples who both work full time was $36,431. [48]

Working wives led many of American families into affluence. Below is a table of the percentage of families at all income levels in which the husband and wife were both employed in 1985: [49]

Income	% of families with two paychecks
Under $10,000	20%
$10,000–$15,000	25%
$15,000–$20,000	37%
$20,000–$25,000	46%
$25,000–$30,000	53%
$30,000–$35,000	57%
$35,000–$40,000	61%
$40,000–$45,000	65%
$50,000–$55,000	69%
$60,000–$75,000	69%
Over $75,000	63%

WHAT AMERICANS OWN

The assets of all Americans at the end of 1985 totaled over $15 trillion. Below is a breakdown of those assets: **[50]**

Asset	% of total worth
Physical assets	32.8%
Real estate	21.7%
Household goods	8.3%
Automobiles	2.8%
Financial assets	67.2%
Cash, bank accounts	15.2%
Stocks, bonds, etc.	23.1%
Equity in business	15.9%
Life insurance, pension fund	13.0%

Subtracted from the total assets was $2.37 trillion in debts, including $1.45 trillion in home mortgages. The net worth of all Americans was $12,963,000,000,000.

YOUR NET WORTH

When it came to accumulating assets, there was a tremendous gap between the very wealthy and the rest of Americans. The wealthiest 10% of American families owned: **[51]**

51% of all money deposited in banks

72% of all stock

70% of all bonds

86% of all tax-free bonds

50% of all property

78% of all businesses

This concentration of wealth at the very top makes talking about "average" net worth very misleading. Instead, we'll take a look at "median" net worth—that is, the point where 50% of people had more and 50% had less.

In terms of total net worth, half of American families had a net worth of $24,574 or under in 1984. **[52]**

For most of you, that net worth consisted primarily of the equity in your home. The dramatic effect of home ownership is graphically demonstrated by the following two statistics: **[53]**

Median net worth of home owning families $50,125

Median net worth of families who rent $ 15

That's right—half of all families who rented had a net worth of under $15, about the cost of a good haircut.

As you'd expect, net worth increased with income (families who earned over $50,000 year had a median net worth of $130,851) and age (people age 55–64 had a median net worth of $55,587). One factor that may surprise you is the dramatic effect graduating from college had on accumulating wealth—the net worth of college graduates was almost three times as great as the average net worth of all other Americans, even those with 1–3 years of college. **[54]**

YOUR FINANCIAL ASSETS

While your net worth is interesting, you tend to be more concerned with your financial assets—how much money you have in checking accounts, savings accounts, money market funds, mutual funds, stocks, bonds, etc.

In 1984, half of all American families had under $3,500 in financial assets. One in eight families had absolutely no financial assets, and another 27% had less than $1,000. On the other end of the spectrum, 10% of American families had financial assets of more than $50,000 and 5% had assets over $100,000. **[55]**

The most common type of asset you had was a checking account—nearly four out of every five American families had one. Below is a table showing the percentage of American families who had various types of assets, and the median value of those assets: **[56]**

Type of asset	% of people owning	Median dollar value for those who own that asset
Checking account	79%	$ 500
Savings account	62%	$ 1,151
Money market account	14%	$ 8,900
Certificates of deposit	20%	$ 10,000

Type of asset	% of people owning	Median dollar value for those who own that asset
IRA or Keogh account	28%	$ 4,000
Savings bonds	21%	$ 325
Stocks	19%	$ 4,076
Bonds	3%	$ 10,000
Tax-free bonds	3%	$ 14,125
Investment property	19%	$ 35,000
Business	14%	$ 50,000

The percentage of people owning all assets rose dramatically with income, as the table below shows: [57]

Income	% of people with			
	Checking account	Savings account	Stocks	Business
Under $ 10,000	53%	39%	5%	5%
$ 10,000–$ 19,000	77%	59%	13%	8%
$ 20,000–$ 29,000	88%	72%	20%	16%
$ 30,000–$ 49,999	94%	78%	31%	21%
Over $ 50,000	97%	72%	51%	37%

Of the 19% of all Americans who owned stock, only a small portion traded actively, or, in other words, "played the market." Only 27% of current shareholders bought or sold stock in the last 12 months. [58]

WOMEN'S SAVINGS AND INVESTMENTS

As women's income rose, so did the percentage of women who owned substantial financial assets. Increasingly, women became not only savers, but investors. Between 1980 and 1984, according to the New York Stock Exchange, the number of new women shareholders outnumbered new men shareholders 3 to 2, and the number of women owning stock rose 44%. The average portfolio for women was $4,100, compared with $7,400 for men.

The following table shows the percentage of women who had the following types of assets: [59]

Type of asset	Percent of women
Checking account	85%
Regular savings account	67%
Certificates of deposit	24%
IRA accounts	21%
Money market accounts	21%
U.S. savings bonds	19%
Stocks	15%
Gold/precious metals	8%
Mutual funds	7%
Tax-free municipal bonds	3%
Coins/stamps/other collectibles	3%
Corporate bonds	2%
Keogh accounts	1%
Treasury bills	1%

WHAT THE VERY RICH OWN

In 1982, 1,965,100 Americans owned gross assets totaling $500,000 or more—that was about 8 out of every 1,000 of you. When debts and mortgages were subtracted, 13% of these people had net worths of under $250,000, 22% were worth between $250,000 and $500,000, 44% were worth between one half million and one million dollars, and a lucky 21% (or 17 out of every 10,000 Americans) were millionaires. [60]

A 1987 study of these "upper affluent" Americans commissioned by CIGNA Individual Financial Services Company revealed that 42% of those with annual incomes of $100,000 or more or assets of $500,000 or more were either self-employed or owned their own businesses. The average age of these wealthy Americans was 48. 83% of them were married, and 56% had spouses who worked.

According to the Internal Revenue Service, in 1982 the average millionaire had a net worth of $2,750,000. [61]

Their assets consisted of:

Real estate	24%
Corporate stock	31%
Business assets	10%
Cash	6%
Bonds	8%
Notes and mortgages	5%
Other	16%

If you were looking for millionaires, you have been most likely to find them in Florida. Other states with the top number of millionaires per 1,000 population were, in order, Connecticut, California, Arizona, Hawaii, Vermont, Nevada, Kansas, Iowa, Illinois, Oregon, New York, and Texas.

U.S.A. Today analyzed Forbes Magazine's 1986 list of the 400 richest people in American and discovered that 174 of the listees primarily built their own fortunes, 168 primarily inherited their money, and the rest combined the two. The list included 323 men and 77 women. Ten people on the list were high school dropouts, 33 were high school graduates only, 266 had college diplomas, and 71 had post-graduate degrees. Half of the very rich made their money in financial operations or media enterprises, 20% in oil and gas, 11% in New York City real estate, and the rest in retailing, agriculture, or high-tech.

WHO IS POOR?

In 1985, 14.0% of the American population was listed by the Bureau of the Census as "poor", or living below the poverty line. The poverty line was defined as incomes below: [62]

$10,989   for a family of four
$ 8,573   for a family of three
$ 7,231   for a couple
$ 5,593   for a single person

The percentage of Americans living in poverty was below the 22.4% recorded in 1960, but was 29% higher than the 1973 poverty rate. The 14.4% of Americans living in poverty translated into 33,700,000 people. The percentage of single people who were poor was 21.5%, the percentage of poor families was 12.6%, and the percentage of children who were living in poverty was 20.1%. [63]

One interesting way to look at poverty is that developed by American Demographics Magazine, which exploded a number of myths about poverty and the poor by comparing the myths with the facts of poverty in 1984, as described below:

Myth #1: Most poor people are black and most black people are poor.

68.2% of poor people were white. The number of whites in poverty was growing 61% faster than the number of blacks. Two-thirds of blacks were not poor.

Myth #2:   Most poor people live in inner-city ghettos.

14% of poor people lived in ghettos.

26% lived in the suburbs and 39% in rural areas.

Myth #3:   Poor people live off government welfare.

40% of poor people didn't get a cent in government money in 1984. Only 43% got food stamps, 33% received welfare payments, and only 26% lived in subsidized housing. 30% of non-poor Americans received some sort of cash government benefits.

Myth #4:   People are poor because they refuse to work.

Over half of poor families had at least 1 worker, and 20% had two workers. A family of four with one person working 40 hours per week at the minimum wage and one person working 20 hours per week at the minimum wage did not earn enough to get above the poverty level.

Myth #5:   Welfare payments are a large part of the federal deficit.

Welfare expenditures in 1984 totaled less than 1% of federal spending. They were only 4% of the defense budget and 5% of payments for social security.

Myth #6:   The poor remain poor.

The University of Michigan's Panel Study of Income Dynamics showed that while 25% of American families were poor for one or more years over a 10 year period, only 2.6% were poor for 8 or more years of that decade.

WHY THE REST OF YOU AREN'T RICHER

Americans increasingly became borrowers rather than savers. By the end of 1985, the Federal Reserve Board found that you were spending an average of 19.2% of your after-tax income on monthly payments for charge-card accounts, automobile loans, and other forms of installment credit other than home mortgages. That was up from 14% of your after tax income just a year before.

At the same time, the percentage of after-tax income that you saved plummeted to just 1.9%, down from over 6% in 1984 and 11.5% in 1977.

YOUR TOTAL INSTALLMENT DEBT

According to the Federal Reserve Board, of all U.S. families in 1983, 59% had debts other than their home mortgages. By family income, the percentage of Americans in debt and the average debt owed were:

Family income	% in debt	Average owed
Under $10,000	39%	$ 3,205
$10,000–$19,999	61%	$ 3,723
$20,000–$29,999	73%	$ 4,725
$30,000–$39,999	78%	$ 5,687
$40,000–$49,999	78%	$ 7,432
$50,000 or more	73%	$15,629

YOUR CREDIT CARDS

By the end of 1987, almost 1 billion credit cards were in the hands of over 100 million Americans, an average of nearly 10 cards per person for the 81% of adult Americans who had credit cards.

The percentage of Americans who had various types of cards in 1987, by family income, was: [64]

Credit card	$50,000 & over	$35,000–$49,999	$25,000–$34,999	$15,000–$24,999	Under $15,000
Had cards	98%	93%	91%	78%	58%
Retail cards	81%	79%	74%	63%	43%
Sears	63%	61%	56%	36%	29%
JC Penny	46%	47%	41%	30%	22%
Montgomery Ward	19%	20%	19%	15%	8%

Credit card	$50,000 & over	$35,000–$49,999	$25,000–$34,999	$15,000 $24,999	Under $15,000
Bank cards	94%	81%	73%	50%	36%
Visa	77%	66%	52%	37%	29%
Mastercard	65%	47%	46%	31%	19%
Gasoline cards	54%	40%	33%	20%	19%
Telephone cards	49%	39%	27%	19%	14%
Third party cards	39%	16%	14%	13%	4%
Am. Express Green	26%	11%	9%	9%	2%
Am. Express Gold	14%	5%	3%	3%	1%
Diner's Club	3%	2%	1%	1%	—
Carte Blanche	1%	.5	.5%	1%	1%
Discover	17%	12%	10%	6%	8%
Airline cards	8%	3%	2%	2%	1%
Car rental cards	9%	1%	2%	2%	1%

On the average, Americans have charged over $200 billion in purchases on their credit cards every year, an average of over $2,000 per person, according to studies done by the Bankcard Holders of America. Only about a third of you who used bank cards—Visa and Mastercard—paid off all of your balance every month. Below is a table showing how much Americans owed on each bank card after making their monthly payment:

Amount owned	% of card holders
Over $500	38%
$250–$500	15%
$100–$250	8%
$1 –$100	8%
Paid in full	31%

The people who charged the most on their credit cards were those with high incomes and those with a college education. People with a family income of over $50,000 charged an average of $4,100 a year, twice the average of those with incomes from $35,000 to $50,000. The average college graduate charged $391 a month on his or her credit cards, compared with $159 a month for people with some college and just $83 a month for high school graduates. [65]

WHO GETS TOO FAR INTO DEBT?

Between 1982 and 1985, according to the Federal Reserve Board, consumer debt increased an average of $5 billion per month, while after-tax income posted little gain. The result was that the percentage of people who were unable to meet their credit card payments jumped from about 1% to 2.25%. In 1985, 300,000 individuals declared bankruptcy, a 50% increase from 1975.

One in five Americans worried a great deal about his or her debt, and 14% were actually in trouble, spending over 25% of their take home pay on installment bills. Maybe that's why 11% of parents admitted to taking money out of their kids' piggy banks to meet bills.

YOUR OTHER INSTALLMENT LOANS

Consumer installment debt includes bank cash lines and other unsecured personal loans, home equity loans (second mortgages), and automobile loans. The average amount borrowed for these loans in 1984, according to the Federal Reserve Board, was:

Unsecured personal loans	$ 1,996
Home equity loans	$16,606
Automobile loans	$ 9,654

Automobile loans accounted for an increasing proportion of consumer debt. As the cost of new cars soared, the average term of automobile loans increased. In 1970, just 5% of auto loans were for periods over 36 months. In 1985, that figure was 62%, and the average auto loan period was 51 months.

WHAT YOU HAVE LEFT IN YOUR POCKET

A Federal Reserve Board survey showed that the average adult walked around with $104 in his pocket or her pocketbook in 1986.

WHAT YOU SPEND

Since 1888, the Bureau of Labor Statistics has been periodically conducting the Consumer Expenditure Survey, a comprehensive look at how you spend your money. The most recent survey, conducted in 1984, showed that the average household spent $21,788 a year. That figure was 88% of pre-tax household income, up from a spending level of 76% of pre-tax income in 1972–1973.

The reason for the jump was that inflation outstripped personal income in that decade. So most of you dipped into your savings to maintain the same standard of living. That's why the way you spent your money changed little in that decade. Housing and transportation consumed 51% of your expenditures (up from 47% in 1972–3) and food ate up 16% (down from 18% in 1972–73).

The most important factor in determining how much you spent was how much you made. Below is a table of average expenditures for 5 different income levels, from the poorest 20% of Americans to the richest 20%. As you can see, the poorest families spent more than they made, forcing them to rely on borrowing, charity, gifts, or public assistance.

	Poorest 20%	Second 20%	Third 20%	Fourth 20%	Richest 20%
Pre-tax income	$ 3,577	$10,828	$19,297	$30,370	$58,639
Total expenditures (excluding taxes)	$11,347	$13,864	$18,981	$25,525	$40,935
Food	$ 2,130	$ 2,448	$ 3,119	$ 3,843	$ 5,371
Away from home	381	666	998	1,420	2,034
Alcoholic beverages	166	209	277	347	519
Housing	3,916	4,447	5,866	7,367	11,570
Mortgage/rent	2,219	2,449	3,296	4,171	6,588
Heat/utilities	1,114	1,340	1,618	1,821	2,454
Household operations	155	185	244	388	712
Furniture/equipment	428	473	708	987	1,817
Clothing/laundry	612	670	988	1,272	2,503
Transportation	1,948	2,759	4,002	5,297	8,270
Health care	571	842	902	919	1,293
Insurance/pensions	435	704	1,505	2,951	5,378
Other (entertainment, personal care, etc.)	1,566	1,784	2,324	3,528	6,029
Taxes	39	661	1,797	3,144	7,682

Now, let's take a look at the same expenditures as a percentage of total expenditures, by major spending categories: **[66]**

	Poorest 20%	Second 20%	Third 20%	Fourth 20%	Richest 20%
Food	19%	18%	16%	15%	13%
Housing	35%	32%	31%	29%	28%
Clothing/laundry	5%	5%	5%	5%	6%
Transportation	17%	20%	21%	21%	20%
Health care	5%	6%	5%	4%	3%
Insurance/pensions	4%	5%	8%	12%	13%
Other	14%	13%	12%	14%	15%
Alcoholic beverages	1%	1%	2%	2%	2%

These figures show that lower income Americans spent a much "higher portion of their money (54%) on food and shelter than did highest income Americans (41%). Wealthy Americans put most of the difference into retirement plans and insurance, which gave them the ability to maintain their standards of living when crises occurred and allowed them a comfortable life style in their later years.

HOW MUCH YOU CAN SPEND ON 'THE GOOD LIFE'

What really matters to most of us is not how much money we make, but how much we have left over for "fun" after we take care of taxes, mortgage, food, clothing, utilities, car payments, and the other "necessities" of life. Because a lot of corporations are interested in who has money left over after all the important bills are paid, the Bureau of the Census and the Conference Board have done a comprehensive study of what they call "discretionary income."

What they found was that only 31% of American households had any discretionary income at all. Those 31% of households, however, accounted for 55% of all the income earned in the U.S. Following is a table showing how many of you had money left over for the good life, and the average amount you could spend: **[67]**

Household income	% of Americans with discretionary income	Average amount available
Under $15,000	5.0%	$ 1,940
$15,000–$19,999	15.3%	$ 2,874
$20,000–$24,999	27.4%	$ 3,402
$25,000–$29,999	45.9%	$ 3,684
$30,000–$34,999	66.5%	$ 4,829
$35,000–$39,999	79.2%	$ 6,303
$40,000–$49,999	92.3%	$ 8,563
$50,000–$74,999	99.6%	$15,841
$75,000 or more	100.0%	$33,888

WHO'S INSURED?

According to a 1985 survey by Money Magazine, 94% of Americans had some kind of insurance. By type, the percentage of insured people was: [68]

Type of insurance	% insured
Health insurance	85%
Life insurance	82%
Homeowners/renters insurance	81%
Disability insurance	30%
Mortgage insurance	26%
Excess liability (umbrella)	8%

About 30% of Americans had $50,000 or more in life insurance. By income, the average amount of life insurance you had was:

Household income	Average amount of life insurance
$50,000+	$154,300
$35,000–$50,000	$ 94,600
$25,000–$35,000	$ 70,800
$15,000–$25,000	$ 44,300
Under $15,000	$ 35,500

What are your chances of collecting on insurance and how much will you receive? According to research conducted by *U.S.A. Today* in 1985, the average American would file an auto theft claim once in every 25 years, but the average claim yielded only $448. One out of a hundred people files a claim for fire damage each year and receives $4,500. Once every 5 years, Americans receive $4,000–$6,000 for damage and injuries in an auto accident. 1% of Americans file a flood damage claim every year and receive an average $7,379. Your chances of filing a claim for hurricane damage are 1 in 7 years if you live in South Florida, 1 in 15 years if you live on the Gulf Coast, and 1 in 50 years if you live in the Northeast.

YOUR CHARITABLE CONTRIBUTIONS

Americans are very generous people. According to the American Association of Fund Raising Counsel, $79.8 billion—83% of it by individuals—was donated to over 300,000 charitable organizations in 1985. A little under half of this money (47%) was given to religious organizations, 14% went to hospitals, another 14% to colleges and other educational institutions, 11% went to social service groups, and the rest to the arts and humanities, civic/public organizations, and other groups.

Individual contributions averaged about 2% of personal income. More than half of Americans gave away less than 1% of their income, but over 25% gave more than 3%. Middle-aged people gave the most money, as the table below shows:

Age	Average contribution
Under 30	$390
30–34	$500
35–49	$910
50–64	$890
65 and over	$405

People who regularly attended church donated about three times as much money as people who didn't attend church. And the 83 million Americans who volunteered some of their time for non-profit work donated 38% more money that Americans who didn't serve as volunteers.

HOW YOU PAY
FOR WHAT YOU BUY

A 1984 survey by the Federal Reserve Board showed that most Americans walked around with a checkbook rather than a wad of bills. 83% of American families had checking accounts, and the average family paid for 57% of its purchases by check. Cash was used in 36% of transactions. Although 62% of American families used credit cards, they charged only 6% of their expenditures.

Check usage was highest for families with incomes over $50,000 (72% of expenditures) and lowest for families with incomes under $10,000 (44% of expenditures).

The average family wrote 16 checks a month. About 1 in 9 families had a second checking account, on which they wrote an average of 9 more checks a month.

YOUR FEDERAL INCOME TAX

In 1985, the Internal Revenue Service received 101,700,000 individual income tax returns showing $2.3 trillion dollars in adjusted gross income earned by Americans. Taxes paid on that income amounted to $329 billion, 14.17% of the adjusted gross income.

Of all returns filed in 1985: [69]

Adjusted gross income	% of returns	% owing no tax	% of income paid in tax
Under $5,000	16.4%	77.1%	2.7%
$5,000–$9,999	16.2%	27.3%	4.1%
$10,000–$14,999	13.7%	5.5%	7.8%
$15,000–$19,999	11.4%	2.4%	8.4%
$20,000–$29,999	16.1%	1.1%	10.8%
$30,000–$39,999	11.5%	.8%	12.7%
$40,000–$49,999	6.6%	.4%	13.9%
$50,000–$74,999	5.5%	.2%	16.8%
$75,000–$99,999	1.2%	.2%	20.3%
$100,000–$199,999	.9%	.4%	25.2%
$200,000 or more	.3%	.4%	35.0%

39,497 taxpayers had adjusted gross incomes of over one half million dollars and 19,106 had adjusted gross incomes of over one million dollars. Just 36 lucky people who reported million dollar plus incomes paid no federal income taxes.

YOUR TAX FORM

Of all filers, almost two-thirds (65%) used the "long form", form 1040 in 1986. 19% used the short form 1040A and 17% used the short form 1040EZ.

Of those who filed from 1040, 65% hired a tax preparer to do their return. 23% of those who filed form 1040A hired a professional, and only 4% of those filing form 1040EZ used a tax preparer. **[70]**

YOUR MARITAL STATUS AND YOUR TAXES

47% of the returns in 1985 were married couples filing jointly. A little over half of those returns (52%) listed at least some wages earned by both husband and wife. Below is a table showing the comparative taxes at certain incomes between a single person with no dependents and a married couple with two dependents: **[71]**

Income	Tax paid by single person	Tax paid by married couple
$ 5,000	$ 177	0
$ 10,000	$ 888	$ 132
$ 20,000	$ 2,845	$ 1,682
$ 25,000	$ 4,125	$ 2,566
$ 35,000	$ 6,916	$ 4,916
$ 50,000	$ 12,067	$ 9,086
$ 75,000	$ 22,195	$ 17,649

YOUR DEDUCTIONS

39,857,181 Americans, 39.1% of filers, itemized deductions on their 1985 tax returns. Those deductions totaled $401 billion–$73 billion more than the total federal income taxes paid. By income, the average deductions in major categories were: **[72]**

	ADJUSTED GROSS INCOME					
	$10,000 to $19,999	$20,000 to $29,999	$30,000 to $39,999	$40,000 to $49,999	$50,000 to $99,999	$100,000 or more
% of returns itemizing	23.9%	52.0%	78.0%	89.7%	95.4%	98.1%
Average deductions	$6,107	$6,864	$8,293	$10,857	$14,936	$24,293
Average interest	$2,806	$3,420	$4,121	$5,234	$8,302	$18,576
Average taxes paid	$1,441	$1,991	$2,696	$3,484	$5,158	$17,638
Average contributions	$805	$804	$891	$1,105	$1,175	$9,972
Average medical expenses	$2,117	$1,554	$1,639	$1,727	$3,234	$4,310

HOW LONG YOU WORK TO PAY YOUR TAXES

The Tax Foundation calculated that in 1986, you had to work an average of 121 days to pay your federal, state, and local taxes. That is, if all your wages went to pay taxes, May 1 would have been your "Tax Freedom Day," when you started putting money in your pocket. That meant you were a little better off now than you were 5 years ago, when Tax Freedom Day was May 4. But we all can look back in envy to 1930, when all taxes were paid off by February 13.

Another way to look at how long you have to work to pay your taxes is to break down your eight hour work day. In 1986, you had to work 1 hour, 43 minutes to pay your federal taxes and 55 minutes to pay your state and local taxes.

WHAT DO THE RICH PAY IN TAXES?

With all the talk of tax shelters and other tax avoidance schemes, it's easy to assume that the rich pay very little in taxes. The truth is that in 1985, Americans with an adjusted gross income of $50,000 per year or more made up just 8% of all taxpayers. However, this 8% paid 48% of all taxes collected by the I.R.S. The 26% of Americans who had adjusted gross incomes of $30,000 or more paid 76% of all taxes. [73]

WHEN YOU FILE YOUR TAX RETURN

I.R.S. records show that the percentage of taxpayers who filed by the following dates in 1985 were: [74]

January 31	2% filed
February 28	27% filed
March 31	54% filed
April 15	92% filed
Requested extension	4%
Filed late	4%

YOUR TAX REFUND

About two-thirds of tax payers receive refunds in 1985, with the average refund being a little over $800. [75]

YOUR TOTAL TAX BURDEN

In 1985, the average American tax payer paid a total of $6,947 in taxes, 22.5% of his or her income. [76] The tax burden consisted of: [77]

Federal income tax	$4,675	13.2% of income
Social security tax	$1,894	5.6% of income
State income and sales	$1,330	3.8% of income
Local property taxes	$ 814	2.3% of income

YOUR STATE AND LOCAL TAXES

In 1984, state governments collected $832 for every man, woman and child in the country. The five states with the highest per capita taxes were: [78]

Alaska	$3,787
Wyoming	$1,563
Minnesota	$1,220
Hawaii	$1,203
Delaware	$1,161
Wisconsin	$1,074

The five lowest tax burdens were:

Tennessee	$531
Florida	$644
Arkansas	$657
Mississippi	$670
Alabama	$677

On the average, a family of four living in a U.S. city paid 8% of their income in state and local taxes. The most heavily taxed city dwellers in the country were the residents of Newark, New Jersey, who paid about 17% of their income in state and local levies in 1985. The cities in which the tax burden was highest for a family of four earning $25,000 per year were: [79]

Newark, NJ	17.0%
Bridgeport, CT	16.7%
Detroit	12.3%
Philadelphia	12.3%
Wilmington, DE	12.1%
Milwaukee	11.6%
Baltimore	11.5%
Boston	11.5%
Portland, OR	11.1%
New York City	9.8%

WHO GOOFS?

About 10 million Americans made some sort of mistake on their federal tax returns in 1985. Half the mistakes were math errors, of which the number one boo—boo was copying the wrong figures from the tax tables. The other 50% of the mistakes included failing to sign the return, forgetting to enclose a check, and mis-writing social security numbers. [80]

WHO CHEATS?

The Internal Revenue Service estimated that tax cheating by individuals cost the government at least $75 billion in 1985. That total broke down to:

Taxes on unreported income	$ 52.2 billion
Uncollected balances due	$ 6.8 billion
Overstate personal deductions	$ 6.6 billion
Overstated business expenses	$ 6.2 billion
Taxes owed by non-filers	$ 2.9 billion

In anonymous surveys, about 4 in 10 Americans admitted cheating on their taxes. The most common types of cheating were: [81]

Exaggerated expenses or deductions	32%
Did not file return	28%
Did not report all income	21%
Counted too many dependents	18%

Those most willing to cheat on their taxes were the young and the rich. A public opinion survey sponsored by Merit cigarettes found that 50% of those aged 18–34 considered it easy to cheat on taxes, compared with 41% of those 35–49 and 31% of those 50 and older. 47% of people earning over $25,000 considered cheating easy, compared with 36% of those earning less than $15,000.

WHO GETS AUDITED?

The I.R.S. audited a little under 2% of all returns in 1984. Most likely to be audited are those earning over $50,000 per year—8.9% of people in that bracket were audited. [82]

HOW THE GOVERNMENT SPENT YOUR TAX MONEY

In fiscal year 1986, the average worker paid $6,867 in federal taxes. The government spent your money as follows: [83]

Activity	Worker's share	% of total
Income security*	$2,150	31.32%
National defense	$1,797	26.17%
Interest, national debt	$ 965	14.05%
Health	$ 705	10.27%
Education, social service	$ 207	3.02%
Transportation	$ 183	2.67%
Veterans programs	$ 180	2.62%
Agriculture	$ 175	2.55%
International affairs	$ 116	1.69%
Natural resources	$ 87	1.27%
Science, technology	$ 60	.87%
Community development	$ 54	.78%
Law enforcement	$ 46	.67%
Administrative costs	$ 42	.61%
Assistance to states	$ 42	.61%
Energy	$ 30	.44%
Other	$ 28	.39%

* Includes social security, welfare, and unemployment compensation

In 1984, state governments spent an average of $1,537 per capita, according to the Census Bureau. Major per capita expenditures were: [84]

Education	$493
Public welfare	$266
Highways	$122
Health and hospitals	$106
Corrections	$ 33
Natural resources	$ 25
Police protection	$ 13
Housing	$ 6

According to the U.S. Census Bureau, American cities in 1985 spent the following per resident: [85]

$85.71 for police protection

$77.93 for education

$77.20 for general administration

$59.36 for highways

$51.78 for sewers

$46.34 for fire protection

$39.28 for public welfare

$34.76 for housing and community development

$34.17 for hospitals

$34.03 for parks and recreation

$26.24 for trash collection and street cleaning

CHAPTER THREE NOTES

1. U.S. Bureau of the Census, Current Population Reports
2. U.S. Bureau of the Census, Current Population Reports
3. U.S. Bureau of the Census, Current Population Reports
4. U.S. Bureau of the Census, Current Population Reports
5. U.S. Bureau of the Census, Current Population Reports
6. U.S. Bureau of the Census, Current Population Reports
7. U.S. Bureau of the Census, Current Population Reports
8. U.S. Bureau of the Census, Current Population Reports
9. U.S. Bureau of the Census, Current Population Reports
10. U.S. Bureau of the Census, Economic Characteristics of Households in the United States
11. U.S. Bureau of the Census, Current Population Reports
12. U.S. Bureau of the Census, Current Population Reports
13. U.S. Bureau of the Census, Current Population Reports
14. U.S. Bureau of the Census, Current Population Reports
15. U.S. Bureau of the Census, Current Population Reports
16. U.S. Bureau of the Census, Current Population Reports
17. U.S. Bureau of Labor Statistics, Employment and Earnings
18. Monthly Labor Review, September, 1986
19. U.S. Bureau of Labor Statistics, unpublished data

20. U.S. Bureau of Labor Statistics, Employment and Earnings
21. U.S. Bureau of the Census, Current Population Reports
22. U.S. Office of Personnel Management, Occupations of Federal White Collar and Blue Collar Workers
23. U.S. Postal Service, Annual Report of the Postmaster General
24. U.S. Department of Defense, Office of the Controller
25. U.S. Department of Defense, Office of the Controller
26. U.S. Bureau of the Census, Public Employment
27. National Education Association, Estimates of School Statistics
28. U.S. Department of Education, Faculty, Salaries, Tenure, and Benefits
29. American Association of University Professors
30. Federal Reserve Board
31. American Medical Association
32. U.S. Bureau of Labor Statistics, Employment and Earnings
33. U.S. Bureau of Labor Statistics
34. American Dental Association, 1987 Dental Statistics Handbook
35. The Conference Board
36. College Placement Council, Inc., A Study of Beginning Offers
37. U.S. Bureau of Labor Statistics, Handbook of Labor Statistics
38. U.S. Bureau of the Census, Current Population Reports
39. U.S. Bureau of the Census, Current Population Reports
40. U.S. Bureau of the Census, Current Population Reports
41. U.S. Bureau of the Census, Current Population Reports
42. U.S. Bureau of the Census, Current Population Reports
43. U.S. Bureau of the Census, Current Population Reports
44. U.S. Bureau of Labor Statistics, Employment and Earnings
45. U.S. Bureau of the Census, Current Population Reports
46. U.S. Bureau of the Census, Current Population Reports
47. U.S. Bureau of the Census, Current Population Reports
48. U.S. Bureau of the Census, Current Population Reports
49. U.S. Bureau of the Census, Current Population Reports
50. Federal Reserve Board
51. Federal Reserve Board
52. Federal Reserve Board
53. Federal Reserve Board
54. Federal Reserve Board
55. Federal Reserve Board
56. Federal Reserve Board
57. Federal Reserve Board
58. New York Stock Exchange
59. Money Magazine, "Americans and Their Money, 1987"
60. U.S. Internal Revenue Service, Statistics of Income
61. U.S. Internal Revenue Service, Statistics of Income
62. U.S. Bureau of the Census, Current Population Reports
63. U.S. Bureau of the Census, Current Population Reports
64. Money Magazine, "Americans and Their Money, 1987"
65. Bankcard Holders of America
66. U.S. Bureau of Labor Statistics, 1984 Consumer Expenditure Survey
67. U.S. Bureau of the Census and The Conference Board, A Marketer's Guide to Discretionary Income
68. Money Magazine, "Americans and Their Money-1985"

69. U.S. Internal Revenue Service, Statistics of Income
70. U.S. Internal Revenue Service, Statistics of Income
71. U.S. Department of the Treasury, unpublished data
72. U.S. Internal Revenue Service, Statistics of Income
73. U.S. Internal Revenue Service, Statistics of Income
74. U.S. Internal Revenue Service, Statistics of Income
75. U.S. Internal Revenue Service, Statistics of Income
76. U.S. Internal Revenue Service, Statistics of Income
77. U.S. Bureau of the Census, Current Population Reports
78. U.S. Bureau of the Census, State Government Finances
79. Government of the District of Columbia, Tax Burdens in Washington, D.C. Compared With Those in the Largest City in Each of the 50 States
80. U.S. Internal Revenue Service
81. Compiled by USA Today
82. U.S. Internal Revenue Service, Statistics of Income
83. Government Accounting Office
84. U.S. Bureau of the Census, State Government Finances
85. U.S. Bureau of the Census, City Government Finances

CHAPTER
FOUR

YOUR JOB

WHO WORKS IN AMERICA?

Of the 184,490,000 adult Americans in 1987, 121,602,000 (65.9%) were in the labor force, either working or looking for work. 62,888,000 Americans (34.1%) were not in the labor force.

Why weren't these 63 million people looking for work? 90.5% said they didn't want a job. Of these, 48% were keeping house and 13% had a disability that prevented them from working. About 10% said they would like to find a job, but weren't looking, most of them because they were either in school or were discouraged about their prospects for finding work.

Who was in the labor force? In 1987, 76.2% of adult men and 56.0% of adult women. For women, that was a whopping 49% increase from the 37.7% of women who were in the labor force in 1960. [1]

WORK AND AGE

Below is a table of the percentage of labor force participation by sex and age in 1987: [2]

Age	Male	Female
16-17	45.6%	44.6%
18-19	67.4%	62.2%
20-24	85.2%	73.0%
25-34	94.6%	72.4%

Age	Male	Female
35-44	94.6%	74.5%
45-54	90.7%	67.1%
55-64	67.6%	42.7%
65+	16.3%	7.4%

WORK AND RACE

By sex and race, the most industrious of Americans were Hispanic males of Mexican origin, 82.7 of whom were in the labor force. By far the lowest participation rate was that of Hispanic females of Puerto Rican origin, just 39.3% of whom worked. Below is a table of labor force participation for adults age 20 and over by sex and race in 1987: [3]

	Male	Female
White	76.8%	55.7%
Black	71.1%	58.0%
Hispanic	81.0%	52.0%
Mexican origin	82.7%	52.4%
Puerto Rican origin	72.3%	39.3%
Cuban origin	77.6%	55.8%

MEN AND WORK

Between 1950 and 1987, the percentage of men in the labor force dropped a rather substantial 10.1%, from 86.4% to 76.2%. The reason was that greatly increased social security disability payments, social security retirement payments, and private pensions allowed many American men to retire early. Between 1960 and 1987, the percentage of married men age 45-64 in the labor force dropped from 93.0% to 82.4%, and the percentage of married men age 65 and over plummeted from 37.1% to just 17.5%.

The Americans most likely to be working or looking for work were married men under age 45, less than 4% of whom were out of the labor force. In contrast, nearly 15% of single men under 45 and 11% of divorced or widowed men under 45 were not in the market for a job. [4]

WOMEN AND WORK

Perhaps the most dramatic demographic change in America since 1960 has been the flood of women into the work force. In 1965,

52% of American women were keeping house full time and only 37% were in the labor force. In 1987, 34% of American women (the majority of whom were over age 45) kept house full time and 56% were working or looking for work.

The most important component of this change was the number of young women who continued to work after marriage. Historically, marriage for women meant leaving the work force. The origin of the word "spinster" was that all women who worked as spinsters in textile mills in the 19th century were unmarried. In 1890, only 3% of married women in America worked, and as late as 1940, 64% of the female work force was either single, widowed, or divorced. [5]

Between 1960 and 1987, however, the percentage of married women age 25-34 who worked went from 27.7% to 68.6%, and the Bureau of Labor Statistics has projected that figure will reach 80% by 1995. In 1987, women's labor force participation by marital status was: [6]

| | PERCENTAGE OF WOMEN WORKING | | |
Age	Married	Single	Divorced or widowed
20-24	65.7%	74.8%	67.7%
25-34	68.6%	81.8%	76.3%
35-44	72.7%	81.5%	81.5%
45-64	52.7%	65.2%	62.6%
65+	7.4%	10.9%	8.2%

Even having young children didn't prevent an increasing percentage of women from returning to the labor force. The percentage of married women with children under age 6 who worked climbed from 18.6% in 1960 to 53.8% in 1986. In 1986, labor force participation for women by marital status and age of children was: [7]

| | PERCENTAGE OF WOMEN WORKING | | |
	Married	Separated	Divorced or widowed
No children under 18	48.2%	60.4%	72.1%
Children 6–17	68.4%	70.6%	84.7%
Children under 6	53.8%	57.4%	73.8%

The number of children a woman had had an affect on labor force participation, particularly if the age range of those children was wide, as shown in the table below: [8]

Children	% of women working
1 under 18	61.1%
2 under 18	56.4%
3 under 18	49.0%
4 under 18	46.1%
5 under 18	34.3%
6 or more under 18	31.3%
All under 6	50.0%
Some under 6, some 6–17	46.4%
All 6–17	63.3%

According to the Bureau of Labor Statistics, a majority of working women with children under age 18 were in the labor force for economic reasons, as the table below shows:

Husband's income	% of wives working
Unemployed	60.7%
Under $20,000	54.6%
$20,000–$25,000	49.1%
$25,000–$35,000	46.2%
$35,000–$50,000	38.9%
Over $50,000	29.3%

The other extremely significant factor that increased women's participation in the labor force in 1985 was education: [9]

Education	% of women working
Elementary	
Less than 5 years	15.7%
5 to 7 years	22.2%
8 years	21.5%
High school	
1–3 years	40.7%
4 years	58.8%

Education	% of women working
College	
1 to 3 years	66.8%
4 years	71.1%
5 or more years	77.5%

PROBLEMS WOMEN FACE IN THE WORK FORCE

A study of 57,000 women and 56,000 men by the Urban Institute's Program of Policy Research on Women and Families revealed that 72% of America's working women had dropped out of the work force for six months or more, compared with 26% of men. The difference was due entirely to family responsibilities—54% of working women had taken at least a six month hiatus from work to take care of a home or child, compared with just 1% of men. As a result, professional women had spent an average of 23% of their potential work years away from the work force, compared with just 2% of potential work years for professional men.

Time away from the work force meant difficulty getting a job when coming back. A survey of the Fortune 500 companies by the Economic Policy Council showed that only 38% of women got their old job back after they had a baby. 43% got comparable jobs, 6% got some job, and 13% couldn't find any job at all.

Aside from pregnancy and family responsibilities, the other major problem that has forced women to leave jobs more frequently than men has been sexual harassment. A survey of 694,000 female government workers revealed that 42% had experienced some form of sexual harassment on the job and 10% had suffered serious career consequences (poor evaluation, demotion, etc.) because of their refusals to have sex with a supervisor.

WHO'S UNEMPLOYED?

In 1985, 7,425,000 Americans who were actively looking for work were unemployed, and they represented 6.1% of the work force. The reasons they were unemployed were, by sex: [10]

Reason	% of men	% of women
Lost previous job	60.8%	36.7%
Left previous job voluntarily	9.0%	12.3%
Re-entering job market	19.5%	36.4%
Entering job market for first time	10.7%	14.6%

Who was unemployed?

	Unemployment rate
White males	5.4%
White females	5.2%
Black males	12.7%
Black females	13.2%
White married men	4.0%
Black married men	8.0%
Women maintaining families	10.4%
White teen-agers	14.4%
Black teen-agers	34.7%

During 1987, the average unemployed worker was without a job for about 16 weeks, although 65% of job seekers found a new job in less than 2.5 months. The percent of Americans without work for the following periods were: [11]

4 weeks or less	43.7%
5–10 weeks	21.6%
11–14 weeks	7.9%
15–26 weeks	12.7%
Over 26 weeks	14.0%

Workers were most likely to be unemployed in agriculture and construction, and least likely to be out of work if their occupations were in finance, insurance, real estate, transportation, utilities, and government. 39% of those unemployed were eligible for unemployment insurance benefits, and those eligible collected for an average of 14 weeks. [12]

YOUR OCCUPATION

Sometime in the middle of the 1970's, America's workforce, for the first time in history, become predominantly white collar. In 1985, 55% of employed Americans held managerial, professional, technical, sales, or administrative support positions. Just 28% held blue collar jobs (down from 35% in 1970). An additional 13% held service positions, and 4% of Americans were employed in agriculture. [13]

The Bureau of Labor Statistics has classified occupations into six major summary groups:

1. Managerial and professional specialty occupations (white collar)

2. Technical, sales, and administrative support occupations (white collar)

3. Precision production, draft and repair occupations (blue collar)

4. Operators, fabricators, and laborers (blue collar)

5. Service occupations

6. Farming, forestry, and fishing

By sex and race, the occupational categories of working Americans in 1986 were: [14]

	PERCENTAGE OF EMPLOYED			
Occupation	White males	White females	Black males	Black females
Managerial/ professional	29.2%	28.1%	14.7%	18.8%
Technical, sales administrative	20.4%	45.2%	17.2%	35.5%
Precision prod., repair	21.3%	2.4%	17.3%	3.1%
Operators, fabricators	18.1%	8.5%	32.2%	13.6%
Service	7.1%	14.9%	15.1%	28.9%
Farming	4.2%	1.1%	3.5%	.1%

Below is a more specific look at the percentage of females and percentage of blacks in various occupations in 1985: **[15]**

Occupation	% female	% black
TOTAL WORKFORCE	44.1%	9.8%
MANAGERIAL/PROFESSIONAL	42.7%	5.9%
Executive, administrative, managerial	35.6%	5.3%
Public officials	40.7%	8.7%
Financial managers	35.7%	3.1%
Personnel/labor relations	44.5%	5.6%
Purchasing	24.4%	4.0%
Marketing/P.R.	23.8%	3.9%
Education administrators	48.2%	9.4%
Managers, medicine/health	59.2%	8.1%
Accountants/auditors	44.1%	5.9%
Professional specialties	49.1%	6.3%
Architects	11.3%	3.1%
Engineers	6.7%	2.6%
Mathematics/computer science	31.1%	5.6%
Physicians	17.2%	3.7%
Dentists	6.5%	2.6%
Registered nurses	95.1%	6.8%
College teachers	35.2%	3.9%
Elementary teachers	84.0%	11.1%
High school teachers	54.0%	7.6%
Counselors	55.9%	11.7%
Librarians	87.0%	6.6%
Social scientists	42.6%	5.2%
Social workers	66.7%	17.6%
Lawyers and judges	18.2%	3.3%
Writers/artists/entertainers	44.5%	4.7%
	64.7%	8.4%
TECHNICAL, SALES, ADMINISTRATIVE SUPPORT		
Technicians	47.2%	8.9%
Practical nurses	96.9%	19.6%
Science technicians	33.3%	8.1%
Computer programmers	34.3%	6.4%
Sales occupations	48.1%	5.5%
Supervisors/owners	31.2%	3.8%
Sales reps, financial	41.0%	3.4%
Sales reps, commodities	17.5%	2.3%
Retail sales workers	68.5%	8.2%

Occupation	% female	% black
Administrative support/ clerical	80.2%	10.4%
Supervisors	53.4%	12.3%
Computer operators	66.5%	13.5%
Secretaries	98.4%	6.5%
Receptionists	97.6%	6.7%
File clerks	81.0%	17.4%
Bookkeepers	91.5%	4.7%
SERVICE OCCUPATIONS	60.6%	17.5%
Private household	96.2%	28.9%
Police/detectives	10.1%	13.5%
Firefighters	1.4%	5.9%
Guards	20.9%	20.2%
Waiters/waitresses	84.0%	4.7%
Cooks	51.3%	18.4%
Nursing aides/orderlies	89.9%	29.2%
Janitors/cleaners	29.4%	24.0%
Hairdressers/cosmetologists	89.9%	8.2%
PRECISION PRODUCTION/REPAIR	8.4%	7.1%
Mechanics/repairers	3.4%	6.9%
Construction trades	2.0%	6.7%
Precision production	22.3%	8.1%
OPERATORS/LABORERS	25.4%	14.7%
Machine operators/assemblers	40.3%	14.3%
Transportation/moving	8.3%	13.7%
Helpers/laborers/cleaners	16.7%	16.3%
FARMING/FORESTRY/FISHING	15.9%	7.8%

The Bureau of Labor Statistics also reported on employment by average educational level achieved by workers in each occupation in 1986: [16]

	AVERAGE YEARS OF SCHOOLING			
Occupation	Non-H.S. graduate	H.S. grad.	1–3 year college	4+ years college
Professional/ managerial	2.9%	16.7%	18.6%	61.8%
Technical sales/ administrative	6.6%	47.0%	26.2%	20.1%
Service	29.4%	47.5%	16.5%	6.6%

Occupation	Non-H.S. graduate	H.S. grad.	1–3 year college	4+ years college
Production/craft/ repair	23.1%	52.1%	18.3%	6.4%
Operators/fabricators/ laborers	34.2%	49.6%	12.5%	3.6%
Farming	36.1%	43.3%	12.1%	8.5%

YOUR JOB, NOW AND IN THE FUTURE

What does the American economy make best? A very good answer would be, jobs. Despite all we read and hear about unemployment and plant closings, a record 107,150,000 Americans were at work in 1985. Even more impressive is the U.S. Bureau of Labor Statistics' projection of a 25% increase in jobs by 1995—a rate double the projected 13% population growth.

More good news. You don't have to have be a computer whiz or have a college degree to take advantage of this employment boom. While "high-tech" job growth has been faster than average, they will still only make up 1 out of every 25 new jobs created by 1995. Six of the top seven occupations with the largest projected employment growth do not require a college education: building custodian, cashier, secretary, general office clerk, sales clerk, and waiter and waitress.

40 OCCUPATIONS WITH LARGEST JOB GROWTH BY 1995

Occupation	Number of new jobs
Building custodian	779,000
Cashiers	744,000
Secretaries	719,000
General office clerks	696,000
Salesclerks	685,000
Registered nurses	642,000
Waiters and waitresses	562,000
Elementary teachers	511,000
Truckdrivers	425,000
Nursing aides and orderlies	423,000
Sales reps, technical	386,000

Occupation	Number of new jobs
Accountants and auditors	344,000
Automotive mechanics	324,000
Supervisors, blue collar workers	319,000
Kitchen helpers	305,000
Guards and doorkeepers	300,000
Fast food restaurant workers	297,000
Store managers	292,000
Carpenters	247,000
Electrical technicians	222,000
Licensed practical nurses	220,000
Computer systems analysts	217,000
Electrical engineers	209,000
Computer programmers	205,000
General maintenance repair	193,000
Helpers, trade	190,000
Receptionists	189,000
Electricians	173,000
Physicians	163,000
Clerical supervisors	162,000
Computer operators	160,000
Sales reps, non-technical	160,000
Lawyers	159,000
Stock clerks	156,000
Typists	155,000
Delivery and route workers	153,000
Bookkeepers	152,000
Cooks. restaurant	149,000
Bank tellers	142,000
Cooks, short order	141,000

20 FASTEST GROWING OCCUPATIONS BY 1995

Occupation	Percent growth
Computer service technicians	96.8%
Legal assistants	94.3%
Computer systems analysts	85.3%
Computer programmers	76.9%
Computer operators	75.8%
Office machine repairers	71.7%
Physical therapy assistants	67.8%
Electrical engineers	65.3%
Civil engineering technicians	63.9%
Peripheral EDP equipment operators	63.5%
Insurance clerks, medical	62.2%
Electrical technicians	60.7%
Occupational therapists	59.8%

Occupation	Percent growth
Surveyor helpers	58.6%
Credit clerks	54.1%
Physical therapists	53.6%
Employment interviewers	52.5%
Mechanical engineers	52.1%
Mechanical engineering technicians	51.6%
Compression and injection mold machine operators, plastics	50.3%

20 MOST RAPIDLY DECLINING OCCUPATIONS BY 1995

Occupation	Percent decline
Railroad conductor	−32.0%
Shoemaking machine operatives	−30.2%
Aircraft structure assemblers	−21.0%
Central telephone office operators	−20.0%
Taxi drivers	−18.9%
Postal clerks	−17.9%
Private household workers	−16.9%
Farm laborers	−15.9%
College faculty	−15.0%
Roustabouts	−14.4%
Postmasters and mail superintendents	−13.8%
Rotary drill operator helpers	−11.6%
Graduate assistants	−11.2%
Data entry operators	−10.6%
Railroad brake operators	− 9.8%
Fallers and buckers	− 8.7%
Stenographers	− 7.4%
Typesetters and compositors	− 7.3%
Farm owners and tenants	− 7.3%
Butchers and meatcutters	− 6.3%

WHERE YOU WORK

Of all working Americans in 1984: [17]

39% worked for companies with over 500 employees

35% worked for companies with less than 500 employees

15% worked for governments

8% were self-employed

3% worked in agriculture

The following 10 companies had the most employees in 1986: [18]

1.	General Motors Corp.	811,000
2.	Sears Roebuck & Co.	408,800
3.	IBM	405,500
4.	Ford Motor Co.	369,300
5.	AT & T	337,000
6.	General Electric Co.	304,000
7.	ITT Corp.	232,000
8.	K-mart Corp.	210,000
9.	United Technologies Corp.	184,000
10.	GTE Corp.	183,000

WHO WORKS FOR STATE AND LOCAL GOVERNMENTS?

In 1985, state and local governments employed 13,669,000 people, 12.7% of working Americans. 3,984,000 worked for state governments and 9,685,000 for local governments. The services these workers provided were: [19]

Education	52%
Teachers	29%
Health and hospitals	10%
Police protection	5%
Highways	4%
Public welfare	3%
Fire protection	2%
Financial administration	2%

WHO WORKS FOR THE FEDERAL GOVERNMENT?

In 1985, the Federal Government employed 3,020,531 people in civilian jobs. Of these people, 35.9% worked for the Department of Defense, 24.8% worked for the Postal Service, and 8.2% worked for the Veterans Administration. Only 12% of Federal Government employees worked in Washington, D.C. [20]

About one-quarter of all Federal workers (excluding the Postal Service) were either black or Hispanic in 1984. However, minorities made up only 6.5% of all executive jobs and 10.6% of jobs at the highest civil service grades (GS 13–15). [21]

WHO'S IN THE U.S. MILITARY?

At the end of 1986, 2,167,000 Americans were serving on active military duty, and these jobs made up about 2% of all U.S. employment. In addition, the military services employed 1,085,000 civilians. [22]

The breakdown of our forces by service and rank was: [23]

Service	Strength	% officers
Army	781,000	14.1%
Navy	581,000	12.4%
Marines	199,000	10.1%
Air Force	606,000	18.0%

About 90% of both officers and enlisted personnel were men, and about 10% were women. The ratio of women to men in the armed services fell from 70 to 1 in 1962 to 10 to 1 in 1985. 18% of military men and 27% of military women were black. 4% of military men and 3% of military women were of Hispanic origin. [24]

73% of U.S. military personnel were stationed in this country. Only 9 of every 100 members of the armed services had combat-related jobs, down from 40 of every 100 in World War II. 30% of today's military personnel have been re-enlisting. [25]

In 1985, 504,000 men and women were discharged from military service, 10% other than honorably. Of every 1,000,000 military personnel on active duty in 1985, 17,000 were absent without leave on an average day and 6,000 were listed as deserters. [26]

In 1985, 2,390,000 Americans served in national guard and military reserve units. [27]

WHO HOLDS ELECTIVE OFFICE?

Of the 434 members of the House of Representatives in the 99th Congress (1985–1987), 22 were women and 20 were black. 84% were married. 52% were under 50 years old, while 19 members were age 70 or older. [28]

The 100 member Senate in the 99th Congress included 2 women and no blacks. 31 senators were age 60 and over, while only 4 were under age 40. [29]

The occupations of the members of the House and Senate before their elections were: [30]

Agriculture	31
Business or banking	174
Education	47
Journalism	29
Law	251
Public service or politics	76

In January, 1986, there were 6,384 black elected officials on the state and local levels, compared with just 1,472 in 1970. [31] In 1986, there were 17,291 women holding state and local elective office. In 1985, women held 15% of all state legislature seats, up from 8% in 1975. In 1985, on the state government level, there were 11 female Secretaries of State, 11 State Treasurers, 5 Lieutenant Governors, 2 Attorneys-General, and 2 Governors. [32]

YOUR UNION MEMBERSHIP

Between 1980 and 1985, the number of full-time workers who belonged to labor unions fell from 20,968,000 to 16,996,000. The percentage of all workers who belonged to unions was 18.8% of the full-time labor force, a steep drop from 28.9% in 1975. [33]

The table below shows the percentage of workers who belonged to unions by industry in 1985: **[34]**

Industry	% union members
Mining	17.3%
Construction	22.3%
Manufacturing	24.8%
Transportation/utilities	37.0%
Wholesale/retail trade	7.2%
Finance/insurance/real estate	2.9%
Services	6.6%
Government	35.8%
Agriculture	2.6%

Overall, union members averaged $419 per week in wages, compared with $315 a week for non-union members. The largest wage difference was in the construction industry, where union workers averaged $556 a week and non-union workers averaged $315 a week. Smallest difference was in mining, where union members earned $507 a week and non-union members made $499. **[35]**

Perhaps because of the drop in union memberships, unions were much less aggressive in the 1980's. During the 1970's, the annual average number of strikes was 289; between 1981–1985, the average annual number of strikes was just 88. Union contracts negotiated between 1974 and 1981 contained average first year wage hikes of 9.7%; average wage hikes contained in contracts negotiated between 1982 and 1985 averaged just 3.2%. **[36]**

WHO'S KILLED OR HURT ON THE JOB?

In 1986, 10,700 people were killed on the job. Although more people were killed in construction accidents (2,100), the most lethal industries by percentage of deaths were agriculture (52 deaths per 100,000 workers) and mining (50 deaths per 100,000 workers). **[37]**

In 1986, 1,800,000 workers suffered disabling injuries, 60,000 of which resulted in permanent disabilities. **[38]**

In 1984, 8.0% of workers were hurt on the job. 46% of injuries were serious enough for the employee to miss one or more days of work. The U.S. Department of Labor reported that, by industry, the percentage of injured workers was: [39]

Industry	% of workers injured annually
Construction	15.5%
Manufacturing	10.6%
Transportation/utilities	8.8%
Retail	7.4%
Services	5.2%

In terms of specific jobs, the most dangerous place to work in 1985 was meatpacking plants, where 30.4% of all workers suffered job related injuries or illnesses. Next on the list was sawmills, where 28.8% of workers were injured or became ill. [40]

HOW YOU GET TO WORK

According National Decision System, the majority of America's 110,000,000 commuters spent less than an hour traveling to and from work in 1986. 34.5% got to work in less than 15 minutes, 37.0% in 15 to 29 minutes, and only 28.5% had a trip that was 30 minutes or longer one way. However, according to the American Association of State Highway and Transportation Officials, most Americans faced rather heavy traffic on the way. The average commuter was on the road 21 minutes to travel 10 miles, an average speed of just 28 miles per hour.

The daily commute was more of a grind for those in big cities and for those with higher incomes—men earning over $50,000 lived twice as far from work as those who earned under $20,000. Average annual commuting cost in 1985 was $1,355. [41]

According to the Hertz Corporation, the way you got to work in 1985 was:

Type of transportation	% of people
Drive alone	64.5%
Car pool	19.8%
Public transportation	6.3%
Walk	5.5%
Other	3.8%

Car-pooling increased greatly in the last 15 years. The percentage of people taking public transportation fell 50%. The reason may have been lack of service—on the average, people who took public transportation to work traveled 2.5 times as long as those who drove.

YOUR BUSINESS TRAVEL

According to studies by the U.S. Travel Data Center, about 30% of all working Americans, 33,000,000 people, traveled on business or to attend a convention in 1986. The total number of business trips was 141 million, 21% of all trips of 100 miles or more away from home. 59% of travelers took one or two trips during the year, while 10% took 10 or more trips. 90% of trips involved overnight stays, with the average duration being 4.2 days. The average trip was 1,180 miles round trip.

Half of all business travelers made the trip in personal automobiles, while 42% flew to their destinations. 72% stayed in hotels or motels, and 20% rented a car. Only 5% of business trips were out of the country. Women made up one−third of all business travelers, up from just 1% in 1970.

American companies spent $61 billion on business travel, 29% of all travel spending in the U.S. Business travelers accounted for 48% of all airline trips and up to 80% of the revenue of the major hotel and car rental chains.

40% of business travelers loved to travel and another 25% could take it or leave it. A third, however, hated traveling and 5% had emotional problems stemming from their business trips.

HOW LONG YOU'VE HELD YOUR JOB

In 1985, 44.7% of employed men and 54.7% of employed women women had been in their jobs 4 years or less. Only 13% of men and 6% of women had worked for the same company for twenty years or more. [42]

The major factor in how long you'd held your job was your age. Following is a table showing the duration of employment of male and female workers by age: [43]

Men	5 years or less	5–10 years	10–20 years	Over 20 years
18–24	94.9%	4.8%	.3%	—
25–34	69.5%	22.6%	7.9%	—
35–44	42.0%	22.7%	30.3%	6.0%
45–54	28.8%	17.1%	24.1%	30.0%
55–64	24.0%	15.2%	20.2%	40.6%
65+	29.4%	11.8%	15.8%	43.0%
Women				
18–24	97.1%	2.8%	.1%	—
25–34	78.2%	17.5%	4.3%	—
35–44	65.2%	20.0%	12.5%	2.3%
45–54	46.7%	23.7%	20.8%	8.8%
55–64	33.8%	23.4%	24.7%	18.1%
65+	38.0%	17.0%	23.4%	21.6%

About 1 in 5 women and 1 in 6 men leave their jobs in the course of a typical year. The main reasons they leave are: [44]

Got another job	34%
Layoff	11%
Fired	9%
Moving to another city	8%
Retirement	8%
Other	30%

As you'd expect, the greatest job turnover has been among the youngest and lowest paid workers, as the table below shows: [45]

Age	% LEAVING JOB DURING 1 YEAR		
	Earn under $5.00/hr.	Earn $5.00–$10.00/hr.	Earn over $10.00/hr.
Men			
18–24	40.7%	26.1%	*
25–44	25.3%	11.9%	11.3%
45–59	13.5%	6.3%	6.2%
Women			
18–24	33.8%	23.5%	*
25–44	18.8%	11.3%	*
45–59	9.4%	6.2%	*

* Under 2% of 18–24 year old men and under 2% of all women earn more than $10.00/hr., too small a sample to measure in this survey.

WHEN PEOPLE ARE FIRED

In survey of executives at Fortune 1,000 companies, 37% of executives reported that they most commonly fired employees late on Friday afternoon. 48% had no set time, and 8% preferred handing out pink slips on Monday morning. [46]

A word of warning to smokers: 5 studies by pre-employment testing counselor Steven Stanard have revealed that smokers have been fired up to three times as often as non-smokers.

GETTING YOUR NEXT JOB

About 1 in 6 men and 1 in 4 women find themselves having to change occupations to find another job after they've quit or been fired. [47]

When they apply for another job, people sometimes give in to the temptation to cheat on their resumes. According to a survey by Robert Half International,

> 17% of applicants lied about their job qualifications
>
> 9% of applicants lied about their salary history
>
> 7% of applicants lied about their education
>
> 5% of applicants lied about all three above

The Stanton Corporation, which has administered honesty tests to nearly 3 million job seekers, found that 18–31% were untrustworthy in the 1980's, compared with only 10–12% in the 1960's. They also found that women were more honest than men, minorities were more honest than whites, and honesty increased with age. Most honest applicants (88%) were those applying for busboy, dishwasher and waiter jobs. Least honest were sales people (61%) and engineers (66%).

When you look for a new job, you're also increasingly likely to be forced to submit to drug testing. A survey done by the consulting firm of Noel Dunivant & Associates in 1986 found that 18% of the *Fortune* 500 companies currently required drug testing, and another 20% were planning to institute drug testing sometime in the next two years. The overwhelming majority of these companies rejected all job applicants testing positive for drug use.

Finally, another note to smokers: in a 1987 survey of 1,000 executives, Accountemps found that 73% of executives wouldn't hire a candidate who smoked during a job interview.

HOW MANAGERS GOT THEIR JOBS

When 300 managers at companies of all sizes were asked how they obtained their present job, they replied as follows: [48]

Friends, relatives	24%
Placement firm	23%
Want ad	21%
Source at company	13%
Sent unsolicited letter/resume	7%
Cold call	7%
Other	5%

TEMPORARY WORK

In 1986, about 700,000 people worked for temporary help firms on temporary job assignments on the average workday. Of all temporary assignments: [49]

16% lasted less than 1 week

33% lasted 1 to 2 weeks

20% lasted 3 to 4 weeks

15% lasted 1 to 2 months

11% lasted 3 to 6 months

5% lasted more than 6 months

WHO WORKS FULL TIME?

Of all employed men and women in 1985: [50]

	Male	Female
% who worked full time (35+ hours per week)	86.1%	67.9%
% who worked full time, year around (50+ weeks)	66.8%	49.2%

	Male	Female
% who worked full time, 26–50 weeks per year	11.2%	10.3%
% who worked full time, less than 26 weeks per year	8.1%	8.4%

You may be surprised that only 2 out of 3 working men and 1 out of 2 working women had jobs that kept them busy full time, all year around. About 1 in 5 men and women were in occupations that provided full time employment only some of the year.

Of those who worked full time, over one-third of men and one-fifth of women worked an average of 41 hours a week or more. Men who worked over 40 hours a week accumulated so much overtime that they lifted the average work week for full time male workers to 44.3 hours per week. The average work week for female full time workers was 40.7 hours.

SETTING YOUR OWN SCHEDULE

In 1986 about 30% of U.S. companies offered "flextime," which allowed workers to set their own hours, within pre-defined limits. About 16% of corporations allowed two people to share one full time job. The overwhelming proportion of workers who took advantage of job-sharing were mothers of small children. Only 4.1% of full time workers had a four day work week. [51]

Partly as a result of more flexible time schedules, the time-honored "9 to 5" workday has become a relic. A survey by Adia Personnel Services found that only 4% of U.S. employees reported to work at 9:00 a.m.

YOUR PART TIME EMPLOYMENT

Of people in the labor force in 1985, 13.9% of men and 32.1% of women worked part time, or less than 35 hours per week. 4.7% of men and 12.7% of women worked part time all year, while 9.2% of men and 19.4% of women worked part time part of the year. [52]

About one quarter of the female part time workers and 40% of the male part time workers were trying to find full time jobs. The remaining 75% of women and 60% of men worked only part time because they want to. An overwhelming 85% of part time workers put in between 15 and 34 hours per week, while 15% worked less than 15 hours. [53]

WORK AND OLDER AMERICANS

In 1985, 15.2% of men age 65 and older and 6.8% of women age 65 and older were in the labor force. The participation rate for men was less than half the participation rate for men 65 or older in 1960. The labor force participation rate for women 65 and older was virtually unchanged during that same 25 year period. [54]

WHEN WE STAY HOME FROM WORK

The Bureau of Labor Statistics found that on the average work day in 1985, 5.4% of employees were not at work. 58% of those absent were on vacation, 23% were ill, 2% couldn't get to work because of bad weather, 1% were on strike, and 16% had other reasons. [55]

The National Center For Health Statistics reported that in 1985, on the average, male workers missed 4 days a year because of sickness, while women missed 5. [56] Over half of all workers, however, admitted to calling in sick when they were perfectly healthy. [57]

One common reason was that they were "under the weather"— in a literal sense. A study of 6,000 employees of the Department of the Interior revealed that between 3 and 10% of employees called in sick if it rained during the morning rush hour. [58]

GOOFING OFF ON THE JOB

A survey of 120 medium-size and large corporations by Accountemps, a temporary service agency, showed that the average worker spent 34% of his or her day goofing off. That added up to about 4 months of extra paid vacation a year.

Even top executives had a lot of wasted time, according to a detailed time study by the consulting firm of Booz, Allen and Hamilton. The firm compiled detailed diaries of the time spent on various activities during the work days of 90,000 executives. They discovered that the average executive wasted 25% of his or her time every day. The rest of the day was spent as follows:

> 46%   Meetings
>
> 13%   Reading
>
> 8%   Editing
>
> 8%   Analysis and problem solving

A significant part of that wasted time was evidently spent on the phone. Accountemps found that the average employee made or received 3 personal calls a day, spending about 5 minutes on each call. That added up to 62 hours—or over 1 and 1/2 weeks—of work per year.

The personnel firm of Robert Half International found that employees wasted an average of 2 and 1/2 weeks a year getting ready to start and stop work. They spent 35.8 hours a year starting in the morning, 13.9 hours getting ready for lunch, 15.5 hours getting started after lunch, and 27.7 hours getting ready to go home at night. Annual cost to employers was $170 billion.

The management consulting firm Priority Management found that the average U.S. office worker had 36 hours of work piled on his or her desk.

MORE ABOUT THOSE BUSINESS MEETINGS

A survey by MIS, a computer information magazine, revealed there were 12 million business meetings on the average day in North America. Executives spent an average of 16 hours a week in meetings, or a total of 21 weeks a year. Executives earning $45,000 a year were paid $18,500 to sit in meetings. Those surveyed considered a third of meetings to be totally unnecessary and felt that 30% of the time in necessary meetings was wasted.

WHO TAKES WORK HOME

To make up for that time lost in meetings, 52% of Americans took work home at least occasionally. 13% took home work nearly every day, and another 17% carried a briefcase home at least twice a week. [59]

YOUR EMPLOYEE BENEFITS

The slogan "money isn't everything" is an important consideration when evaluating your present or prospective job. In 1985, the average private employer spent $8,200 per year per employee for benefits. By industry, the cost of benefits as a percentage of payroll by industry was: [60]

Industry	% paid in benefits
Services	27.0%
Wholesale/retail	31.2%
Manufacturing	37.9%
Transportation	39.7%
Government	40.8%

The percentage of employees receiving the following benefits in firms employing at least 100 people in 1985 were: [61]

Benefit	Professional & adminis.	Technical & clerical	Production
Paid			
Holidays	99%	100%	96%
Vacations	99%	100%	99%
Personal leave	33%	37%	18%
Lunch period	3%	3%	17%
Rest time	58%	70%	81%
Sick leave	93%	92%	41%
Funeral leave	87%	89%	87%
Military leave	77%	75%	63%
Sickness & accident insurance	30%	38%	70%
Long term disability insurance	64%	61%	32%
Health insurance	97%	96%	96%
Life insurance	97%	96%	96%
Pension	81%	82%	78%
Severance pay	61%	57%	31%

Benefit	Professional & adminis.	Technical & clerical	Production
Profit sharing, savings & stock plans			
Profit sharing	19%	22%	16%
Savings	39%	33%	17%
Stock bonus	1%	1%	—
Stock purchase	3%	3%	2%
Stock ownership	29%	28%	19%
Miscellaneous benefits			
Employee discounts	54%	61%	56%
Gifts	14%	14%	14%
In-house infirmary	47%	38%	50%
Recreational facilities	37%	31%	32%
Subsidized meals	28%	26%	13%
Educational assistance	86%	84%	68%
Parking	82%	77%	92%

About 20% of newly hired employees become eligible for vacation after three months of employment, about 40% after six months, and the remaining 40% after one year. At almost every company, the amount of vacation was also tied to length of employment: [62]

PERCENTAGE OF EMPLOYEES RECEIVING:

Length of employment	1 week	2 weeks	3 weeks	4 weeks	5 weeks	6 weeks
1 year	30%	63%	5%	1%	—	—
3 years	4%	81%	13%	1%	—	—
5 years	1%	47%	49%	2%	—	—
10 years	1%	6%	69%	22%	1%	—
15 years	1%	3%	28%	63%	4%	1%
20 years	—	3%	9%	57%	28%	1%
25 years	—	3%	8%	30%	50%	7%
30+ years	—	3%	8%	29%	44%	14%

92% of technical, administrative, professional and clerical employees received paid sick leave in 1985, as did 41% of production workers. Following is a table of the average number of paid sick days, by years of employment: [63]

Length of employment	Average paid sick days
1 year	17.0
3 years	21.8
5 years	28.5
10 years	37.6
15 years	43.0
20 years	45.9
25 years	47.9
30 years	48.4

The soaring costs of health care has made health insurance perhaps the most vital of all employee benefits. The table below shows what percentage of employees were insured for the following types of medical care, according to the National Center for Health Statistics:

Type of medical care	% of employees
Hospital room and board	100%
Hospital services	100%
Outpatient care	100%
Extended care facilities	62%
Home health care	46%
Surgical	100%
Physician visits—in hospital	100%
Physician visits—office	96%
Diagnostic X-ray and laboratory	100%
Prescription drugs-non-hospital	98%
Private-duty nursing	96%
Mental health care	99%
Dental	77%
Vision	30%

59% of employers paid the total cost of health insurance for an employee in 1986, and 41% required an employee contribution. 41% of companies paid the total cost of coverage for an employee's family, with 56% requiring employee contributions. [64]

YOUR PENSION

About four out of every five full-time workers at firms employing more than 100 people were covered by some sort of pension plan in 1983. Below is a table showing the average annual income a pensioner would receive from his or her pension and social security by the length of service at retirement and the salary earned in the final year before retirement:

Final annual earnings	YEARS OF SERVICE AT RETIREMENT			
	10 years	20 years	30 years	40 years
$15,000	$ 8,085	$ 9,600	$11,070	$12,270
$20,000	$ 9,800	$11,600	$13,300	$14,680
$25,000	$10,600	$12,775	$14,825	$16,425
$30,000	$11,250	$13,890	$16,290	$18,120
$35,000	$11,830	$14,945	$17,719	$19,740
$40,000	$12,360	$15,920	$19,080	$21,320

WHO FARMS?

At the end of 1985, according to the Department of Agriculture, about 5.3 million Americans lived on 2,285,000 farms. Farmers and their families accounted for just 2.2% of the American population, down from 30.2% in 1930 and 8.7% in 1960. About 400,000 people left farms during 1985, the biggest decrease in a decade. [65]

Individuals and families owned 86.9% of the nation's farms, and 68.9% of the nation's farm lands. The average size of the family farm was 416 acres, which produced average gross sales of $58,800. The average net income of farm families was $18,925, 24% less than the average income of non−farm families. [66]

Farms owned by corporations accounted for just 2.2% of all farms, but 13.6% of all farm lands and 23.9% of all farm sales. Corporate farms averaged sales of $527,000, nearly 10 times the average sales of family farms. [67]

In 1986, 21.3% of farms were considered to be in financial trouble because they carried debt greater than 40% of their assets. 8.6% of farmers were on the verge of bankruptcy, with debt greater than 70% of their net assets. [68]

WHO WORKS FOR THEMSELVES?

9.3 million Americans were self-employed in 1984, an increase of 24% since 1974. The increase was largely due to a 50% rise in the number of self-employed women. Women owned 23% of the nation's small businesses. The leading types of businesses owned by women were direct sales operations, real estate firms, and beauty shops. [69]

WHO WORKS AT HOME?

A 1986 national poll conducted by Electronic Services Unlimited, a research firm, produced an estimate of 13 to 14 million people who worked out of their own homes. About 6 million of these people were self-employed.

Surprisingly, the percentage of people working at home who were linked to their offices by computer has been very small. The Yankee Group, a Boston marketing research firm, estimated only 30,000 people worked at home full time while linked to the office by computer. Another 100,000 people were linked informally to the office, doing primarily part-time or overtime work.

THE EDUCATION OF CEO'S

A survey of the chief executive officers of 220 of *Fortune* Magazine's top 1,000 corporations revealed that 52.9% held bachelor's degrees, and 5.9% had just a high school diploma. 18.3% were M.B.A.'s, 10.1% were lawyers, 7.3% had other master's degrees, and 5.9% held doctorates. [70]

One striking characteristic of the school days of top executives was sports participation. In a 1987 survey conducted by Paul R. Ray & Company, 95% of top executives polled had played sports in school, while just 43% had been members of the National Honor Society.

LIFE AT THE TOP

A 1986 survey by *Chief Executive Magazine* revealed that the average CEO:

Earned $288,910 before taxes

Owned $1,987,689 in stock in his own company

Owned $826,014 of stock in other companies

Owned $1,009,511 in real estate outside his own home

The average CEO made 24 business trips and 6 personal trips a year. He or she dined out 108 times on business and 114 times for pleasure.

The average CEO owned or leased 2 or 3 cars. By make they were:

Cadillac	21%
Buick	18%
Oldsmobile	17%
Mercedes	11%
Toyota	6%
BMW	5%
Honda	5%
Jaguar	5%

CHAPTER FOUR NOTES

1. Bureau of Labor Statistics, Employment and Earnings
2. Bureau of Labor Statistics, Employment and Earnings
3. U.S. Bureau of the Census, Current Population Reports and Bureau of Labor Statistics, Employment and Earnings
4. Bureau of Labor Statistics, Bulletin 2096
5. U.S. Bureau of the Census, Current Population Reports
6. Bureau of Labor Statistics, Bulletin 2096
7. Bureau of Labor Statistics, Special Labor Force Reports
8. U.S. Bureau of the Census, Current Population Reports
9. Compiled by author from Bureau of Labor Statistics, unpublished data
10. Bureau of Labor Statistics, Employment and Earnings
11. Bureau of Labor Statistics, Employment and Earnings
12. Bureau of Labor Statistics, Geographic Profile of Employment and Unemployment
13. Bureau of Labor Statistics, Employment and Earnings
14. Bureau of Labor Statistics, unpublished data
15. Bureau of Labor Statistics, Employment and Earnings
16. Bureau of Labor Statistics, unpublished data
17. U.S. Bureau of Labor Statistics, Handbook of Labor Statistics
18. Ward's Business Directory
19. Bureau of the Census, Public Employment
20. U.S. Office of Personnel Management, Monthly Release of Federal Workforce Employment Statistics
21. U.S. Office of Personnel Management, Affirmative Action Statistics
22. U.S. Department of Defense, Selected Manpower Statistics
23. U.S. Department of Defense, semi-annual statistics
24. U.S. Department of Defense, Office of the Deputy Assistant Secretary of Defense
25. U.S. Department of Defense, Selected Manpower Characteristics

26. U.S. Department of Defense, unpublished data
27. U.S. Department of Defense, Official Guard and Reserve Manpower Strengths and Statistics
28. U.S. Congress, Congressional Directory
29. U.S. Congress, Congressional Directory
30. U.S. Congress, Congressional Directory
31. Joint Center for Political Studies
32. Center for the Study of American Women and Politics
33. Bureau of Labor Statistics, Employment and Earnings and Industrial Relations Data and Information Service, U.S. Union Sourcebook
34. Bureau of Labor Statistics, Employment and Earnings
35. Bureau of Labor Statistics, Employment and Earnings
36. Bureau of Labor Statistics, Current Wage Developments
37. National Safety Council, Accident Facts-1987
38. National Safety Council, Accident Facts-1987
39. Bureau of Labor Statistics, Occupational Injuries and Illnesses in the United States by Industry
40. U.S. Bureau of Labor Statistics, Occupational Health and Safety, 1985
41. Hertz Corp.
42. U.S. Bureau of the Census, Current Population Reports
43. U.S. Bureau of the Census, Current Population Reports
44. U.S. Bureau of the Census, Current Population Reports
45. U.S. Bureau of Labor Statistics, Employment and Earnings
46. Accountemps
47. Bureau of Labor Statistics, unpublished data
48. Administrative Management Society
49. Administrative Management Society
50. U.S. Bureau of the Census, Current Population Reports
51. Administrative Management Society
52. U.S. Bureau of the Census, Current Population Reports
53. U.S. Bureau of the Census, Current Population Reports
54. U.S. Bureau of Labor Statistics, Employment and Earnings
55. Bureau of Labor Statistics, Employment and Earnings
56. National Center for Health Statistics, Vital and Health Statistics
57. Psychology Today
58. Government Accounting Office
59. USA Today survey
60. U.S. Chamber of Commerce
61. Bureau of Labor Statistics, Employee Benefits in Medium and Large Firms
62. Bureau of Labor Statistics, Employee Benefits in Medium and Large Firms
63. Bureau of Labor Statistics, Employee Benefits in Medium and Large Firms
64. Employee Benefit Research Institute
65. U.S. Department of Agriculture, Farm Population Estimates
66. U.S. Bureau of the Census, Census of Agriculture
67. U.S. Bureau of the Census, Census of Agriculture
68. U.S. Department of Agriculture, Financial Characteristics of Farms
69. U.S. Department of Commerce
70. Heidrick and Struggles

CHAPTER
FIVE

YOUR LOVE LIFE

LOVE AND YOUR LIFE

If you were to look at the results of appropriate public opinion surveys, you'd be totally convinced that Americans are, first and foremost, "people who need people." 96% of adult Americans have said that love and romance is very important to their lives. 86% of you listed having a "traditional marriage" as a "most important life goal." When asked what you looked for in a relationship, 53% of you said "love," 32% said "companionship," and only 1% said "sex." When people were asked to list the "great sources of satisfaction" in their lives, more than twice as many people listed "marriage" as listed "friends," "sex," "career," or "money." [1]

Of course, people don't always do what they say, and if you had a nickel for every husband and wife who acted like sex, career, money, or friends were more important than marriage, you'd be the richest person on earth. Still, there's no doubt that love is a fundamental need of all of us. Below are some facts about love compiled by Nancy Biracree for her 1986 book, *Lover's Quotient*.

- The average American had his or her first "puppy love" at 13, and the first serious love 4 years later.

- Americans fall in love an average of 6 times in their lives.

- About 25% of Americans are "love prone," having fallen in love at least 10 times.

- Women fall in love more frequently, but they also end 70% of relationships.

- About 12% of Americans have had 3 or more unrequited loves.

WHO'S SINGLE?

In 1985, there were 45,480,000 unmarried adults age 20–64. By age and sex, these singles were: [2]

Age	# of men	# of women	Men per 100 women
20–24	7,746,000	6,458,000	120
25–29	4,669,000	3,724,000	125
30–34	2,960,000	2,689,000	110
35–44	3,079,000	3,656,000	84
45–54	1,752,000	2,739,000	64
55–64	1,665,000	3,534,000	47

Another 3,129,000 Americans age 25–54 (3.2% of men and 4.5% of women) were separated from their spouses at the time of the Census Bureau's 1985 survey. [3]

The number of divorced women surpassed the number of never-married women at age 32, while the number of divorced men didn't overtake the number of never married men until age 38.

HOW DO SINGLE MEN AND WOMEN MEET?

The results of the nationwide survey of singles commissioned by Jacqueline Simenauer and David Carroll for their book *Singles: The New Americans* showed that today only 60% of singles met most of their dates in "traditional ways"—through friends, family, social events, and work. The breakdown for men and women was:

How they met dates	% of men	% of women
Through friends	30%	36%
At social gatherings	22%	18%
At bars, discos, etc.	24%	18%
At singles functions	14%	18%
At work	10%	9%
Through newspaper ads	1%	1%
Other/don't know	1%	2%

The people most likely to have met dates through friends were college students and young never-married working people. Career women were the least likely to have met dates through friends and the most likely to have met men at work. Singles bars were the primary source of contacts for divorced men, twice-divorced women, and blue collar workers of both sexes.

According to a five year study of singles by Philadelphia biologist Timothy Perper, associate editor of the *Journal of Sex Research*, women most often made the first move and controlled how far the flirtation went. Perper found that two-thirds of the time, women made the first approach through eye contact or body language. The "courtship sequence" of approach, talk, touch lasted 15 minutes to 3 hours, with men often making the mistake of going too fast. In only 10% to 20% of the contacts, however, did a woman complete the flirtation by asking the man for a date.

WHAT ATTRACTS WOMEN TO MEN?

Sex: A Users Manual by the Diagram Group reported a study of the parts of man's body women found most attractive:

Face	55%
Hair	8%
Shoulders	7%
Chest	6%
Hands	4%

The same book also reported that the personal qualities women found most attractive in men, in order, were:

1. Achievement
2. Leadership
3. Occupational ability
4. Economic ability
5. Entertaining ability
6. Intellectual ability
7. Observational ability
8. Common sense
9. Athletic ability
10. Theoretical ability

WHAT ATTRACTS MEN TO WOMEN?

The studies reported by the Diagram Group included the parts of a woman's body men found most attractive:

Face	27%
Legs	24%
Bust	18%
Hair	5%
Bottom	4%

The book also reported how men rated a woman's personal qualities, in order of importance:

1. Physical attractiveness
2. Erotic ability
3. Affectional ability
4. Social ability
5. Domestic ability

6. Sartorial ability

7. Interpersonal understanding

8. Art appreciation

9. Moral-spiritual understanding

10. Art-creative ability

HOW YOU THINK
YOU LOOK TO OTHERS

It probably doesn't surprise you that 50% more men than women consider themselves better than average looking. Following are the results of a study on how men and women rated their appearances: [4]

Men	
Extremely handsome	5%
Very attractive	9%
Handsome	28%
Average good looks	33%
"Interesting" looking	11%
Plain	6%
Don't know	8%
Women	
Very beautiful	3%
Very attractive	12%
Pretty	13%
Average good looks	47%
"Interesting" looking	12%
Plain	4%
Don't know	9%

Further breaking down the results of the survey yields some very interesting nuggets of information:

- Men and women who had never married were 5 times more likely to consider themselves much better than average looking than men and women who were or had been married.

- College educated men and women were 2–1/2 times more likely to consider themselves better than average looking.

- Bisexual and homosexual men and women were more than more than twice as likely to call themselves "extremely handsome" or "very beautiful."

- 20% of women earning over $25,000 a year considered themselves "very attractive," compared with 10% of women earning under $15,000 a year.

HOW OTHERS RATE YOUR LOOKS

Two sociologists from Virginia Polytechnic Institute & State University interviewed a carefully chosen sampling of 3,600 adults and rated their looks. The results of their ratings were:

Strikingly beautiful or handsome	3.0%
Above average looks	30.6%
Average looks	54.9%
Below average looks	9.7%
Very unattractive	1.8%

The study found that both men and women whose looks were striking or above average made more money and had more education than those whose looks were average or below average.

DO YOU LOOK YOUR AGE?

The research firm of Cadwall Davis reported that in a nationwide poll of adults, 57% of those surveyed thought they looked younger than their actual age, 33% thought they looked older, and only 8% thought they looked their actual age.

Even though a majority of you thought you looked younger than you were, you were still not totally happy with your appearance. The "1985 *Psychology Today* Body Image Survey" found that only 18% of men and 7% of women were totally satisfied with their appearance. 34% of men and 38% of women were dissatisfied with their looks in general. In terms of specific parts of the body, 50% of men and 57% of women were dissatisfied with the appeance of their stomachs, 41% of men and 55% of women were dissatisfied with their weight, 32% of men and 45% of women didn't like their overall body tone, and 21% of men and 50% of women were dissatisfied with their hips and thighs.

Your view of your appearance, however, is likely to be distorted, especially if you're a woman. Psychologist J. Kevin Thompson found that women thought they were 25% larger than they actually measured, while men overestimated themselves by 13%.

THE ROMANTIC IN YOU

Although most of you don't see movie star good looks when you stand in front of the mirror, most of you do see a romantic. A national survey commissioned by Korbel Champagne found that 80% of American men and 77% of American women considered themselves romantic. 26% considered themselves very romantic and 52% somewhat romantic. 42% thought romance was on the rise.

When asked to list the most appropriate items to celebrate a romantic occasion, the responses, in order, were: flowers, wine, romantic meals, champagne, food in general, candles, perfume and cologne, jewelry, candy, and clothing.

SOME FACTS ABOUT SEX

Because sex is by nature a private activity, it's difficult to compile statistics on sexual preferences and activities that are as accurate to the decimal point as statistics on such public activities as the number of marriages. However, in the last three decades, there has been a vast increase in the quantity and quality of academic sex research. This research provides a fairly clear idea of what we'd see if we were given the opportunity to peek into the bedrooms of a representative sample of our neighbors.

For the *Book of Sex Lists*, the Association for Research, Inc. examined a number of academic studies to compile list of the sexual activities preferred by men and women. Those activities, in order of preference were:

Sexual activities preferred by women:

1. Gentle cunnilingus by a man.

2. Gentle finger stimulation of clitoris by a man.

3. Sexual intercourse on top of a man.

4. Sexual intercourse in a variety of changing positions.

5. Receiving cunnilingus while performing fellatio ("69").

6. Massaging a man all over.

7. Masturbating a man.

8. Being petted and kissed by two men.

9. Masturbation.

10. Performing fellatio.

Sexual activities preferred by men:

1. Fellatio by a woman to orgasm.

2. Intercourse with a woman in a variety of positions.

3. Nude encounters with two women.

4. Petting the breasts of a woman.

5. Anal intercourse with a woman.

6. Performing cunnilingus while receiving fellatio ("69").

7. Performing mild sadomasochistic acts upon a woman.

8. Being masturbated by a woman.

9. Performing cunnilingus.

10. Masturbation.

What do people actually do in bed? For their 1982 book, *How Big is Big?: The Book of Sexual Measurements*, Dr. Zev Wanderer (former Clinical Professor of Psychology at UCLA) and Dr. David Radell (professor, California State University at Los Angeles) examined all current academic sexual research to come up with the following figures:

Of all women:

60% made love most frequently in the missionary position, while 25% most frequently used the woman-on-top position

93% had received oral sex, 91% had given oral sex

43% had tried anal intercourse

5% have had sexual contact with animals

5% had played the passive role in sadomasochistic sex, 2% had played the aggressor

83% masturbated, with the average frequency once every 3 weeks

Of all men:

97% masturbated

79% had performed oral sex on a woman

60% had heterosexual anal sex

30% had sex with prostitutes

5% had participated in sadomasochistic sex

5% had sexual contact with animals

For the average married couple, foreplay lasted 14 to 17 minutes, and the man had an orgasm after an average of 6 minutes of copulation. About 63% of women regularly had orgasms when making love.

FIRST SEXUAL EXPERIENCES

Despite all the publicity in the last few years about the dangers of teen-age pregnancy and sexually transmitted diseases, research showed that more teen-agers were becoming sexually active in their early teens. Research studies commissioned by the National Institute of Child Health and Human Development showed that between 1970 and 1980, the percentage of girls age 15–19 who'd had intercourse soared from 30% to 50%. The following percentages of unmarried teen–age girls who reported having had intercourse were: [5]

Age	Total % of non-virgins	% of white non-virgins	% of black non-virgins
15	18.4%	16.9%	28.0%
16	28.5%	26.7%	40.8%
17	40.1%	36.4%	55.4%
18	53.8%	49.7%	76.1%
19	65.6%	63.2%	80.5%

A study done for *Rolling Stone* Magazine), conducted in 1984, came up with virtually identical results (53.0% of 18 year old girls having had sex). [6]

The study commissioned by the National Institute of Child Health and Human Development, which was conducted by Melvin Zelnik and Farida Shah of Johns Hopkins University, showed that the average age at which boys had sex for the first time was 15.7 years, half a year younger than the average age at which girls had sex for the first time. The same study showed that 66% of 18 year old boys and 81% of 20 year old men had had sex.

Sexual intercourse is the last step in a progression of exploration that begins with "kissing games" played at parties by 11 and 12 year olds. By age 13, according to the *Rolling Stone* study, 73% of girls and 66% of boys had kissed. (87% of teen-age boys and 90% of teen-age girls had kissed.) Next step was breast play—54% of 14 year old boys and 31% of 14 year old girls had participated in breast play. By age 15, 46% of boys and 37% of girls had experienced vaginal play. [7]

The earlier teen-agers begin to date, the earlier they have sex. A study of 2,400 teens by Brent C. Miller of Utah State University and Terrance D. Olson of Brigham Young University showed the following relationship between dating and sex:

Age girl starts dating	% having sex before H.S. graduation
12	91%
13	56%
14	53%
15	40%
16	20%

70% of high school freshman boys who had a "steady" girlfriend had had sex, compared with 52% of boys who dated occasionally. Miller and Olson also found that more teen-agers with "not very" strict and "very" strict parents had experienced sexual intercourse than teen-agers with "moderately strict" parents.

Very few first sexual experiences of both boys and girls were casual encounters. Following is a table showing the relationship of girls and boys to their first sexual partners, as compiled by Zelnik and Shah of Johns Hopkins University:

Relationship	% of girls	% of boys
Engaged	9.3%	.6%
Going steady	55.2%	36.5%
Dating	24.4%	20.0%
Friends	6.7%	33.7%
Recently met	4.4%	9.3%

Although few first sexual experiences took place with casual "pickups," the vast majority were spur-of-the-moment decisions. Zelnik and Shah found that only 17% of girls and 25% of boys planned their first intercourse.

That's one of the reasons that only 49% of girls and 44% of boys used any contraceptive method the first time they had sex. The situation was even worse than the figures show, because 35% of the time the contraceptive method was "withdrawal," which is very unreliable.

The figures on contraceptive use by teen-agers don't get much better with sexual experience. Planned Parenthood found that only one-third of teen-agers who were sexually active always practiced birth control, while 27% said they *never* used any type of birth control.

The inevitable result is pregnancy—4 out of 10 teen-agers have been pregnant by the time they're 20. The rate of teen-age pregnancy in the United States has been the highest of any Western nation, with about 8% of unmarried teen-age girls age 15 to 19 becoming pregnant in 1984. About 46% of those 892,000 pregnancies ended in abortion. Of the 480,000 babies born to teen-agers, 56% were out-of-wedlock, compared with just 16% in 1960. [8] The Center for Population Options estimated that the Federal Government spent over $16 billion a year supporting teen-age mothers and their children.

There appears to be a strong correlation between sex education and use of birth control. Planned Parenthood found that teen-agers who had received sex instruction at home or school were 60% more likely to use contraceptive methods. But a *U.S.A. Today* poll revealed that only 20% of American teens learned most of what they knew about sex from their parents and only 12% listed school sex education as their primary source of information. Sources for the other 68% of teens were friends, dating partners, and magazines such as *Playboy* and *Penthouse*.

One more interesting way to look at teen-age sexual activity is to look the relationship between sex and academics. *Rolling Stone* found that over half of all teens with "well below average" and "below average" grades were sexually experienced, compared with just 21% of teens whose grades were "well above average." Three-quarters of teen-agers who planned to go to college were virgins, while only 24% of sexually active teens were interested in any kind of higher education. [9]

A final note: only 13% of teen-agers who had never used alcohol had had sex, compared with 47% of teen-agers who drank. A similar relationship existed between marijuana use and sex.

SEX AND TELEVISION

According to a study by Planned Parenthood of Greater Kansas City, children see nearly 60,000 references to sex on television in the average year, but only 104 references to birth control.

SEX AND COLLEGE STUDENTS

A comparison of surveys of college students commissioned by *Forbes* Magazine that were conducted in 1966, 1976, and 1986 show that today's college students have turned very conservative in all areas, including sex. In 1986, only 19.6% of students age 18–22 said they thought an occasional one-night stand was all right, compared with 40.7% in 1976 and 48.1% in 1966. Only 13% approved of extra-marital affairs, less than half the approval rate of college students in 1966 and 1976.

Since the 1960's, colleges have been viewed as hotbeds of sexual promiscuity, but recent studies of college women don't back that image. A representative example was a study by Harvard University that found that 57% of coeds were sexually active, about the same percentage as young single women who weren't in college and about the same percentage as high school seniors.

Unfortunately, a substantial percentage of college men don't handle the freedom of being away from home as well. At least four separate studies have revealed that 20%–25% of college women have been the victims of rape or attempted rape. In 90% of the cases, the women victims of forced sex were dates or acquaintances of their assailants. More than a third of the victims didn't discuss the rape with anyone, and less than 1 in 10 reported the rape to the police.

These shocking reports were not solely based on interviews with coeds. A 1982 survey of college men by Karen Rapaport and Barry Burkhart of Auburn University found a wide pattern of coercive sexual behavior. 61% of college men said they'd placed a hand on a woman's breast against her will, 53% had kissed a woman against her will, 42% had "disarranged or removed" a woman's clothing without her permission, and 15% said they'd had intercourse with a woman against her will—in other words, they'd raped a woman. Over half the men admitted they would rape a woman if they were guaranteed not to be prosecuted.

SEX AND SINGLES

The National Survey of Family Growth, conducted by the National Center for Health Statistics, found that 73% of never married women age 20–24 and 82% of never–married women age 25–44 had had sexual intercourse. The same study also found that 50.4% of never married women age 15–44 described themselves as "sexually active."

The National Survey of Unmarried Women conducted by Planned Parenthood of America also found that 82% of never-married women age 20–29 had had sex. The Planned Parenthood survey further revealed that 53% of single women in their twenties were sexually active, having had intercourse in the last 4 weeks. They also found that 32% of white single women and 70% of black single women had been pregnant; 14% of whites and 62% of blacks had had a baby. Despite the risk, only 78% of the women had used some form of contraception during their sex act. Surprisingly, the most careful of all single women were devout Catholics, 98% of them having used contraception despite the Church's strict prohibition of artificial birth control.

The Simenauer/Carroll survey of singles found that single women were not as sexually promiscuous as single men, with half of all single women having had 4 or fewer sex partners while single. By marital status, the response were: [10]

Number of sex partners	Never married	Divorced once	Divorced twice
None	10%	9%	3%
One	13%	16%	12%
2–4	23%	28%	21%
5–9	20%	15%	22%
10–19	15%	15%	9%

Number of sex partners	Never married	Divorced once	Divorced twice
20-49	12%	10%	19%
50 or more	5%	4%	19%
Don't know	2%	3%	4%

Simenauer and Carroll found that half of single women had slept with a man on the first through third date at least once. Other studies showed that casual sex was declining dramatically, largely due to fear of herpes, AIDS, and other sexually transmitted diseases.

Heterosexual single men have been more sexually active and more likely to engage in casual sex than have single women. About two-thirds had had sex in the past four weeks, and only 5% of men over age 20 were virgins. [11]

Simenauer and Carroll found that the average single man had had 16 sex partners while single. The breakdown by marital status was: [12]

Number of sex partners	Never married	Divorced once	Divorced twice
None	5%	3%	2%
One	4%	10%	1%
2-4	14%	18%	9%
5-9	14%	14%	12%
10-19	19%	23%	26%
20-49	21%	17%	21%
50 or more	22%	14%	27%
Don't know	1%	1%	2%

HOMOSEXUALITY

Famous sex researcher Alfred Kinsey found that 37% of males and 19% of females reported at least one homosexual experience, most commonly when young. The percentage of adults who are homosexual, however, depends primarily on the definition of homosexuality. [13]

A number of recent surveys have found that about 4% of adult men had had exclusively homosexual sex, 4% had had almost exclusively homosexual sex, and another 9% had had adult homosexual sex more than twice. Famous sex researcher John Money of Johns Hopkins University defined a homosexual as a man who has had 6 or more sex experiences with other males. By that definition, Money's research showed that 13% of adult males were gay. By the same definition, about 7% of adult females were lesbians.

Homosexual men have traditionally been much more sexually active than heterosexual men. Studies by Alan P. Bell and Martin S. Weinberg for their book *Homosexualities* showed that 93% of homosexual men had sex at least once a month and 70% had sex at least once a week. The recent AIDS epidemic, however, may have drastically altered these percentages, but that has yet to be documented by research.

Bell and Weinberg also studied the attitudes of homosexuals. They found that 73% of males and 84% of females had little or no regrets about their homosexuality. They also found, however, that many homosexual men and women were still very secretive about their homosexuality. In terms of the people in their lives:

Of fathers,
53% of males/46% of females said he didn't know or suspect

16% of males/17% of females said he was suspicious

31% of males/37% of females said he knew

Of mothers,
38% of males/32% of females said she didn't know or suspect

21% of males/19% of females said she was suspicious

42% of males/49% of females said she knew

Of employers,
53% of males/68% of females said they knew

18% of males/17% of females said they were suspicious

29% of males/15% of females said they knew

Of fellow workers,
31% of males/48% of females said nobody knew

31% of males/28% of females said few knew

29% of males/15% of females said most knew

In their landmark study *American Couples*, conducted under a grant by the National Science Foundation, Dr. Philip Blumstein and Dr. Pepper Schwartz of the University of Washington found that gay cohabiting couples had sex more frequently than heterosexual couples and lesbian couples had sex much less frequently. The results of their study were:

Years together	3 times a week +	1–3 times per week	Once/week to once/month	Once/month or less
SEXUAL FREQUENCY				
Gay men				
0–2	67%	27%	3%	2%
2–10	32%	41%	14%	13%
10+	11%	34%	22%	33%
Lesbians				
0–2	33%	43%	19%	5%
2–10	7%	30%	35%	28%
10+	1%	26%	26%	47%

WHO LIVES TOGETHER?

Between 1970 and 1986, the number of unmarried couples who lived together quadrupled, from 523,000 to 2,220,000. The Census Bureau projected the number of unmarried couples living together will remain at about 2 million over the next five years. [14]

By marital status, the people who lived together in 1984 were: [15]

	% of men	% of women
Never married	54%	51%
Divorced	34%	33%
Separated	8%	8%
Widowed	4%	8%

Only 37% of cohabiting couples consisted of a man and a woman who had never been married. 17% were two divorced people, 11% were a never married woman and a divorced man, and 12% were a never married man and a divorced woman. There was at least one child 15 or younger in about 30% of cohabiting households. [16]

Men who cohabited tended to be older than women—61% of men were between ages 25–44, while 73% of the women were between ages 18–34. The older a woman was, however, the more likely she was to be living with a younger man—9,000 women over age 65 lived with men under age 45. [17]

An analysis of Census Bureau statistics showed that the average cohabitation lasted a little more than a year and a half, making it the most temporary of living arrangements—the average marriage lasted 27 years. [18] In the absence of any definitive studies, most experts have "guessed" that between one-third and one-half of cohabitations lead to marriage. One widely reported study of couples who got married in Oregon between 1970 and 1980 showed that 53% of them were living together when their marriage licenses were issued. Another study of 459 Detroit area women by Professor Whyte of the University of Michigan Sociology Department found that 40% of women married between 1980 and 1985 had lived with their husbands before marriage.

According to the study *American Couples*, the sexual frequency of cohabiting couples was: [19]

	SEXUAL FREQUENCY			
Years together	3 times a week +	1–3 times per week	Once/week to once/month	Once/month or less
0–2	61%	31%	7%	1%
2–10	38%	38%	17%	7%

Couples living together for less than two years (more than half of all cohabiting couples), had a somewhat more active sex lives than couples married for less than two years—93% had sex at least 1–3 times per week, compared with 83% of married couples. Cohabiting couples were also more likely to "cheat"—both men and women who cohabited were 60% more likely than married men and women to have had an affair in the first two years together and more than twice as likely to have had an affair during the second through tenth years.

METHODS OF BIRTH CONTROL

The National Center for Health Statistics found 36.9% of all women age 15–44 reported that they or their partners used some method of birth control. The reasons for not using birth control varied dramatically by marital status of the women: [20]

Of never-married women:

3.2% were sterile
2.5% were either pregnant or had just had a baby

1.2% were trying to get pregnant

49.6% were not sexually active

10.1% had no reason for not using birth control

Of married women:

40.9% were either sterile or had sterile husbands, primarily because the man had had a vasectomy or the woman had had a tubal ligation

7.2% were either pregnant or had just had a baby

6.7% were trying to conceive

.2% were not sexually active

4.8% had no reason for not using birth control

Of formerly married women:

38.0% were sterile

2.6% were either pregnant or had just had a baby

2.1% were trying to get pregnant

15.1% were not sexually active

10.4% had no reason for not using birth control

The methods of birth control used by these women were:

Method used	Never married	Currently married	Formerly married
Total users	33.3%	40.1%	31.8%
Pill	18.7%	13.4%	15.8%
IUD	1.9%	4.8%	6.4%

Method used	Never married	Currently married	Formerly married
Diaphragm	4.7%	4.5%	3.7%
Condom	4.1%	9.8%	.8%
Foam	1.3%	2.0%	1.1%
Rhythm	.9%	3.2%	1.4%
Other	2.6%	2.3%	2.7%

One in four couples decided they wanted to have children after the husband or wife had been surgically sterilized, according to a study reported in the September/October, 1986 issue of *Family Planning Perspectives*. Those most likely to regret their operation were women who were unmarried and under age 30 when they were sterilized.

SEXUALLY TRANSMITTED DISEASES

The federal Centers for Disease Control estimated that there were about 11 million new cases of sexually transmitted diseases in 1986:

Diseases	1986 new cases
Chlamydia	4,600,000
Trichomoniasis	3,000,000
Gonorrhea	1,800,000
Venereal Warts	1,000,000
Herpes	500,000
Hepatitis	200,000
Syphilis	90,000
AIDS	15,000

The most prevalent complication of these disease was pelvic inflammatory disease (PID) in women. About 1 million cases of PID occurred in 1986, about half of them caused by chlamydia. As a result, 200,000 women were hospitalized and between 50,000 and 100,000 became sterile. [21]

The more sex partners a person has had, the higher the risk of contracting a sexually transmitted disease. The National Center for Health Statistics estimated that half of all 25 year old single men who had been sexually active since their teens had contracted at least one sexually transmitted disease. [22]

Despite dangers of contracting diseases, many women are reluctant to quiz their partners before sex. *Cosmopolitan* Magazine found that only 13% of its readers always asked men if they had a contagious disease, and 64% never asked.

No sexually transmitted disease is more feared than AIDS, which to date has been 100% fatal. Through the end of 1987, 50,000 Americans had contracted the disease, with new cases being diagnosed at the rate of 400 per week. The distribution of the AIDS victims in the United States was: [23]

Homosexual/bi-sexual men	73%
Intravenous drug users	17%
Heterosexuals	4%
Blood transfusion recipients	2%
Hemophiliacs	1%
Unknown	3%

6.6% of the victims of AIDS were females. Of these women, 297 had been infected through heterosexual contact.

WHAT LOVERS WEAR TO BED

A survey by R.H. Bruskin Associates revealed that about 1 in 8 of you reveal everything when you slip between the sheets. The results:

Sleep attire	% of men wearing	% of women wearing
Nude	19%	6%
Pajamas	37%	19%
Nightgown/nightie	—	63%
Underwear	33%	4%
Long johns	2%	1%
Nightshirts	—	3%

SEX AND AGING

A Duke University study of older people in North Carolina found that about 60% of those age 60–74 were sexually active. That percentage dropped to about 26% of those age 75 and over.

About 50% more older men than women were sexually active, largely because so many more older women lived alone. 59% of women age 50–70 admitted masturbating, compared with 25% of men over age 60.

Men over age 60 commonly required about 5 times the time to attain an erection as did teen-age men. Impotence was a problem for about 22% of 65 year old men, 50% of men age 70–80, and about 98% of men age 90.

WHO'S MARRIED?

Below is a table of the marital status of Americans by age and sex in 1985: [24]

Age	% single	% married	% divorced	% widowed
Male				
18–19	97.1	2.9	—	—
20–24	75.6	23.0	1.4	—
25–29	38.7	55.2	6.0	—
30–34	20.8	69.7	9.5	.1
35–44	9.4	79.9	10.3	.4
45–54	6.3	83.8	8.7	1.2
55–64	6.1	83.9	6.2	3.7
65–74	5.2	81.3	4.2	9.3
75+	5.3	69.3	2.7	22.7

Age	% single	% married	% divorced	% widowed
Female				
18–19	86.7	12.5	.7	.1
20–24	58.5	38.0	3.3	.2
25–29	26.4	65.2	7.9	.5
30–34	13.5	73.1	12.4	1.0
35–44	6.8	77.1	14.0	2.0
45–54	4.6	76.3	12.1	7.0
55–64	3.7	70.0	8.9	17.4
65–74	4.4	51.1	5.6	38.9
75+	6.2	23.8	2.4	67.7

It's impossible to glance at the above statistics without drawing the conclusion—the very accurate conclusion—that marriage has been extremely popular in America. Over the past 30 years, about 95% of men and women have been married during their adult lives. Behind the figures above, however, are trends that show the marital patterns of Americans have been undergoing a pronounced change since 1970.

The first of these trends is that more and more men and women have been marrying later. Between 1970 and 1985, the median age at which people married increased from 20.8 years to 23.1 years for women and from 23.2 years to 25.7 years for men. In the same time period, the percentage of single women age 25-29 nearly tripled 151% (from 10.5% to 28.8%) and the percentage of single men age 25-29 doubled (from 19.1% to 42.2%). [25]

One major reason why so many women delayed marriage was their pursuit of higher education and a career. 65% more women attended college in 1987 than in 1970, and, as the table below shows, college graduate women were almost three times as likely to be single into their early thirties as women who had only a high school degree: [26]

Women age 25–34

Education	% never married
Elementary school	10.0%
1–3 years high school	6.6%
High school graduate	8.5%
1–3 years college	12.1%
College graduate	22.5%
Postgraduate degree	29.9%

Increased education and pursuit of a career are major factors in a second trend in marriage in America: for women in their 20's in 1985, the percentage who never marry is projected to soar from 5% to an estimated 10 to 12%. Almost all of this increase will be made up of women with four or more years of college.

The third trend in American marriage patterns is the increased acceptance of divorce that has lead to a huge increase in the number of people moving in and out of marriages in their adult life. In 1985, only 54% of all weddings were first marriages for both the bride and groom. From 1960 to 1987, the number of divorced people per 1000 married people jumped from 35 to 130, and the percentage of marriages that were the third or more marriage for one of the partners increased 50%. [27]

TEEN MARRIAGE

Although American women have been generally marrying at an older age, wedding guests in the South were more than twice as likely to find a teen−age bride than in the Northeast in 1984. 36% of marriages in the South in 1983 involved a bride under 20, and 12% of brides were younger than 18. In contrast, 18% of Northeastern brides were teen-agers, and only 4% were under 18.

Most eager to tie the knot were Kentucky girls, 45% of whom married as teen−agers. Other states with over 40% teen−age brides were Tennessee, Alabama, West Virginia, Mississippi, South Carolina, Idaho, Wyoming, and Utah. That compared with a national average of 19% teen-age brides, a precipitous drop from the 1970 figure of 33% teen-age brides. [28]

MARRIAGE AND COLLEGE-EDUCATED WOMEN: IS THERE A "MAN SHORTAGE"?

In 1986, two Yale University sociologists and a Harvard University economist issued a report entitled "Black and White Marriage Patterns: Why So Different?" which immediately made front page news. The reason wasn't the report's analysis of racial marriage patterns. Rather, the report made headlines because the authors projected that single, college−educated women born in the 1950's had only a 20% chance to ever marry at age 30, a 5% chance at age 35, and a tiny 2.6% chance at age 40.

At the same time this bleak report was made public, Money Magazine published its estimates of the number of "eligible" single men per 100 women in major U.S. cities. Their figures, arrived at by subtracting from the actual number of single men estimates of gay men and others not interested in marriage, told marriage-minded women that even in the top rated cities in the U.S., there were only 75 "eligible" men age 20–64 for every 100 single women. The national average, according to Money, was less than 60 men per 100 women, and in some cities the ratio was less than 1 eligible male for every 2 females.

These reports were based not only on the demographic fact that single women began to outnumber single men in their thirties (as shown above), but also heavily relied on the assumption that the following marriage patterns would continue in the future:

PATTERN ONE: Men, on the average, marry a woman 2.5 years younger the first time, and remarry a woman 4 years younger. Between the start of the baby boom in 1946 and 1957, more female babies were born each year than male babies the year before, so women must compete for a smaller group of older "eligible" men.

PATTERN TWO: Women have been "fussier" than men in choosing spouses—they have strongly tended to marry men with more education, higher incomes, and higher status jobs. Today, when women make up more than half of all college students and vastly increased percentage of higher paying managerial and professional jobs, the number of men with "better" credentials is very much smaller.

If you assume these trends will continue, you can readily see how the Yale sociologists and Harvard economist reached their bleak conclusions.

Other experts, however, including the U.S. Census Bureau, have taken a position that is much more optimistic about the marriage chances of college-educated older women. Instead of assuming that old marriage patterns will continue, these experts pointed out trends that suggest college-educated women are creating new marriage patterns. For example, although young women still marry older men, in 1985 only 54% of women 30-34 and 52% of women 35-39 married older men. If this trend continues, the "baby boom" would work for women instead of against them, making the pool of "eligible" men vastly larger. Secondly, experts believe that the earning power and job status college-educated women have begun to attain will make them more emotionally secure about marrying men with less education and lower incomes. At the same time, the income of college-educated women has made them more desirable as marriage partners.

So what are the real chances of a woman's eventually getting married if she's unmarried at age 25, 30, etc.? Below are the projections of both the Census Bureau and the Harvard-Yale researchers. [29]

PROBABILITIES OF NEVER-MARRIED
WOMEN MARRYING BY AGE 65

Age	Census Bureau study		Harvard/Yale study	
	4 yrs H.S.	4 yrs Col.	4 yrs H.S.	4 yrs. Col.
25	65%	85%	56%	52%
30	47%	58%	22%	20%
35	32%	32%	6%	5%
40	21%	17%	1%	1%
45	12%	9%	0%	0%

The same Census Bureau report estimated the percentage of all women in different age ranges in 1986 who would eventually marry before age 65. Those projections were:

Age in 1986	Percentage married by 1986	Percentage of women who will marry by 65
15–19	0	88%
20–24	24%	88%
25–29	65%	90%
30–34	83%	92%
35–39	91%	94%
40–44	94%	96%
45–49	94%	95%

WHOM YOU MARRY

Information collected by the National Center for Health Statistics revealed the following information about who you chose as a spouse: [30]

Your Spouse's Marital Status

54.4% of marriages were between two people marrying for the first time. Of all brides who were marrying for the first time:

91.2% married single men

8.5% married divorced men

.3% married widowed men

Of all grooms who married for the first time:

90.2% married single women

9.5% married divorced women

.3% married widowed women

Your Spouse's Age

Of all marriages involving women age 18-29, 67.1% of women married older men, 10.8% married men of the same age, and 22.1% married younger men. But the older a women was at the time of her marriage, the more likely that her partner was younger, as shown in the table below:

Age of bride	Married older man	Married same age man	Married younger man
21	76.7%	13.1%	10.2%
25	64.8%	13.2%	21.9%
29	56.6%	9.7%	33.7%

Your Spouse's Education

People tended to marry others at or near their own educational level. Of all marriages, 55% were between people of the same educational level, 26% included husbands with more education, and 19% included wives with more education. A more detailed look is provided in the table below:

Husband's education	WIFE'S EDUCATION				
	Elem. school	1−3 yrs. H.S.	4 yrs. H.S.	1−3 yrs. college	4+ yrs. college
Elem. school	38.3%	24.1%	31.1%	4.4%	2.1%
1−3 yrs.	9.7%	35.7%	43.3%	5.5%	1.8%
4 yrs. H.S.	3.1%	13.8%	65.5%	11.2%	4.2%
1-3 yrs. H.S.	2.5%	6.9%	49.2%	29.2%	12.2%
4 yrs. col.	1.1%	2.1%	34.5%	27.0%	35.2%
5+ yrs. col.	.5%	1.2%	19.4%	24.3%	54.6%

Your Spouse's Religion

Overwhelmingly, both sexes tended to choose spouses of the same religion, as shown in the table below:

Religion of husband	
Protestant	91.1% Protestant brides
Roman Catholic	82.0% Roman Catholic brides
Jewish	85.1% Jewish brides
Religion of wife	
Protestant	87.0% Protestant husbands
Roman Catholic	76.0% Catholic husbands
Jewish	85.3% Jewish husbands

The tendency to intermarry was very strong even within Protestant denominations. Over 85% of Baptists and Lutherans of both sexes married within their denomination, as did over 80% of Methodists and Presbyterians.

Your Spouse's Ethnic Background

In terms of marriage, America has been a melting pot. Of all marriages:

27% were between people of entirely same ethnic background

47% were between people of entirely different backgrounds

26% were between people of overlapping backgrounds

In terms of specific ethnic groups, 72% of Italian men and 64% of Italian women married non-Italians, over 80% of Polish men and woman married non-Poles, and 75% of French men and 66% of French women married people with non-French ancestry. The only exception was Americans of Hispanic background, 71% of whom married other Hispanics.

Your Spouse's Race

Although interracial marriages more than doubled between 1970 and 1982 (from 310,000 to 719,000), they still made up only 1.3% of all U.S. marriages. 99% of whites, 98% of black women, and 97%

of black men married within their race, and only 164,000 American newlyweds were black-white couples. Most likely to marry out of their race were Asians (28%) and American Indians (53.7).

Your Spouse's Name

If you were named Barbara and you had a chance to marry one of three identical brothers, Alan, Barry or Charles, who would you marry?

A study of the first names of over 40,000 couples showed that you were 12% more likely than chance to marry a person whose name began with the same first letter. It appears that alliteration sounds good to people, which is why Mickey Mouse was paired with Minnie and Donald Duck was paired with Daisy. [31]

REMARRIAGE

About 21% of all American adults in 1985 had been married two or more times—up from 15% in 1981. Of all marriages in 1983: [32]

11.6% were remarriages for grooms, first marriage for bride

10.5% were remarriages for brides, first marriages for grooms

23.5% were remarriages for both bride and groom

Most divorced persons remarried—78% of divorced men and 60% of divorced women. Divorced men who did remarry did so, on the average, 3.1 years after the divorce; the average interval for women who remarried was 3.4 years. The remarriage rate for divorced men was relatively constant for all age groups to age 75. As a result, the percentage of all men who were married varied only 3 percentage points between men age 35 and age 74. [33]

However, as shown by the table below, the chances of a divorced woman remarrying decreased with age: [34]

Age of women at divorce	% who remarried
Under 30	76.3%
30–39	56.2%
40–49	32.4%
50+	11.5%

There have been two major reasons for this disparity. One, the ratio of unmarried women to unmarried men increased dramatically over age 35. In 1984, of people age 40–44, there were 133 unmarried women for every 100 unmarried men; of people age 45–54, there were 247 unmarried women for every 100 unmarried men.

Secondly, men who remarried were even more likely to marry younger women than men who married for the first time. The average age advantage of men increased from 2.2 years for first marriages to 3.7 years for remarriages. 61% of men remarried younger women, and over half of these men found a bride more than 5 years younger. In contrast, only 21.7% of women remarried younger men.

WIDOWS

Nine out of ten married women become widows at some point in their lives, and in 1984, widows outnumbered widowers 6 to 1. 32.9% of widows lost their husbands before they themselves reached age 40, and the remarriage rates for these women were very similar to those for divorced women above. The remarriage rate for widows over age 40 dropped dramatically, to a low of only 2% of widows over age 65 who remarried. The widowed man who remarried waited an average of 3.7 years after the death of his spouse, while the average interval to remarriage for widows who remarried was 6.2 years. **[35]**

YOUR MARRIAGE CEREMONY

75.9% of first marriages and 58.8% of remarriages were religious ceremonies, according to the National Center for Health Statistics. The percentage of religious ceremonies for first marriages peaked at 80.0% for brides age 20–24 and dropped lowest (51.6%) for brides age 45–54.

Nearly half of all first marriages took place between May 1 and August 31. Below are the percentage of marriages that took place in:

June	13.1%
August	12.5%
May	10.8%
September	8.9%
July	8.6%

October	8.5%
November	7.6%
April	7.2%
March	6.5%
December	6.4%
February	5.4%
January	4.4%

Remarriages were spread out much more evenly throughout the year, with June and August still the most popular months. Over half of all marriage ceremonies (53%) took place on Saturday. 20% took place on Friday, 8% on Sunday, and the rest were spread out evenly among the other four weekdays.

According to a survey conducted by *Modern Bride*, the average honeymooning couple spent about $2,000 on an 8 day honeymoon in 1986–87. Top destinations, in order, were: Florida, Hawaii, Mexico, California, and the U.S. Virgin Islands. [36]

WHAT MEN AND WOMEN THINK OF MARRIAGE

The Virginia Slims American Woman's Opinion Poll has asked a nationally representative sample of men and women the same questions for over 15 years, and this study has shown a steady change in the concept of marriage in this country.

In 1974, 50% of women and 48% of men said the most satisfying lifestyle was a "traditional" marriage with the man working and the woman staying home. In 1985, only 37% of women and 43% of men favored the traditional marriage. 57% of women and 50% of men picked a marriage in which both husband and wife shared work, housekeeping, and child care. 53% of women and 43% of men approved of a mother with young children working, and only 30% of working women would stop working if they were financially secure.

90% of Americans thought that marriage was the best way to live, and 80% rated marriage and their children as a "great source of satisfaction" in their lives, more than twice the percentage of any other source of satisfaction—work, sex, money, etc.

When asked what was most important in a marriage, Americans responded:

	Women	Men
Being in love	91%	89%
Fidelity	83%	77%
Keeping romance alive	75%	74%
Good sexual relationship	69%	72%
Financial security	58%	53%
Children	46%	45%

Do Americans think they made the right choice in marriage? It seems that more men than women were happy with their partners. A 1986 survey by *Woman's Day* found that only half of women in their first marriages and 63% of women in their second marriages would choose their current husband, if they had to do it all over again. But a Chicago *Sun-Times* poll found that 77% of men in their first marriages and 82% of men in their second marriages said, "I'd marry her again."

WHEN COUPLES ARGUE

R.H. Bruskin Associates found that American couples argued about the following:

Subject	% of couples
Money	78%
Indifference to feelings	30%
Sex/adultery	25%
Irresponsibility	20%
Drinking	11%

The *General Mills American Family Report* found that when Americans argued about money, the arguments revolved around:

Subject	% of couples
Money in general	59%
Need to economize	47%
Wasting money	42%
Unpaid bills	38%
Keeping track of spending	33%
Saving	25%

Subject	% of couples
Borrowing	17%
Bad investments	10%
Lending	8%

A poll by *Family Circle* revealed the following sources of continuing arguments among married couples:

Subject	% of couples
Supervision of children	39%
In-laws/relatives	38%
Spending leisure time	34%
Politics	32%
Household chores	28%
Showing affection	27%

According to studies conducted by the Institute for Social Research at the University of Michigan, 62% of married people reported that they at least occasionally had trouble getting along with their spouses, up from 48% twenty years ago.

A study funded by the National Institute of Mental Health in 1985 found that in half of all families, arguments had gotten to the hitting or shoving stage at least once. 16% of married couples had at least one violent incident during the course of any given year.

Between 1975 and 1985, the number of wives who suffered severe violence declined by 375,000, or 21%. However, 1.3 million wives were still beaten, kicked, stabbed, or shot during the year— that was 1 out of every 38 married women. [37]

SEX LIVES OF MARRIED COUPLES

The study *American Couples* revealed the following sexual frequency among married couples: [38]

Years together	SEXUAL FREQUENCY			
	3 times a week +	1–3 times per week	Once/week to once/month	Once/month or less
0–2	45%	38%	11%	6%
2–10	27%	46%	21%	6%
10+	18%	45%	22%	15%

Blumstein and Schwartz found that a couple's satisfaction with their sex lives was directly related to the frequency with which they had sex. But they also found that frequency of sex had little relationship to the probability of a marriage breaking up.

In 51% of the marriages, the husbands were more likely to initiate sex, in 12% the wives were more likely to initiate sex, and in a little over a third, initiation was equal. In 53% of marriages, the wife was more likely to refuse sex; the husband was more likely to refuse in 13%.

WHO HAS AFFAIRS?

The results of the study reported in *American Couples* showed that the following percentages of husbands and wives had sex with other people: [39]

Years together	% of men	% of women
0–2	15%	13%
2–10	23%	22%
10+	30%	22%

A survey of 100,000 adults conducted by sociologist Morton Hunt for *Playboy* Magazine found that 48% of men and 38% of women had had affairs. For men, the incidence of "cheating" rose dramatically with income: [40]

Income	% of husbands unfaithful
Under $5,000	16%
$5,000–$10,000	23%
$10,000–$20,000	31%
$20,000–$30,000	47%
$30,000–$40,000	54%
$40,000–$50,000	64%
$50,000–$60,000	68%
$60,000 or more	70%

Hunt found the infidelity rate for women to be more closely tied to employment status than income. About 20% of non-working women were unfaithful, compared to 40% of women who worked full time.

43% of the unfaithful women and 29% of the unfaithful men in the *American Couples* study had only one extramarital sex partner; 7% of the men and 3% of the women had more than 20 partners. According to a study by Professor Frederick Humphrey of the University of Connecticut, only 20% of men and 8% of women had extramarital sex with a "pick-up" date that they hadn't known before. Humphrey found that the average man's affair lasted 29 months, and the average woman's lasted 21 months.

Although a significant percentage of married men and women have affairs, the overwhelming percentage of married Americans trusted their spouses. In a survey conducted by the American Psychiatric Association in 1986, only 8% of married Americans suspected that their spouses had had or were having an affair. Of the people who discovered that their spouses had cheated, half learned from a friend or vindictive love, 15% were told by their mates, and the rest discovered the affair on their own. About half the marriages in which cheating was discovered were still intact two years later.

Who is the "other woman?" Laurel Richardson, a sociologist at Ohio State University, found that between 18% and 32% of single women had had an affair with a married man. 90% knew the man was married; only 10% wanted to marry the man. But in 70% of the cases, the married man broke off the affair.

WHEN IT'S TOUGH TO FIND TIME

1 out of 5 men and 1 out of 8 women who work full time do not work the day shift. [41]

HOW LONG MARRIAGES LAST

With all you hear and read about divorce rates, you may be surprised—and pleased—that for the average American, marriage has been a long term commitment: [42]

- The average marriage lasted 23 years

- The average first marriage lasted 27 years

- The average marriage ending with the death of one of the partners lasted 43 years

- 1 out of every 8 couples celebrate their 50th anniversary

DIVORCE

More good news. While the divorce rate soared 227% between 1960 and 1980, that rate dropped 4% over the next 5 years. Because divorce has become more socially acceptable and readily available, the rate will probably never descend to the levels of pre-1960 America, when millions of people stayed trapped in unhappy marriages. But recent reports indicate that the extremely high rates of recent years were a reflection of social changes that hit hardest at Americans now in their thirties.

The proof of this is a 1986 U.S. Census Bureau study that projected: **[43]**

- 45% of first marriages by women now age 45–49 have or will end in divorce.

- 60% of first marriages by women now age 35–39 have or will end in divorce.

- 51.7% of first marriages by women now age 25–29 have or will end in divorce.

Reinforcing this projection were divorce statistics from 1984 (the last year available), which showed a 10% increase in divorce ratio for people age 35-44 and a 43% drop in divorce ratio for people under age 30. **[44]**

It is still true, however, that the highest risks of divorce were in the early years of marriage. One indication is that the average duration of marriage before divorce stayed constant between 1980 and 1985. The following table is further confirmation: **[45]**

Years of marriage	% of all divorces	Cumulative percentage
Under 1	4.1	4.1
1	7.9	12.0
2	8.9	20.9
3	8.9	29.8
4	7.8	37.6
5	6.7	44.3
6	5.7	50.0
7	5.0	55.0
8	4.4	69.4
9	4.1	63.5
10–14	15.7	79.2

Years of marriage	% of all divorces	Cumulative percentage
15–19	9.1	88.3
20–24	5.6	93.9
25–29	3.0	96.9
30+	3.1	100.0

This table shows that a fifth of all couples divorced before their third anniversary, half before their seventh, two-thirds before their ninth anniversary.

This timetable of divorce varied sharply, however, for marriages and remarriages, as shown below: [46]

	Median years at divorce
First marriage	7.5
Second marriage	4.8
Third or more marriage	3.5

The median years before divorce was also a function of the age at which people married. [47]

Age at marriage	Median years at divorce	
	Husband	Wife
Under 20	7.2	7.8
20–24	7.9	7.5
25–29	7.0	5.7
30–34	5.7	4.9
35–39	5.2	4.6
40–44	4.4	4.1
45+	3.4	3.1

While women who married in their teens had the highest median years of marriage before divorce, they also had the highest divorce rates. Following is a table of the percentage of men and women who will divorce, by age at marriage, according to projections by the Census Bureau:

Age at marriage	Median years at divorce	
	Husband	Wife
Under 20	69.6	66.9
20–24	50.6	45.3
25–29	54.0	51.5
30–34	55.5	52.5
35–44	48.3	41.0
45+	23.4	21.1

The average couple who divorced had been separated a little more than a year, and about 6% of couples were separated at any given time. [48]

Data from a study of 5,000 families by the University of Michigan Panel Survey of Income Dynamics found that married women averaged 744 work hours a year. In the year before a separation, however, the hours of work jumped to 1,024, because women sought to protect themselves economically from the effects of divorce.

Still, divorce had a catastrophic economic affect on women, especially in states with new "no-fault" divorce laws. The University of Michigan Panel Survey of Income Dynamics found that the average divorced woman's income dropped 30% in the first year after termination of the marriage. According to a study of women in "no-fault" divorce states by Lenore Weitzman of Stanford University, men's standard of living went up an average of 42% in the year following divorce, while women's standard of living plummeted 73%—even counting alimony and child support.

Remarriage solved most of the problem, however. A second husband was worth about $15,000 a year to white women and about $9,000 a year to black women, according to the University of Michigan's Panel Survey of Income Dynamics.

WHY COUPLES DIVORCE

All couples have disagreements, but certain problems are more likely to become so serious that couples seek therapy or seek a divorce.

According to a survey conducted by *Marriage and Divorce Today*, a newsletter for family therapists, the reasons couples most commonly sought therapy were (answers add up to more than 100% because most couples had more than one reason):

Poor communication	90%
Problems with children	80%
Alcohol/drug abuse	50%
Sexual problems	47%
Unrealistic expectations	40%
Money conflicts	39%
Inequality	30%
Problems with in-laws	16%

It's interesting to match that survey with extensive studies on the causes of divorce reported in the February, 1985 issue of the *Journal of Marriage and the Family*:

Divorce cause	% females citing	% males citing
Poor communication	69.7%	59.3%
Basic unhappiness	59.9%	46.9%
Incompatibility	56.4%	44.7%
Emotional abuse	55.5%	24.7%
Money problems	32.9%	28.7%
Sexual problems	32.1%	30.2%
Alcohol abuse-spouse	30.0%	5.8%
Infidelity-spouse	25.2%	10.5%
Physical abuse	21.7%	3.6%
In-laws	10.7%	11.6%
Children	8.9%	4.4%
Religious differences	8.6%	6.5%
Mental illness	5.0%	6.9%
Drug abuse-spouse	3.9%	1.4%
Infidelty-self	3.9%	6.2%
Women's lib	3.0%	14.5%
Alcohol abuse-self	.9%	9.4%
Drug abuse-self	.3%	1.1%

The above comparison produces two points worth emphasizing. First, problems with children were common in marriages, but they appeared to be largely solvable with therapy—they were listed as causes of less than 1 in 10 divorces. Secondly, physical and emotional abuse were serious marital problems, but few abusing partners agreed to seek counseling before the marriage was irreparably harmed.

ANNULMENTS

Between 1% and 2% of marriages ending each year were annulments. The average length of marriage before the annulment was 1.2 years. [49]

CHILDREN AND DIVORCE

Every year since 1972, between 1 million and 1.2 million children have been involved in divorces. The percentage of divorces that involved children in 1984 were: [50]

None	44.8%
1 child	25.7%
2 children	20.3%
3 children	6.7%
4 or more children	2.5%

DOES HAVING A BABY SAVE A MARRIAGE?

Over the long run, the answer has been no—couples with children divorced at approximately the same rate as childless couples. But Census Bureau statistics show that significantly fewer couples divorced during pregnancy and the first two years of the child's life. Less than 2% of couples got a divorce while the wife was pregnant, 4% in the child's first year, and 8% by the child's second birthday The divorce rate for childless couples over this same time period was 3 times higher. [51]

DIVORCE AND STEPCHILDREN

The presence of stepchildren greatly increased a couples' chances of divorcing early in marriage, according to a study by Lynn White and Alan Booth of the University of Nebraska. In looking at the first three years of marriage, they found divorce rates of:

6% for two people marrying for the first time

7% for marriages in which one partner had been married before, but with no stepchildren

9% for marriages in which one partner had been married before that had at least one stepchild

10% for marriages in which both partners had been married before, but with no stepchildren

17% for marriages in which both partners had been married before that had at least one stepchild

CHAPTER FIVE NOTES

1. Psychology Today, "Love and Romance Survey," July, 1983
2. U.S. Bureau of the Census, Current Population Reports
3. U.S. Bureau of the Census, Current Population Reports
4. Singles: The New Americans, by Jacqueline Simenauer and David Carroll
5. National Center for Health Statistics, Understanding U.S. Fertility: Findings from the National Survey of Family Growth
6. Sex and the American Teen-Ager, Harper & Row/Rolling Stone Press, 1985
7. Sex and the American Teen-Ager, Harper & Row/Rolling Stone Press, 1985
8. National Center for Health Statistics, Vital and Health Statistics
9. Sex and the American Teen-Ager, Harper & Row/Rolling Stone Press, 1985
10. Singles: The New Americans, by Jacqueline Simenauer and David Carroll
11. National Center for Health Statistics, Understanding U.S. Fertility: Findings from the National Survey of Family Growth
12. Singles: The New Americans, by Jacqueline Simenauer and David Carroll
13. Alfred Kinsey, Sexual Behavior in the Human Male and Sexual Behavior in the Human Female
14. U.S. Bureau of the Census, Current Population Reports
15. U.S. Bureau of the Census, Current Population Reports
16. U.S. Bureau of the Census, Current Population Reports
17. U.S. Bureau of the Census, Current Population Reports
18. U.S. Bureau of the Census, Current Population Reports
19. American Couples by Dr. Philip Blumstein and Dr. Pepper Schwartz
20. National Center for Health Statistics, Vital and Health Statistics
21. Centers for Disease Control
22. National Center for Health Statistics, Understanding U.S. Fertility: Findings from the National Survey of Family Growth
23. Centers for Disease Control
24. U.S. Bureau of the Census, Current Population Reports
25. U.S. Bureau of the Census, Current Population Reports
26. U.S. Bureau of the Census, Current Population Reports
27. National Center for Health Statistics, Vital Statistics
28. National Center for Health Statistics, Vital Statistics of the United States
29. U.S. Bureau of the Census, The History and Future of the Relationship Between Education and Marriage, and Neil G. Bennett, David E. Bloom, and Patricia H. Craig, "Black and White Marriage Patterns: Why So Different?"
30. National Center for Health Statistics, Vital Statistics
31. Richard Kopelman and Dorothy Lang

32. National Center for Health Statistics, Vital Statistics of the United States
33. National Center for Health Statistics, Vital Statistics of the United States
34. National Center for Health Statistics, Vital Statistics of the United States
35. National Center for Health Statistics, Vital Statistics
36. Modern Bride, 1986/1987 Honeymoon Market Report
37. National Institute of Mental Health
38. American Couples by Dr. Philip Blumstein and Dr. Pepper Schwartz
39. American Couples by Dr. Philip Blumstein and Dr. Pepper Schwartz
40. Playboy Magazine, January, 1983
41. U.S. Bureau of the Census, 1980 Census of the Population
42. National Center for Health Statistics, Vital Statistics of the United States
43. U.S. Bureau of the Census, Current Population Reports
44. National Center for Health Statistics, Vital Statistics of the United States
45. National Center for Health Statistics, Vital Statistics of the United States
46. National Center for Health Statistics, Vital Statistics of the United States
47. National Center for Health Statistics, Vital Statistics of the United States
48. National Center for Health Statistics, Vital Statistics of the United States
49. National Center for Health Statistics, Vital Statistics of the United States
50. National Center for Health Statistics, Vital Statistics of the United States
51. U.S. Bureau of the Census, Current Population Reports

CHAPTER
SIX

YOUR CHILDREN

AMERICA'S CHILDREN

In July, 1987 there were 63,542,000 children under the age of 18 in the United States. While that might seem like a large number, it was 2.3% less children than there were in 1960. Because the U.S. population climbed while the number of children fell, the percentage of the U.S. population that was under age 18 dropped from 34.2% in 1960 to 26.1% in 1987. [1]

The decline in the number of children would have been far steeper except for the higher fertility rates among minorities. For example, in 1984, 35.0% of Hispanic Americans were under age 18, 33.3% of blacks, and just 25.2% of whites. [2]

The Census Bureau reported that the number of American children by sex and age group in 1985 were: [3]

Age	Number	% of population
Under 5	18,252,000	7.5%
Male	9,341,000	
Female	8,910,000	
5-9	17,661,000	6.9%
Male	9,037,000	
Female	8,625,000	
10-13	13,162,000	5.4%
Male	6,747,000	
Female	6,414,000	

Age	Number	% of population
14-17	14,467,000	5.9%
Male	7,414,000	
Female	7,053,000	

BABIES

In 1986, there were 3,756,000 babies born in the United States. About 2% of babies were multiple births (primarily twins), which meant about 3,701,000 women became mothers. [4]

The most births ever recorded in one year was 4,300,000 in 1957—15% more babies than entered the world in 1986. [5]

Those 1986 births averaged: [6]

313,000   births a month

72,230   births a week

10,319   births a day

430   births an hour

7   births a minute

The birth rate—that is, the number of babies born per 1,000 women age 15-44—plummeted since its peak in the late 1950's. In 1986, the birth rate was 65.4, less than half the 1957 rate. Most of the drastic decline in childbearing took place between 1960 and 1970, with the rate virtually unchanged since 1975. [7]

If you were to compare the birth rate to the death rate, you'd find that women of childbearing age must produce an average of 2.1 children to keep the population from declining (assuming no immigration, of course.) In 1985, women averaged just 1.8 children, which means the population would be decreasing at a rate of 5.2% without immigration. [8]

The birth rate for blacks was 33% higher than for whites; although 12% of the population was black, black babies accounted for 17% of all birth. [9]

WHO'S HAVING BABIES?

It may surprise you to know that the median age of all mothers in 1985 was 25.9 years, less than 5 months older than the median age of mothers in 1960. Although there's been a great deal publicity about women in their 30's having babies, the percentage of all babies born to women age 30 and over in 1984 was 26.2%, compared with 26.6% in 1960.

By age of the mother, the percentage of babies born was:

Under 18	6.7%
18–24	35.7%
25–29	31.3%
30–34	18.8%
35–39	6.1%
Over 40	1.4%

The major age difference between 1960 and the 1980's was that women—especially college-educated women—waited longer to have their first babies. The median age of women giving birth to first babies was 23.3, compared with 22.0 in 1960. The median age of women with 4 or more years of college at first birth, however, was 28.8 years in 1984. 44% of all mothers with four years of college or more had their first babies at age 30 or older, compared with just 11% of mothers with a high school diploma. Although women with at least one year of college made up only 40% of all women age 30–44, they accounted for 71% of the first babies born to that age group.

Family income had the same relationship to age of childbirth as did education. Women age 18–29 with incomes of $35,000 or more had the lowest childbirth rate of any income group, while women age 30–44 with family incomes of $35,000 or more had the highest birth rate of any income group. 42% of first births to families with incomes over $35,000 were to women age 30–44.

HOW MANY BABIES YOU'RE HAVING

Of all babies born in 1984: [10]

42%   were first babies

33%   were second babies

15%   were third babies

6%   were fourth babies

4%   were fifth or higher number

In 1960, only 26% of births were first babies, and a whopping 20% of births were at least their mothers' fifth baby. Between 1970 and 1984, the percentage of married couples with no children increased 34%, the percentage with one child increased 18%, but the percentage of married couples with 3 or more children dropped 44%. [11]

The Census Bureau projected in 1983 that about two-thirds of married women age 18–34 would have either one or two children in their lifetime. By race, the expected lifetime births of married women 18–34 years old were: [12]

Number of children	White	Black	Spanish origin
None	6.4%	3.6%	4.1%
One	12.6%	14.1%	9.1%
Two	49.8%	46.1%	40.2%
Three	22.2%	21.8%	26.0%
Four or more	9.0%	14.5%	20.5%

MULTIPLE BIRTHS

The natural occurance of multiple births has been: [13]

Twins	1 in 90 births
Triples	1 in 9,000 births
Quadruplets	1 in 900,000 births
Quintuplets	1 in 85,000,000 births

WHO WANTED THEIR BABIES?

In the 1982 National Survey of Family Growth, the National Center for Health Statistics found that 89.2% of mothers said their babies were wanted at the time of conception, and only 10.8% said they were unwanted. 29%, however, said that their pregnancies were mis-timed.

WHEN BABIES
WERE CONCEIVED

The following study by the Census Bureau of babies born over a five year period showed when they were conceived, by age of the mother: [14]

Conception	Age of mother			
	15–17	18–19	20–24	25–29
Premarital births	57.4%	39.6%	15.5%	4.2%
Premarital conception	24.2%	24.1%	10.4%	4.9%
Postmarital conception	18.4%	36.3%	74.1%	90.9%

WHO HAS TROUBLE HAVING BABIES?

According to research compiled by *U.S.A. Today* in 1986, half of all American couples trying to have a baby were having trouble. Infertility—defined as the inability to have children after a year of trying—affected about 1 in 7 couples. Excluding couples in which one or both partner were sterile because of voluntary surgery, infertile couples included 21.8% of childless couples and 11.1% of couples who had at least one child. The risk of remaining childless increased from 6% for couples in their early twenties to 15% for couples in their early thirties, then soared for older couples.

Physical causes for infertility were found in 9 out of 10 couples, with the physical problem being the woman's in 60% of the cases and the man's in 40%. Women's problems increased with age, with the average time it took to conceive went from three months for women in their early twenties to a year for women in their mid-thirties and older. The percentage of women who were infertile by age group was: [15]

Age	% of women infertile
15–19	2.1%
20–24	10.6%
25–29	8.7%
30–34	13.9%
35–39	24.6%
40–44	27.3%

Medical or surgical treatments were available for about half the physical problems. Pregnancy rates after treatment ranged from 20% to 70%. [16]

MISCARRIAGES

The National Center for Health Statistics found that 1 in 6 pregnancies ended in miscarriage during the first 20 weeks after conception. The miscarriage rate was 15% for women age 15–24, 17% for women age 25–34, and 31% for women age 35–44. [17]

UNMARRIED MOTHERS

In 1984, 21.0% of all babies were born out-of-wedlock. That figure included 13.4% of white babies and 59.2% of black babies. [18]

The percentage of single women who had had babies was also very different for blacks and whites. In 1985, 42.9% of single black women age 18–29 and 69.6% of black single women age 30–49 had had babies, compared with 7.9% single white women age 18–29 and 11.1% of single white women age 30–49. About a quarter of all black single women have had two or more children. [19]

The percentage of births to unmarried women among Hispanic Americans included 50.8% of births to women of Puerto Rican origin, 24.2% of births to women of Mexican origin, and 16.2% of births to women of Cuban origin. [20]

HOW YOU TIME YOUR BABIES

A Census Bureau study of births over a 5 year period showed the following median intervals in childbearing: [21]

Marriage to first birth	25.0 months
First to second birth	35.8 months
Second to third birth	40.1 months
Third to fourth birth	42.2 months

The same study revealed that 5.5% of married couples had a child before they were wed.

Because substantially more babies have been born in August and September than any other months, you'd think there must be something extra romantic about the Thanksgiving and Christmas holiday seasons. But studies show that a significant majority of parents want to have a baby in the springtime. Unfortunately, they underestimate the amount of time necessary to become pregnant. The result: proportionately, the fewest babies are actually born in April and May. [22]

When you look at days of the week, the most babies have been born on Tuesdays, followed by the other weekdays with approximately the same number of births. 15% to 20% fewer babies have been born on weekends, primarily because doctors don't schedule cesarean sections or induced labor on the weekends. [23]

YOUR BABY'S SEX

Each year there are 105 baby boys born for every 100 baby girls. According to a Media General/Associated Press poll, if parents could chose the sex of their babies, 27% would have a boy, 16% a girl, and 57% would have no preference.

WHO'S CHILDLESS?

In 1985, the percentage of women who were or had ever been married and had never given birth were: [24]

Age	% of childless women
15–19	50.9%
20–24	40.9%
25–29	28.7%
30–34	18.3%
35–39	11.6%
40–44	8.0%

The percentage of women who reached menopause without having born a child dropped dramatically between 1950 and 1985. In 1950, 20% of ever–married women age 40–44 were childless; in 1975, that figure reached the low point of 5.9%, before climbing to 8% in 1985. The major reason for the recent increase in childlessness among married women was that more women were graduating from college. In 1982, 17.7% of college-graduate women age 35–44 were childless, compared with 9.7% of women who were high school graduates. That same year, 14.9% of women college graduates and 19.7% of women with five or more years of college said that they expected to remain childless for life. With more women attending college, the percentage of women who reach age 44 without having had a baby is expected to climb to 10% to 12% by the year 2000. [25]

WHO HAD ABORTIONS

There were 1,573,900 abortions performed in the United States—about 43 abortions for every 100 live births. The abortion rate varied greatly by state, with the District of Columbia topping the list with 150 abortions for every 100 live births, and Utah at the bottom of the list, with just 10 abortions for every 100 live births. [26]

81.1% of women who had abortions were unmarried. 28.5% of abortions were performed on teenagers, and another 55.5% on women in their twenties. 57.8% of women who had abortions had never given birth, while 22.4% had two or more children. About two-thirds of women who had an abortion had never had one before. 51.4% of abortions were performed in the first eight weeks of pregnancy, while 91.2% occured before the end of the first 12 weeks of pregnancy. [27]

HOW BABIES ARE BORN

In 1984, 3,631,000 babies were delivered by physicians in hospitals, 10,000 were delivered by physicians at the mother's home, and 28,000 were delivered by mid-wives or arrived with no professional assistance at all. [28]

In 1984, 21.1% of all babies were delivered by cesarean section, compared with just 5.5% of all babies in 1970. The percentage of cesarean births rose with age of the mother, from a low of 16.5% of babies born to women under age 20 to a high of 28.7% of babies born to women age 35 and older. The National Center of Health Statistics projects that the percentage of cesarean deliveries could rise to 40% of all births by the year 2000. [29]

While some experts believe many cesarean deliveries were un-necessary, this increase may have been one reason the deaths of women during delivery or as a result of post−natal complications dropped from 21.5 per 1000 women in 1970 to 8.0 per 1000 women in 1983. The death rate for infants in the first 28 days of life fell from 15.1 per 1000 in 1970 to 7.3 per 1,000 in 1983. [30]

These rates remained much higher for blacks, however. The

death rate from childbirth was three times higher for black mothers than white mothers, and the death rate in the first 28 days was twice as high for black infants as for whites.

WHO ADOPTS BABIES?

Americans adopted 141,861 babies in 1982, according to the *Adoption Factbook*, prepared and published by the National Committee for Adoption.

64% of all adoptions were by relatives, up from an average of 50% of adoptions during the years 1951–1971. The rise was probably due to the increase in stepparents adopting the children of their new spouses after remarriage.

Children of unwed mothers, the traditional source of babies for adoption, were less frequently given up in 1982 than in 1972. The percentage of babies of unwed mothers given up for adoption fell from 16% in 1972 to 7% in 1982. The percentage varied greatly by race, however. In 1982, 12% of the babies of white unwed mothers were given up for adoption, compared with less than 1% of babies of unwed black mothers.

Keeping the babies, however, was a great sacrifice for the mothers. The National Committee for Adoption found that 40% of women who kept their babies had incomes below the poverty level, compared with 18% of the women who gave up their babies. Only 60% of unwed mothers who kept their children finished high school, compared with 77% of mothers who gave up their children. Half the women who kept their babies eventually married, compared with 75% of the women who gave their babies up for adoption.

8,000 foreign born children were adopted by Americans in 1982, twice as many as in 1972. 62% were from Korea, 7% from Columbia, 5.6% from India, and 4.9% from the Phillipines. 60% of the foreign children adopted were girls.

Mothers who adopted babies were older than the average mother of a first baby, better educated, and had a higher than average income. The vast majority were unable or unwilling to have their own children.

Adopted children tended to be very well off after their adoptions—only 2% lived in families below the poverty level, compared with 13% of all children. That may be one reason why only 2% of adopted children ever searched for their biological parents.

HOW BIG WAS YOUR BABY?

In 1984, the average male baby weighed 7 lb. 9 oz. at birth and measured 20 inches long; the average female baby weighed 7 lb. exactly and measured 19.75 inches long. To be in the highest 10%, male babies had to weigh over 9 lb. 2 oz. and female babies over 8 lb. 10 oz. [31]

In 1984, 5.6% of white babies and 12.4% of black babies were considered "low birth weight babies," weighing 5.5 lb. or less at birth. These babies accounted for between 80% and 90% of all infant deaths. [32]

WHAT YOU NAME YOUR BABY

According to the Facts on File Dictionary of First Names, the most common names given to babies were:

Boys		Girls	
White	Non-white	White	Non-white
Michael	Michael	Jennifer	Tiffany
Matthew	Christopher	Sarah	Crystal
Christopher	James	Jessica	Erica
Brian	Brandon	Amanda	Ebony
David	Anthony	Nicole	Latoya
Adam	Robert	Ashley	Candice
Andrew	Jason	Megan	Jennifer
Daniel	David	Melissa	Brandi
Jason	William	Katherine	Nicole
Joshua	Brian	Stephanie	Danielle

Fashion in selecting names changed most for girls—not a single girl's name on the recent list was on the list of most popular girls' names for 1950 (when Linda and Mary topped the list) or the 1925 list (when Mary and Barbara were on top). Boys' names on the 1950 list that were still popular were Michael and David. The name Robert headed the boys list in both 1950 and 1925.

HOW YOU FEED YOUR BABY

The American Academy of Pediatrics and virtually every other health expert has recommended breastfeeding infants, especially in the first three months of life. The percentage of all mothers who breastfed at birth climbed from 24.3% in 1970 to 62.5% in 1984. 65% of white mothers breastfed their newborns, compared with 33.3% of black mothers. The percentage of mothers breastfeeding increased dramatically with education—50.7% of women without a college education breastfed, compared with 77.5% of women with at least one year of college. [33]

37.0% of all mothers were still breastfeeding their three month old infants, and 27.5% were breastfeeding when their babies were six months old. Of all college educated mothers, 39% were breastfeeding their six month old babies. [34]

HOW CHILDREN GROW

Infants grow very rapidly—on the average, they double their birth weight in the first six months and triple it by their first birthday. According to the medical textbook (*Growth and Development of Children*) by George H. Lowrey, some other rules of thumb about the average child's growth rate: [35]

Height at age 2 is one-half of adult height

At 3 years, the child is 3 feet tall

At 3–1/2 years, the child weights 35 pounds

At age 7, the child weighs 7 times his or her birth weight

Height of a child equals 2.5 times age plus 30 inches

Below is a table of the average weight in pounds and height in inches of boys and girls from birth to age 18, as compiled by the National Center for Health Statistics: [36]

Age	Boys		Girls	
	Weight	Height	Weight	Height
1 mo.	10.0 lbs	21.2 in.	9.7 lb.	21.0 in.
2 mo.	11.5	22.5	11.0	22.2
3 mo.	12.6	23.8	12.4	23.4
4 mo.	14.0	24.7	13.7	24.2
5 mo.	15.0	25.5	14.7	25.0
6 mo.	16.7	26.1	16.0	25.7
9 mo.	20.0	28.0	19.2	27.6
12 mo.	22.2	29.6	21.5	29.2

Age	Boys		Girls	
	Weight	Height	Weight	Height
18 mo.	25.2	32.2	24.5	31.8
2 yr.	27.7	34.4	27.1	34.1
3 yr.	32.2	37.9	31.8	37.7
4 yr.	36.4	40.7	36.2	40.6
5 yr.	40.5	42.8	40.5	42.9
6 yr.	48.3	46.3	46.5	45.6
7 yr.	54.1	48.9	52.2	48.1
8 yr.	60.1	51.2	58.1	50.4
9 yr.	63.1	53.3	63.8	52.3
10 yr.	71.9	55.2	70.3	54.6
11 yr.	77.6	56.8	78.8	57.0
12 yr.	84.4	58.9	87.6	59.8
13 yr.	93.0	61.0	99.1	61.8
14 yr.	100.7	64.0	108.4	62.8
15 yr.	120.1	66.1	113.5	63.4
16 yr.	129.7	67.8	117.0	63.9
17 yr.	136.2	68.4	119.1	64.0
18 yr.	139.0	68.7	119.9	64.0

WHERE CHILDREN LIVE

The high divorce rate has had a very profound affect on the living arrangements of American children. Over 90% of children born in the early 1950's spent the first 18 years of their lives with both biological parents. Today, 42% of white children and 86% of black children will spend part of their childhood living with one parent.

The Child Health Supplement to the National Health Interview Survey revealed the following living arrangements of American children, by race: [37]

Child lived with	White	Black	Hispanic	Total
Both biological parents	73.3%	37.5%	67.1%	67.5%
Biological mother only	12.4%	46.4%	23.4%	18.3%
Biological father only	1.4%	1.9%	1.4%	1.5%
Biological mother/stepfather	7.4%	7.1%	5.0%	7.1%
Biological father/stepmother	1.8%	.7%	.9%	1.6%
Neither biological parent	3.7%	6.4%	2.2%	4.0%
Adoptive parents	2.0%	.9%	.7%	1.7%
Other (relatives, etc.)	1.7%	5.5%	1.5%	2.3%

STEPFAMILIES

In 1984, about 20% of all married couples were remarriages for one or both partners. About 60% of these remarried households had one or more children under age 18, compared with about 50% of all married couple households. About 5.5 million children lived with a stepmother or step father.

In about 1 in 8 remarriages, both the husband and the wife had children under 18 from their previous marriages. Only 3% of remarried couples had children under 18 from previous marriages and a child from their current marriage. [38]

60% of children who lived with their mothers rarely or never see their natural fathers. The National Health Interview Survey revealed the following frequency of contact: [39]

Frequency of contact with father	Children living with single mother	Children living with mother/stepfather
Every day	4.5%	.6%
Several times a week	9.3%	2.1%
Once a week	9.8%	5.3%
2–3 times a month	10.4%	9.8%
Once a month	8.8%	5.2%
Rarely	22.8%	28.7%
Never	31.2%	46.0%

The frequency of contact with the absent parent was slightly better for the much smaller number of children who lived with a single father or a father and stepmother. About half of these children (49%) rarely or never saw their natural mothers. [40]

AMERICA'S ORPHANS

In 1985, 2,330,000 American children, 3.6% of all children, were considered to be orphans. Of these: [41]

1,699,000 had lost their fathers

599,000 had lost their mothers

33,000 had lost both parents

WHO RECEIVES CHILD SUPPORT?

According to the Bureau of the Census, approximately 8,800,000 mothers were raising children without a father present in 1985. 61% of these women were legally awarded child support, including 76% of divorced mothers, 76% of divorced but remarried mothers, 41% of separated mothers, and 18% of single mothers.

74% of the mothers who were entitled to child support received at least some money, but only 48% received the entire amount due. The average child support payment was $185 per month, down 12% from the average payment in 1983. **[42]**

WHO ARE GRANDPARENTS?

According to a study by the Meredith Corporation in 1986, 70% of grandparents were age 55 older. 7% were age 35–44 and 10% were age 45–49. Nearly half of all grandparents had grandchildren age 6–11.

CHILD SUPPORT BY UNWED FATHERS

The percentage of unwed fathers who paid child support, by race, were: **[43]**

Black	36%
Hispanic	24%
White	20%

CHILD ABUSE

The 1985 National Family Violence Survey sponsored by the National Institute of Mental Health showed a sharp drop in severe violence against children between 1975 and 1985. The study also revealed, however, that almost 2 million children a year—1 out of every 33 children under age 18—were very severely abused, and as many as 5,000 died as a result.

The survey of children in two-parent homes showed that some

kind of violence (including spanking) took place in 62% of homes. Severe violence took place in 10.7% of homes (down from 14.0% in 1975, and very severe violence in 1.9% of homes (down from 3.6% in 1975).

About one-third of the victims of very severe violence were under age 1, about one-third were age 1–6, and the remaining third were age 7–17. Child abuse was the cause of 10% of the hospital emergency room visits for all children.

Researchers believe the decline was the result of massive public awareness that has led to a 9% annual increase in the number of reports of child abuse, as well as tougher criminal penalties for parents convicted of abusing their children. Especially significant, say experts, has been the willingness of schools and physicians to report suspected child abuse victims. [44]

Recent studies have revealed that as many as 28% of girls were sexually abused before the age of 14 and 38% by the age of 18. Diana E.H. Russell of Mills College found that a girl who lived with her stepfather had a 1 in 6 chance of being sexually abused. 4.9% of girls had been abused by an uncle, 4.5% by her father, 3% by a first cousin, and 2.2% by a brother.

A national poll conducted by the Los Angeles *Times* in 1985 revealed that 16% of men had been sexually molested as children. A study of undergraduates at 6 New England colleges produced a figure of 9% of men having been sexually abused before age 18.

The Los Angeles *Times* poll indicated that between 10.9 million and 17.6 million American men have sexually abused a child. Overall, about 30% of those who have sexually abused girls were relatives, 60% were known to the victim but unrelated (babysitters, neighbors, teachers, etc.), and only 10% were strangers.

HOW MANY KIDS ARE JUVENILE DELINQUENTS?

In 1982, 1.9 million young people age 10–17 were arrested, about 4.3% of all young people in that age group. Three quarters of those arrested were boys. Juveniles under 18 made up 16% of all males arrested and 22% of all females arrested.

In 1985, 49,322 juveniles were being held in detention centers. Their offenses were: [45]

Car theft/burglary/property crime	45%
Robbery/murder/rape/violent crime	25%
Probation violations	9%
Alcohol/drug offenses	5%
Truancy/running away	5%
No offense—victim of abuse	2%
Other	9%

HOW MANY CHILDREN ARE MISSING?

The estimates of how many children are missing vary widely, from 50,000 to a high of one million. Although as many as 2 million youngsters have run away from home each year, 53% of them went less than 10 miles. Most returned in a few days or stayed with a friend. About 27% were away from home more than six months, and in many of these cases, the parents knew where the child was staying. **[46]**

The fact that kidnapping by strangers is relatively rare is pointed out by taking a look at the 4,418 children recovered with the assistance of the National Center for Missing and Exploited Children between 1984 and 1986. The reasons these children were missing were:

Runaways	3,299
Parental abductions	784
Abducted by family members	217
Abducted by strangers	118
Recovered dead	43

WHAT IT COSTS TO RAISE YOUR CHILD

Expert estimates on what you'll spend to raise a single child born in 1980 to age 18 ranges from $142,700 to $148,642. Three different estimates, with percentages of total expeditures by category are:

Expense	Cost	% of total cost
Urban Institute		
Food	$ 32,600	23%
Housing	$ 32,200	23%
Clothing	$ 8,900	6%
Transportation	$ 36,500	26%
Health	$ 8,500	6%
Other	$ 24,000	16%
Total	$ 142,700	
U.S. Department of Agriculture/ Cornell University		
Food	$ 36,250	25%
Housing	$ 49,300	34%
Clothing	$ 11,600	8%
Transportation	$ 24,650	17%
Health	$ 7,250	5%
Other	$ 15,950	11%
Total	$ 145,000	
COSTS OF CHILDREN by Lawrence Olson		
Food	$ 41,348	28%
Housing	$ 48,435	33%
Clothing	$ 6,700	5%
Transportation	$ 16,727	11%
Health	$ 12,609	8%
Other	$ 22,823	15%
Total	$ 148,642	

These expenses above represently roughly 30% of the after-tax income of the average family. The Urban Institute found that families with 2 working parents spent 23% more than families with 1 working parent. Each subsequent child after the first was less expensive. Bringing up 2 children took about 40% of after tax spending, while 3 children cost 50% of after tax spending.

With baby furniture, hospital bills, etc., the cost of the baby's first year is high. Cost fall, then rise again beginning with age 12. You'll spend about 40% of your child raising money when your child's age 12–18.

According to Lawrence Olson, your costs per year for a baby born in 1980 will be the following:

1980	Birth	$ 7,118
1981	1	$ 6,216
1982	2	$ 5,323
1983	3	$ 4,747
1984	4	$ 4,437
1985	5	$ 4,357
1986	6	$ 4,441
1987	7	$ 4,645
1988	8	$ 4,994
1989	9	$ 5,473
1990	10	$ 7,870
1991	11	$ 8,530
1992	12	$ 9,883
1993	13	$ 9,227
1994	14	$ 10,861
1996	15	$ 11,577
1997	16	$ 12,284
1998	17	$ 12,978
1999	18	$ 13,679

The consolation for parents is that inflation will increase income as well as expenses. Lawrence Olson estimates the average family will earn over $900,000 during those 18 years.

PAYING FOR COLLEGE

Estimates on the cost of sending a baby born in 1980 through four years of college range from $67,000 to $157,000. How can you save that money? To accumulate $100,000, you must put $2,193 a year for 18 years in an investment that nets 10% a year—not an easy thing to find these days.

The difficulty of saving so much money is the reason that over half the money for college expenses in 1984 came from loans, scholarships, and the student's earnings. The Carnegie Foundation found that 1984 college students paid for their education as follows:

Family	39%
Student earnings/savings	33%
Grants/scholarships	15%
Loans	13%

DAY CARE FOR CHILDREN

In 1985, 53.4% of married and separated women and 67.6% of divorced women with children under age 6 were in the work force. [47] Numerous recent surveys show that the availability, quality, and cost of day care was the biggest source of worry and guilt for these women. Surveys also show that a third of non-working mothers would be in the workforce if they could find or afford day care.

In 1985, the Census Bureau found that the 8,686,000 employed mothers with children under age 5 made the following day care arrangements: [48]

Type of care	% of children
Care in child's home	31.0%
By father	15.7%
By other relative	9.4%
By non-relative	5.9%
Care in another home	37.0%
By relative	14.7%
By non-relative	22.3%
Group care center	23.1%
Mother cares for child while working	8.1%

In 1984, the National Education Association found that 2.1 million children age 5–13 had no adult supervision after school.

Employee benefits experts have called assistance with child care the "employee benefit of the 1990's." But in 1985, the Conference Board found that of 44,000 U.S. companies employing 100 or more people, only 2,500 offered some child care assistance and only 150 offered an on-site or near-the-job day care facility.

While the cost of day care varied widely with the over−all cost of living in different parts of the country, *Fortune* Magazine estimated in its February 16, 1987 issue that sitters who came to a child's home during the day charged between $165 and $340 per week, live−in help averaged $150 a week plus room and board, care in another home cost between $50 and $100 a week, and group day care cost between $60 and $120 per week per child.

Even with day care, *Fortune* found that "problems with child care are the most significant predictors of absenteeism and unproductive time at work." 41% of parents missed at least 1 day of work in the preceeding three months to take care of a child, and 10% missed 3 to 5 days.

YOUR CHILD'S DENTAL HEALTH

Thanks to the fluoridation of drinking water, there has been a dramatic improvement in the dental health of children over the last two decades. The most recent dental health survey conducted by the National Center for Health Statistics revealed that the average number of cavities in children under age 18 decreased from 7.06 per child in 1971–1974 to 4.77 per child in 1979–1980. In that same time frame, the percentage of children age 6–11 who'd never had a cavity increased from 43.6% to 56.7% during that same time period. The 1980 survey found that 36.6% of children reached at age 18 without ever having a cavity. Some experts predict that as many as 75% of children born in 1988 may reach 18 without any cavities. [49]

In 1984, 17% of children under age 5 and 67.3% of children age 5–14 visited a dentist. Those needing treatments averaged 2.5 visits per person. [50]

Worried about the cost of braces for your child's teeth? According to the American Dental Association, 13% of children do or will need orthodonic treatment before age 18.

WHO GOES TO PRE-SCHOOL?

In 1985, 28.8% of 3-year-olds and 49.1% of 4-year-olds attended a pre–school program, compared with 13.0% of 3-year-olds and 27.9% of 4-year-olds in 1970. 58% of those in pre-school had mothers who worked. [51]

Pre-school education proved to be very valuable, at least for children of low-income families. In 1985, about $1 billion in federal money funded Head Start pre-school programs for 452,00 children of low-income families. A study of Head Start graduates by New York University education expert Martin Deutsch showed the following results:

	Head Start graduates	Non-Head Start graduates
Graduates from H.S.	57%	36%
Men receiving college degrees	43%	24%
Women with college degrees	37%	31%
Males with full time jobs	55%	29%
Females with full time jobs	48%	17%

WHO ATTENDS KINDERGARTEN?

In 1985, 87.2% 5-year-olds attended kindergartens, up from 69% in 1970. One-third of these tykes were enrolled in full-day kindergarten programs, up from 20% in 1973. [52]

WHO'S IN ELEMENTARY SCHOOL?

In 1985, there were 26,900,000 students enrolled in grades 1–8 in the United States, representing 99.2% of children in the appropriate age group. 88% of these students attended public elementary schools. [53]

The days of the one-room schoolhouse are long gone. The average public elementary school had 468 students, with only 8% having less than 100 children in attendance. [54]

About 71% of all private schools were church-related, and half of these were Catholic schools. The percentage of students who attended private schools rose with education and income—24% of children born to college-graduates and 33% of children in families with an income of $75,000 a year or more attended private school in 1985. The average tuition at a private school in 1985 was $1,218 per year. [55]

In 1986, there were 1,212,000 public elementary school teachers. 84% of all elementary school classroom teachers were female and 89% were white. 86% of all principals, however, were men. [56]

Elementary school teachers were better educated than ever— 64.9% had masters or higher degrees in 1986, up from 25.5% in 1973. They were also more experienced. The average elementary school teacher had 14 years experience in 1986, and 70.7% had ten years or more on the job. [57]

That experience, while greatly benefiting students now in school, represents a serious future problem for American education as the majority of teachers retire. The number of students receiving bachelor degrees in education in 1986 was less than half the number receiving education degrees in 1970. As a result, the National Center for Education Statistics estimated that between 1988 and 1992, there will be 126 job openings for every 100 new teachers.

The major reason for the teacher shortage has been teacher salaries. The average salary for elementary school teachers in 1986 was $25,300 a year. When adjusted for inflation, however, that figure represented a 15% decline in purchasing power since 1970.

In 1985, starting salaries for teachers averaged $15,400, almost 25% lower than the average starting salary for all college graduates. Low pay was the primary reason that 55% of America's elementary teachers in 1986 said they wouldn't become teachers again (compared with just 9% of all teachers in 1965). **[58]**

The average elementary school library had 8,000 books, an average of 17 books per pupil. The library had an additional average of 1,026 audio-visual materials (tapes, films, film strips, etc.). **[59]**

91% of public elementary schools were equipped with at least one micro-commputer in 1985, with a national average of 9 computers per school. The ratio of students to computer was 55, and the average weekly computer instruction time was 30 minutes. **[60]**

WHO ATTENDS HIGH SCHOOL?

In 1985, 14,100,000 teenagers attended American high schools, 91% in public schools. The percentage of teenagers enrolled was 98.1% of 14 and 15 year olds and 91.7% of 16 and 17 year olds. Despite the publicity about the dropout rate in inner-city schools, a slightly higher percentage of blacks than whites age 14–17 were in school. **[61]**

About a quarter of American high schools had 1,000 or more students, and 57% had over 500. **[62]**

WHO GRADUATES FROM HIGH SCHOOL?

In 1986, 2,402,000 students received public high school diplomas. The graduates included about 72% of all 18 year olds, with the rest having dropped out or been held back. **[63]** In 1983, 97.6% of all seniors graduated. An estimated 87% of all teenagers will eventually receive a high school degree. **[64]**

The average high school graduate earned credits for 4 years of English, 2-1/2 years of math, 2 years of science, 3 years of social studies, and 1 year of a foreign language. The National Center for Education Statistics also estimated 17% had an A average in English, 17% had an A average in math, 19% had an A average in science, and 45% had an A average in art. **[65]**

WHO DROPS OUT OF HIGH SCHOOL?

In 1985, 10.6% of people age 14–24 were high school dropouts, according to the National Center for Education Statistics. That included:

7.0% of 16–17 year olds

14.1% of 18–21 year olds

14.1% of 21–24 year olds.

The overall percentage of dropouts declined 1.6% from 1970 to 1985. But the percentage of blacks age 14–24 who were dropouts plunged from 22.2% in 1970 to 12.6% in 1984. There were .6% more blacks age 16–17 in school than whites in the same age range in 1985. **[66]**

Where were the dropout rates the highest?

Louisiana	43%
Mississippi	35%
Tennessee	35%
Florida	35%
Georgia	34%

The states with the lowest rates, on the other hand, were North Dakota (5%) and Minnesota (9%).

The drop out rates by family income were: **[67]**

Low income	22.3%
Low middle income	13.2%
High middle income	10.7%
High income	7.0%

High school drop outs didn't fair well in the labor market. When the Bureau of Labor Statistics compared high school graduates age 16–21 who didn't go on to college with high school dropouts age 16–21, they found that the unemployment rate for graduates was 15.1%, while the unemployment rate for dropouts was 31.1%. **[68]**

WHO TEACHERS
HIGH SCHOOL?

According to the National Center for Education Statistics, 967,000 public secondary school teachers earned an average salary of $26,100 in 1986, 5% more than the average elementary school teacher. 68.5% of senior high school teachers had a masters degree or more education. High school teachers were even more experienced than elementary teachers—54.6% had been on the job 15 years or more and 73% had over 10 years experience. 84% of secondary school teachers were white, 44% were male, and 56% female. Secondary school teachers were generally more satisfied with their career choice, with only 38% saying that they would choose another career if they had to make the choice again. **[69]**

THE COSTS OF
PUBLIC EDUCATION

In 1985, America spent about $138 billion on public education, a little less than 7% of its gross national product.

The average per pupil expenditures for public elemetary and secondary schools was $3,182. The 5 states with the highest per pupil expenditures were:

Alaska	$6,867
New York	$5,226
New Jersey	$5,220
Wyoming	$4,809
Connecticut	$4,477

The 5 states with the lowest per pupil expeditures were:

Utah	$2,182
Mississippi	$2,205
Alabama	$2,241
Idaho	$2,290
Arizona	$2,344

WHO TAKES
COLLEGE ENTRANCE EXAMS?

In 1985, 977,000 high school students took the Scholastic Aptitude Test (SAT). This test has two parts, a verbal test and a math test, both of which have a minimum score of 200 and a maximum score of 800. The average scores in 1985 were: **[70]**

Verbal Test	431
Males	437
Females	425
Math Test	475
Males	499
Females	452

7.9% of those who took the verbal SAT and 17.1% of those who took the math test scored over 600; 39.4% of the verbal scores and 28.2% of the math scores were below 400. High school seniors who ranked in the top 10% of their class averaged 547 on the combined tests. Since 1967, the average verbal score has dropped 35 points and the average math score has declined 17 points.

739,000 students took the American College Testing Program (ACT) examination. The ACT has four parts, English, Math, Social Sciences, and Natural Sciences, each of which has a minimum score of 1 and a maximum score of 36. The average scores in 1985 were: **[71]**

English	18.1
Male	17.6
Female	18.6
Math	17.2
Male	18.6
Female	16.0
Social studies	17.4
Male	18.3
Female	16.6
Natural science	21.2
Male	22.6
Female	20.0

14% of those who took the test had a composite score of 26 or over, while 32% had a composite score of 15 or less.

WHO GOES TO COLLEGE?

In 1985, 54% of high school graduates age 24 or younger were either enrolled in college or had completed at least one year of college. [72] Of all college freshmen: [73]

21% had A averages in high school

59% had B averages

20% had C averages

1% had D averages

41% ranked in top 20% of their high school class

23% ranked in the second 20%

29% ranked in the third 20%

7% ranked in the bottom 40%

One in three college freshmen didn't make it to the sophomore year. Below were the first year dropout rates from a 1983 study of 2,432 schools by the American College Testing Program:

Four year public universities	30%
Four year private universities	26%
Two year public universities	46%
Two year private universities	30%
All institutions	32%

HOW MANY CHILDREN ARE HANDICAPPED?

In 1985, 4,315,000 children were enrolled in educational programs for the handicapped. By the type of handicap, the percentage of enrollees was: [74]

Learning disabilities	42.4%
Speech impairment	26.1%
Mentally retarded	16.1%
Emotionally disturbed	8.6%
Hard of hearing and deaf	1.6%

Orthopedically handicapped	1.3%
Other health impaired	1.6%
Visually handicapped	.7%
Multihandicapped	1.6%
Deaf-blind	.1%

HOW MANY CHILDREN ARE MENTALLY RETARDED?

The commonly used criteria for determining mental retardation—that is, significantly subnormal intellectual capability—is based on the Stanford-Binet IQ test. The average IQ score is 100, with half the population scoring over 100 and half under 100. The American Association of Mental Deficiency defines mental retardation as an IQ score below 70, a range which includes about 3% of the population.

69–52	Mild
36–51	Moderate
35–20	Severe
Below 19	Profound

About 85% of mentally retarded children are classified as "educatable." With special classes, they can achieve a second to seventh grade level education, many can read and write, and almost all are capable of self-support.

HOW MANY CHILDREN HAVE LEARNING DISABILITIES?

A learning disability is any perceptual or communication difficulty that affects a child's ability to absorb or deal with information. Many such disabilities only affect specific skills, such as a child's ability to read or do mathematical calculations—in all other areas, the child may be normal or even well above average.

Because the definition of a learning disability is vague and because many mild disabilities go undetected, it's hard to come up with the exact number of children affected. Experts estimate that up to one-third of U.S. children children have academic difficulties not related to intelligence, physical handicaps, home environment, or emotional disturbances.

Perhaps the most common disability is dyslexia, a disorder in which children have problems reading and understanding what they read. As many as 10% of children may suffer from dyslexia, with boys outnumbering girls 4 to 1. A number of very famous people have suffered from dyslexia, including Nelson Rockefeller and Albert Einstein. **[75]**

HOW MANY CHILDREN ARE GIFTED?

About 5% of children have IQ scores over 120, one definition of "giftedness." About 2 children in every 1000 have IQ's of 145 or over, the "genius" level. **[76]**

YOUR CHILD'S HEALTH

Children today are much less prone to serious illness than they were twenty-five years ago. The infant mortality rate in 1984 was 2.5 times lower than in 1960. The death rate for children ages 1–4 was cut in half in the same time period, and the death rate for children ages 5–15 fell 59%. **[77]**

One major reason for the decline in fatal illness was widespread immunization against serious childhood illnesses. From 1960 to 1985, the number of cases of rheumatic fever fell from 9,022 to 117, the cases of measles from 441,000 to 2,700, the cases of whooping cough from 14,800 to 3,300, the cases of polio from 3,190 to 5, and the cases of diptheria from 918 to 2. In 1985, 73.7% of children under the age of 14 were immunized against whooping cough, tetanus and diptheria, 69.7% against polio, 71.5% against measles, and 71.6% against mumps. **[78]**

Children were, of course, still prone to the common cold, influenza, chicken pox, and other routine illnesses. Information gathered by the National Center for Health Statistics over the last decade shows that the average child under age 15 felt ill about 11 days a year and missed an average of 5 days of school. **[79]**

The average child under age 5 saw a doctor 4 times a year. The average child 5–9 saw a doctor 3 times a year, and children 10–14 averaged 2 yearly visits. About 8% of all visits were in a hospital emergency room. **[80]**

The percentage of children who were hospitalized during 1984 was, by age: **[81]**

Under 1	22.5%
1–4	7.0%
5–14	4.1%

The most common cause of hospitalization for infants under age 1 was respiratory diseases (30% of admissions), followed by infective disease (15% of admissions), and digestive problems (13% of admissions).

Respiratory disease accounted for almost half the hospital admissions of children age 1–4, with injuries from accidents or abuse moving up to be the second leading cause (12% of admissions). For children age 5–14, respiratory diseases were responsible for 28% of admissions and accidents and abuse were next at 20% of admissions. [82]

About 1.2% of babies born in the U.S. died during the first year of life in 1984, with more than half passing away in the first seven days. The death rate for children age 1–4 was 1 in 1754 and for children 5–14, 1 in 3225. Half the deaths of children age 1–14 were caused by accidents, poisonings, or violence. [83]

YOUR CHILD'S SLEEP

A newborn baby sleeps 18–20 hours a day, normally broken up in 7 periods ranging in time from 20 minutes to 4 hours. By age 1, a child normally sleeps 14 hours a day, including morning and afternoon naps. By age 2, the average time sleeping is 12 hours, including 1 nap a day. By age 12, the sleep requirement drops to 10–11 hours a day, with no naps.

Bedtime rituals are important in the lives of almost all families. A survey of parents of children age 3–13 conducted by the firm Public Attitudes found that:

92% kissed their child good night

65% said bedtime prayers

52% often read or told stories at bedtime

15% tucked their child in with a toy or stuffed animal

20% had problems getting their kids to bed

POISONING AND YOUR CHILD

An estimated 1,472,000 children under age 6 required treatment for ingesting poisonous chemicals, household products, drugs, etc. in 1984. According to a study of more than 250,000 poisoning incidents by the American Association of Poison Control Centers, the causes were:

Over the counter/prescription drugs	60%
Aspirin/acetaminophen	10%
Cleaning agents	9%
Toxic plants	9%
Cosmetics	5%
Alcohol	4%
Insecticides/pesticides	3%

The two leading causes of death from poisoning were drugs and alcohol. 83% of all alcohol poisonings were children under age 6.

ACCIDENTS AND YOUR CHILD

In 1983, 6,000,000 children age 5 and under, 31% of all boys and 25% of all girls, were injured in accidents. Accidents hurt 13,000,000 children age 6–16, including 42% of boys and 27% of girls. **[84]**

One cause of injury to infants and toddlers was nursery equipment. The Consumer Product Safety Commission estimated the following annual product-related injuries that resulted in trips to the emergency room:

Walkers	16,000
Strollers/carriages	11,300
High chairs	9,000
Playpens	4,000
Infant seats	3,700
Changing tables	1,330

In 1984, an estimated 189,000 U.S. children needed hospital care for injuries suffered in playgrounds—an increase of 23% from

1980. 72% of the injuries resulted from falls from playground equipment. The equipment involved in the injuries was: [85]

Climbers	42%
Swings	23%
Slides	16%
Merry-go-rounds	8%
Seesaws	5%
Other	6%

591,000 children were treated at hospital emergency rooms in 1986 after injuries with playthings. The number of injuries by cause were: [86]

Bicycles	377,000
Toys	95,000
Skateboards	58,000
Roller skates	44,000
Sled	17,000

The leading cause of deaths to small children were crib injuries. Most of these resulted from use of cribs manufactured before 1974, when federal regulations specified more narrow spacing between crib bars, new safety latches, etc. The second leading cause of deaths were the lids of toy chests falling on children's heads. [87]

71% of accidental deaths of older children were caused by motor vehicle accidents in 1984. Drownings accounted for 8%, fires for 4%, firearms for 3%, and falls and poisonings for 2% each. [88]

YOUR CHILDREN AND DRUGS AND ALCOHOL

The Federal government now believes that drug and alcohol education should start at age 9. This policy stems from a survey of 500,000 young people conducted for the White House Drug Abuse Policy Office. The study found that 25% of fourth graders said they felt pressure from their peers to try beer, wine, liquor, or marijuana. By the sixth grade, 25% of students said alcohol was a "big problem" and 33% said marijuana was a big problem.

A study of 44,326 kids in 1983 conducted by the National Parents' Resource Institute for Drug Education found that 33.4% of sixth graders had tried beer or wine and 9.5% had tried hard liquor. About 3% of sixth graders drank alcohol at least once a week.

Early drug usage has been directly tied to later teenager drug abuse. A study of teenage drug abusers by Straight, Inc., a drug treatment program, showed that half of the abusers got involved with drugs or alcohol before the age of 12. Of these abusers, 61% had used alcohol first and 30% had used pot first.

In 1986, an estimated 93% of students had tried alcohol by the time they were seniors in high school. 70% of high school seniors had used alcohol in the past 30 days, 11.5% drank alcohol at least three times a week, and 6% drank daily. An estimated 500,000 alcoholics were in their teenage or preteen years.

A 1986 study of drug use among high school seniors conducted for the National Institute on Drug Abuse by the University of Michigan Institute for Social Research showed that 58% of high school seniors in 1985 had tried marijuana. Of these students, 3% first smoked in the sixth grade or younger, 15.3% began in the 7th or 8th grade, and 15.3% first tried the drug as a high school freshman.

In 1986, 26% of high school seniors had used marijuana in the previous month, down from the all-time peak of 37% in 1978–79. 5% of seniors used marijuana daily. The only drug showing a marked increase in usage was cocaine. In 1986, 17% of high school senior had tried the drug and 7% had used it in the previous 30 days. Only 10% of 1976 high school seniors had tried cocaine. 4.2% of boys and 3.6% of girls had smoked crack, the powerful cocaine-derived drug.

Parents commonly underestimated their kids' drug and alcohol usage. An Emory University Medical School study of 800 high school seniors and their parents showed that 35% of parents said their children had used alcohol in the previous 30 days, while 67% of students said they had. Only 3% of parents said their children had used marijuana in the previous 30 days, while 28% of the seniors said they'd smoked the drug.

YOUR CHILDREN'S FITNESS

America's school age children are in dismal physical condition, and they've gotten even fatter and less fit in recent years.

A study of 8,800 kids in grades 5–12 conducted by the Department of Health and Human services revealed that less than half of the children were getting enough exercise to maintain adequate cardiovascular fitness. Guy Reiff, a University of Michigan professor who has conducted three national fitness surveys over 25 years, found that 40% of American children had at least one risk factor for cardiovascular disease, with 20% of the children at serious risk.

In 1984, only 2% of 18 million young people passed the Presidential Physical Fitness test. The 1984 Amateur Athletic Union/Nabisco study of 18,000 youths age 6–17 found only 36% met fitness standards for "average healthy youngsters" and only 5% were outstanding. The 1985 School Fitness Survey showed that 40% of boys and 70% of girls age 6–12 couldn't do more than one pull-up. 40% of boys age 6–15 weren't flexible enough to reach beyond their toes. 50% of girls age 6–17 couldn't run a mile in less than 10 minutes.

Researchers gave two major reasons for these very poor results. First of all, they found a strong correlation between fitness and television watching. 30% of teenagers who watched five hours or more of TV daily while they were ages 6–11 were obese, compared with just 10% of teenagers who watched an hour or less daily.

Secondly, kids were getting less and less physical education in school. Only 36% of students in grades 5–12 had a daily gym class. [89]

About 1 in 8 12–14 year olds has had at least one cigarette in the last week. The University of Michigan's Institute for Social Research found that in 1986, 71% of high school students had tried cigarettes and 30% were currently smokers.

EATING DISORDERS

Two 1986 Gallup polls found that 12% of teenage girls and 4% of teenage boys had some sort of eating disorder, including anorexia nervosa, or dieting to the point of starvation. Another 34% of girls reported occasional food "binges," which were followed by vomiting to purge the food, fasting, taking laxatives or diuretics, or strenuous over-exercise.

According to some experts, most teenage girls have the potential to develop eating disorders because of their obsessive preoccupation with weight. Psychiatrist K.A. Halmi, an expert on anorexia, has found that girls began dieting as early as the fourth grade, and by the teenage years, 70% were dieting.

How many children are really obese. Studies show that about 13% of pre-school children, 11%–17% of children 6–12, and 16%–20% of children 13–18 were more than 20% overweight. **[90]**

YOUR CHILD'S TELEVISION VIEWING

In the average household, television watching occupies more of the time of children age 2–12 than any activity except sleeping—including hours spent attending school. Studies show the average child in that age bracket watched 28 hours a week of television, with the range of hours spent in front of the tube ranging from a low of 5 to a high of 100 hours per week. **[91]**

As discussed in our section about kid's fitness above, the likelyhood of a child being overweight increased with the number of hours of television viewing. The National Assessment of Educational Progress found that children who watched 6 or more hours a day of television scored 9% lower on standardized reading tests than kids who averaged 2 hours a day or less. Psychologists S. Gadberry also conducted a number of studies that tied increased television viewing to lower school grades.

Children who watched commercial television were exposed to an average of 9 acts of physical aggression and 8 acts of verbal agression per hour. The U.S. Surgeon General has issued two reports (1972 and 1982) that revealed that children who watch a lot of television violence were more likely to act violently than children who didn't watch a lot of television violence.

The primary positive effects of television watching that have been documented by research result from pre-school children viewing public television programs like *Sesame Street* and *Mr. Roger's Neighborhood*. Three to five year olds who watched these shows had better skills, a more positive attitude toward school, and a more cooperative attitude with adults than non-viewers.

An increase in television viewing, plus the increase in the number of working mothers, has led to a drastic decrease in the amount of "quality time"—time spend talking, reading, and playing—parents spend with their children. A major survey of time use by the Institute for Social Research at the University of Michigan found that working mothers spent an average of 11 minutes of quality time with their children on workdays and 30 minutes a day on weekends. Fathers spent about 8 minutes a day during the week and 14 minutes a day on weekends. **[92]**

CHAPTER SIX NOTES

1. U.S. Bureau of the Census, Current Population Reports
2. U.S. Bureau of the Census, Current Population Reports
3. U.S. Bureau of the Census, Current Population Reports
4. National Center for Health Statistics, Vital Statistics
5. National Center for Health Statistics, Vital Statistics
6. National Center for Health Statistics, Vital Statistics
7. National Center for Health Statistics, Vital Statistics
8. National Center for Health Statistics, Vital Statistics
9. National Center for Health Statistics, Vital Statistics of the United States
10. National Center for Health Statistics, Vital Statistics of the United States
11. U.S. Bureau of the Census, Current Population Reports
12. U.S. Bureau of the Census, Current Population Reports
13. World Book Encyclopedia
14. U.S. Bureau of the Census, Current Population Reports
15. National Center for Health Statistics, National Survey of Family Growth
16. U.S.A. Today
17. National Center for Health Statistics, National Survey of Family Growth
18. National Center for Health Statistics, Vital Statistics of the United States
19. U.S. Bureau of the Census, Current Population Reports
20. National Center for Health Statistics, unpublished data
21. U.S. Bureau of the Census, Current Population Reports
22. National Center for Health Statistics, Vital Statistics of the United States
23. National Center for Health Statistics, Vital Statistics of the United States
24. U.S. Bureau of the Census, Current Population Reports
25. U.S. Bureau of the Census, Current Population Reports
26. National Center for Health Statistics, Vital Statistics of the United States
27. National Center for Health Statistics, Vital Statistics of the United States
28. National Center for Health Statistics, Vital Statistics of the United States
29. National Center for Health Statistics, National Hospital Discharge Survey
30. National Center for Health Statistics, Vital Statistics of the United States
31. National Center for Health Statistics, Vital Statistics of the United States
32. National Center for Health Statistics, Vital Statistics of the United States
33. Ross Laboratories
34. Ross Laboratories
35. George H. Lowrey, Growth and Development of Children
36. National Center for Health Statistics, Health Examination Survey
37. National Center For Health Statistics, National Health Interview Survey
38. National Center for Health Statistics, National Health Interview Survey
39. National Center for Health Statistics, National Health Interview Survey
40. National Center for Health Statistics, National Health Interview Survey
41. U.S. Social Security Administration
42. U.S. Bureau of the Census, Current Population Reports
43. The Socioeconomic Newsletter
44. National Institute of Mental Health, 1985 National Family Violence Survey
45. National Center for Juvenile Justice
46. National Center for Missing and Exploited Children
47. U.S. Bureau of the Census, Current Population Reports
48. U.S. Bureau of the Census, Current Population Reports
49. American Dental Association, 1987 Dental Statistics Handbook

50. American Dental Association, 1987 Dental Statistics Handbook
51. U.S. Bureau of the Census, Current Population Reports
52. U.S. Bureau of the Census, Current Population Reports
53. U.S. Bureau of the Census, Current Population Reports
54. U.S. Department of Education, Digest of Education Statistics
55. U.S. Bureau of the Census, unpublished data
56. National Education Association
57. National Education Association
58. National Education Association
59. School Library Journal, May, 1985
60. Market Data Retrieval
61. U.S. Bureau of the Census, Current Population Reports
62. U.S. Department of Education, Digest of Education Statistics
63. National Education Association
64. National Center for Education Statistics
65. National Center for Education Statistics
66. U.S. Bureau of the Census, Current Population Reports
67. U.S. Department of Education, Digest of Education Statistics
68. U.S. Bureau of Labor Statistics
69. National Education Association.
70. College Entrance Examination Board
71. The American College Testing Program
72. U.S. Bureau of the Census, Current Population Reports
73. The Higher Education Research Institute
74. U.S. Department of Education, Office of Special Education Programs
75. National College of Education
76. National College of Education
77. National Center for Health Statistics, Vital Statistics of the United States
78. U.S. Centers for Disease Control
79. National Center for Health Statistics, Vital Statistics of the United States
80. National Center for Health Statistics, Vital Statistics of the United States
81. U.S. Bureau of the Census, Current Population Reports
82. National Center for Health Statistics, Hospital Discharge Survey
83. National Center for Health Statistics, Vital Statistics of the United States
84. National Center for Health Statistics, Vital Statistics of the United States
85. Consumer Product Safety Commission
86. Consumer Product Safety Commission
87. Consumer Product Safety Commission
88. National Center for Health Statistics, Vital Statistics of the United States
89. U.S. Department of Education
90. National Center for Health Statistics, National Health Interview Survey
91. A.C. Nielsen
92. Institute for Social Research, Time, Goods, and Well-being

CHAPTER
SEVEN

WHAT YOU OWN

YOUR AUTOMOBILE OWNERSHIP

In 1985, Americans owned 137,300,000 passenger vehicles. That came to one car for every 1.7 people in this country, and 10 cars for every 13 Americans age 16 and older. The world average was 12 people for every passenger automobile. [1]

Nine out of ten U.S. households own at least one passenger vehicle (automobile or light truck), and the average household owned 1.8 vehicles, up from 1.4 cars in 1960. [2]

According to the Hertz Corp., the average automobile in the United States in 1986 was 7.6 years old.

YOUR NEW AUTOMOBILE

In 1987, Americans purchased 10.2 million new automobiles. [3] An all-time high 29.8% of new cars sold in 1987 were imports. In total market share, the big story of 1987 was a 20.6% plunge in the sales of General Motors. The market shares of the major automobile companies in 1987 were: [4]

General Motors	36.6%
Ford Motor Co.	20.1%
Chrysler	10.7%
Honda	7.2%
Toyota	6.2%

Nissan	5.2%
Hyundai	2.6%
Mazda	2.0%
Volkswagen	1.8%

According to the Department of Commerce, the price you paid for that new car in 1986 averaged $12,585, more than double the 1976 average price of $5,418. According to a study sponsored by *Newsweek*, sales by type of vehicle and median price in 1986 was:

Type of vehicle	% of total sales	Median price
Sub-compact	24%	$ 8,500
Small specialty	12%	$12,500
Compact	18%	$11,400
High-roofed station wagon	2%	$10,900
Mid-size	20%	$12,700
Domestic mid-size specialty	5%	$14,100
Domestic standard	8%	$16,400
Import sport specialty	2%	$18,200
Luxury	4%	$23,500
Mini-van	5%	$14,300

The 5 best-selling models were: [5]

Model	Number sold
Ford Escort	392,360
Ford Taurus	354,971
Honda Accord	334,876
Chevrolet Cavalier	307,028
Chevrolet Celebrity	306,480

What new automobiles were most satisfactory to their owners? The 1987 customer satisfaction ratings compiled by J.D. Power & Associates showed that more owners were satisfied with their Honda Acuras in the first 12–14 months of ownership than any other model. It's interesting that half of the top ten ranked automobiles sold for less than the average sales price of all new cars. The top ten models in terms of customer satisfaction, with average prices, were:

1. Honda Acura — $10,039
2. Honda Civic — $ 9,038
3. Mercedes-Benz 420 — $54,050

4.	Toyota Tercel	$ 5,848
5.	Mazda 323	$ 8,299
6.	Subaru Station Wagon	$ 9,208
7.	Cadillac Brougham	$22,637
8.	Nissan Maxima	$16,849
9.	Jaguar XJ5	$39,700
10.	Mercury Grand Marquis	$15,163

New automobiles had an increasing percentage of electronic options. According to *Wards Automotive Reports*, 72% of U.S. built cars had rear window defoggers, 76% had electronic radios, half had power door locks or stereo tape decks, two-thirds had tilt steering wheels, and three-quarters had digital clocks. Chilton Company's *Annual Statistical Issue, Automotive Industries* listed the following factory installed equipment in 1984 models:

Transmission	
Automatic	84.0%
Manual	15.0%
V-8 engine	27.0%
6 cylinder engine	25.0%
4 cylinder engine	46.0%
Diesel engine	1.3%
Power brakes	94.0%
Power steering	90.0%
Power windows	39.0%
Air conditioning	83.0%
Tinted glass	90.0%

What were your favorite car colors? A 1987 survey of auto body shop owners and paint suppliers indicated the following: [6]

Color	% of cars
Blue	24%
Red	17%
White	14%
Gray	13%
Black	11%

New car buyers had an average household income of $35,600, 51% higher than the national average. 46% had professional or managerial jobs, 38% were college graduates, and their average

age was 40. 57% of the buyers were men, 43% were women. The average buyer intended to keep his or her car for 5 years.

To pay for that new car, 75% of buyers took out loans stretching out an average of 51 months, up from an average of 45 months in 1980. The average loan payment on a new car sold in 1985 was $238.47. 54% of borrowers obtained their loans from banks or credit unions, 38% used automobile company financing, and the rest used other sources. [7]

YOUR NEW TRUCK OR VAN

Sales of pick-ups, jeeps, and mini-vans, all considered "trucks" by the automotive industry, totaled 4.6 million in 1987, or a record 31% of all passenger vehicles sold. The two best selling passenger vehicles in 1987 were both trucks: the Ford F-series truck (550,125 sold) and the Chevrolet C-K truck (418,221) sold. [8]

In total, by the end of 1987, Americans owned approximately 35 million pick-ups, jeeps, and mini-vans used for personal transportation. [9]

YOUR USED CAR

According to an annual study by the Hertz Corporation, Americans purchased 16.5 million used cars in 1986, 49% more vehicles than the number of new cars sold. The average purchase price for a used car in 1986, including taxes, was $5,833. The average used car sold was 4.5 years old and had 41,140 miles on the odometer. In 1979, the average used car sold was only 2.8 years old and had only 29,090 miles on the odometer.

Almost 30% of the used cars sold were 7 or more years old. The average car had three owners before being retired to the junk heap. 45% of all automobiles built in 1977 were still on the road in 1987.

In 1985, 29% of the buyers of used cars were women, up from just 16% in 1979. Only 46% of used car buyers financed their purchases, compared with 75% of new car buyers.

WHAT IT COST TO OPERATE YOUR CAR

The cost of owning and operating your automobile depended on how many miles you drove and how long you had owned and were planning to own the vehicle. Since depreciation and financing costs are much higher in the first years of ownership, the longer you drove your car, the lower your yearly vehicle operating costs.

One estimate of the costs of owning and operating your car was issued by the U.S. Federal Highway Administration. Based on your owning a 1984 model for 12 years and driving 120,000 total miles, the Highway Administration estimated an overall cost of 30.62 cents per mile for large 4-door sedans and 23.31 cents per mile for compact cars. [10]

A second, and perhaps more realistic estimate, was provided by the Hertz Corporation, which based its figures on ownership of a new 1985 car driven 10,000 miles a year for 5 years. Those figures, by size of car, were:

Sub-compact	40.9 cents per mile
Compact	47.6 cents per mile
Mid-size	47.2 cents per mile
Intermediate	52.8 cents per mile
Full-size	63.0 cents per mile

Hertz estimated the average dollar cost of owning and operating an automobile in 1986 to be $3,002, $51 more than in 1985. Lower fuel costs and better fuel efficiency resulted in a $156 reduction in the average cost of gasoline. But the average age of all cars, 7.6 years, the highest since 1950, meant that repairs and maintenance more than wiped out the fuel savings. The average maintenance and repair costs in 1986 were $1,035.

According to Hertz, new car owners spent an average of 50 cents per mile to operate their vehicles in 1986, while used car owners spent 29 cents per mile.

YOUR AUTOMOBILE SERVICE AND REPAIRS

The most common service you were likely to perform on your car was pumping your own gasoline. In 1986, 78% of Americans usually used self-service pumps, compared with just 17% in 1974. [11]

A study by the Newspaper Advertising Bureau revealed that 48% of Americans had their car serviced at regular intervals, 35% only visited a repair shop when something went wrong, and 17% did their own checkups. According to a study by Mediamark Research Inc., the percentage of people who did the following work for themselves was:

Changed oil	46.8%
Add antifreeze	40.9%
Changed oil filter	33.4%
Changed air filter	29.3%
Installed spark plugs	23.9%
Installed battery	13.6%
Added oil additives	12.0%
Installed shock absorbers	11.4%
Installed muffler	4.7%

Most car owners were loyal when their cars needed work. 70% always took their car to the same place for service, and 48% almost always purchased gasoline at the same station. [12]

According to the Hertz Corporation, the average American automobile used 525 gallons of gas to travel 9,304 miles, an average of 17.7 miles per gallon.

BREAKDOWNS

Figures supplied by the American Automobile Association showed that 45% of their emergency road service calls in 1986 were for problems starting cars, 35% were for mechanical failures requiring towing, 10% were for flat tires, 4% were for cars out of gas or keys locked in car, and 6% had other causes.

YOUR ENCOUNTERS WITH POTHOLES

According to the Road Information Program, there were an average of 56 million potholes in American roads in 1986. The average pothole was 16 inches wide, 5 inches deep, and needed 110 pounds of filler to repair.

WHAT'S IN YOUR GLOVE COMPARTMENT

A survey conducted by Runzheimer and Co. in 1986 revealed the percentage of car owners who kept the following in their glove compartments:

Item	% of glove compartments
Maps	50%
Insurance cards	31%
Sunglasses	23%
Pads of paper	14%
Tissues	13%
Cassette tapes	11%

HOW YOU USE YOUR VEHICLE

The average car was driven 8,894 miles in 1983. According to figures compiled by the Federal Highway Administration, at least one member of the average American household got into a car (the average household has more than one car) 1512 times in 1983, traveling an average of 11,921 miles, or 7.9 miles per trip. By percentage of trips, the reasons were: [13]

Trip to work	27.9%
Work-related business	2.9%
Shopping	20.0%
Family/personal business	18.3%
Trip to school or church	5.9%
Visit friends or relatives	9.9%
Other social/recreational	12.2%
Vacation	.1%
Other	2.8%

WHO HAS A DRIVER'S LICENSE?

In 1985, 158,224,000 Americans were licensed to drive. Those licensed by age were: [14]

Age	% with driver's licenses
16–17	58%
18–21	86%

Age	% with driver's licenses
22–24	94%
25–34	94%
35–44	94%
45–54	92%
55–64	86%
65+	65%

The most recent National Personal Transportation Study by the Federal Highway Administration showed that men drove an average of 13,563 miles per year, while women averaged just 5,943 miles. One reason was that when couples were in the car together, men were 8 times more likely to be driving than women. [15]

You can bet that those couples in the car have had at least one argument about who was the better driver, a man or a woman. A look at who gets traffic tickets would seem to give the nod to America's females. A 1985 survey by R.H. Bruskin Associates revealed that 20% of male drivers received some sort of ticket that year, compared with 10% of women. The breakdown by type of ticket was:

Type of ticket	Men	Women
Speeding ticket	10%	5%
Parking ticket	9%	5%
Moving violation	3%	1%
Running red light	2%	1%

ACCIDENTS

In 1986, according to the National Safety Council, 22% of all drivers were involved in a motor vehicle accident. Americans age 20–24 were most likely to have been involved in an accident (37%), while the most safety conscious drivers were those age 45 to 74. By age of the driver, the percentage of drivers involved in accidents was: [16]

Under 20	36%
20–24	37%
25–34	25%

35–44	18%
45–54	14%
55–64	13%
65–74	14%
75 and over	23%

In 1986, 14% of the accidents were non-collision accidents (car running off the road, etc.), 80% were collisions with another vehicle, 1% were collisions with a pedestrian, and 5% were collisions with a tree or other fixed object. At least one driver received a ticket for improper driving in 62% of all accidents. The average vehicle damage was about $1,600. [17]

About 1,800,000 people were injured in 1,200,000 accidents, or 14.7% of all accidents. That was a rate of 1 injury for every 1,033,000 miles driven. About 140,000 people were injured so badly that they had a permanent disability. In 1986, a person was injured in a motor vehicle accident every 18 seconds. [18]

47,900 people were killed in 42,300 traffic accidents in 1986. The fatality rate per 100 million miles driven was 2.57, half the rate posted in 1960. According to statistics compiled by the Motor Vehicle Manufacturers Association, the U.S. fatality rate per miles driven was the lowest of 14 selected countries. Spain was the most dangerous country, with a fatality rate of 10.6 deaths per 100 million miles driven. [19]

Of those killed, 58% were drivers, 24% were passengers, and 18% were pedestrians or bicyclists. Of the 42,300 fatal accidents, 16,400 (39%) involved collisions between two vehicles, 13,200 (31%) were non-collision accidents such as running off the road, 8,100 involved vehicles striking pedestrians, and 4,600 involved collisions with trees or other objects. [20]

Men were the drivers involved in an amazing 78% of the fatal accidents. 33% of the drivers were under age 25 and 62% were under age 35. In terms of fatal accidents per 100,000 drivers, those most likely to be involved were people age 20–24, followed by drivers under age 20. Least likely to be involved in a fatal accident were drivers age 45–64. [21]

One-third of all fatal accidents occurred between 6 p.m. and midnight, and half occurred between 3 p.m. and midnight. The death rate per 100,000,000 miles driven was three times higher at night than during daylight hours. More than 1 in 5 accidents occurred on a Saturday, and the summer months were, proportionately, the most dangerous times of year. The death rate on rural roads was more than twice as high as the death rate for drivers on urban roads. [22]

In 1986, alcohol consumption was a factor in 52% of all fatal accidents, 27% of all accidents resulting in serious injury, and 8% of all accidents resulting in property damage. However, the percentage of drivers involved in fatal accidents who had alcohol in their bloodstreams dropped 10% between 1980 and 1986. This decline was a major reason for the 24% drop in the rate of fatalities per 100 million miles driven between 1980 and 1986. [23]

A study of the blood alcohol levels of a representative survey of late night drivers showed a significant drop in the number of drinking drivers between 1973 and 1986. In 1973, 14% of late night drivers had a blood alcohol content of .05%, high enough for a charge of driving under the influence of alcohol in some states, and 5% of late night drivers were intoxicated, with blood levels of .10% or higher. In 1986, however, only 8% of late night drivers had blood alcohol contents of .05% or higher, and only 3% were intoxicated. Although their numbers were smaller, late night drunk drivers still caused 69% of all fatal accidents that occurred between midnight and 3 a.m. [24]

WHO WEARS SEAT BELTS?

In July, 1987, 24 states and the District of Columbia had mandatory seat belt use laws. These laws were the reason that the percentage of drivers and front seat passengers wearing seat belts increased from 23% in 1985 to 34% in 1987. Usage was 23% in states without seat belt laws and 49% in states where seat belt use was mandatory. [25]

Studies by the National Highway Traffic Safety Administration has shown that 50% to 65% of people killed in traffic accidents would have survived if they had been wearing seat belts. Another study revealed that traffic fatalities in states with seat belt laws were 11% lower than in states without seat belt laws during the first half of 1986.

One reason for not wearing seat belts has been the fear of being trapped in a burning car. However, University of North Carolina researchers studied 3,500,000 car crashes that occurred over a twelve year period. They found that no belted driver or passenger was killed by fire in a car crash over that period.

WHO SPEEDS?

In 1985, American drivers received 8,449,085 speeding tickets, according to the U.S. Department of Transportation. Californians got 1 out of every 8 tickets issued, while residents of Hawaii received a paltry 7,500 of the unwanted summonses.

While on interstate highways, an estimated 59% of drivers were exceeding the 55 mile per hour speed limit. America's leading ticketed leadfoots were residents of Arizona, Rhode Island, Vermont, and New Hampshire. Least likely to be caught speeding were residents of West Virginia, Virginia, Hawaii, and Kentucky. [26]

If you're speeding at night, you should be more careful, according to a study by psychologists at San Jose State University in California. They found that 71% of motorists stopped by police at night were given tickets, compared with just 58% of motorists stopped during daylight hours.

AUTOMOBILE THEFT

In 1986, according to the Justice Department, 1 out of every 159 cars was stolen in the U.S.A. You were about 10 times more likely to have had your car stolen if you lived in a city with a population over 250,000 than if you lived in the country.

Top city in terms of number of cars stolen was New York, with about 80,000 vehicles swiped in 1986. Next were Los Angeles, Chicago, Houston, Detroit, and Boston. In thefts per 100,000 population, however, Detroit was first by far with a rate of 3,749 cars stolen per 100,000 population, 8 times the national average. Next came Los Angeles, Chicago, New York, and Memphis.

According to the National Highway Traffic Safety Administration, the cars most often stolen, in order, were:

Buick Riviera

Toyota Celica Supra

Cadillac Eldorado

Chevrolet Corvette

Pontiac Firebird

Mazda RX-7

Chevrolet Camaro

Porsche 911

Pontiac Grand Prix

Oldsmobile Toronado

YOUR BICYCLES

You may be surprised that Americans bought more new bicycles and tricycles (11.4 million) in 1985 than new cars. [27] In 1986, Americans owned 111,100,000 pedaled vehicles. About 1,200 bicyclists died in traffic accidents. [28]

YOUR BOATS

In 1985, according to the National Marine Manufacturers Association, Americans owned 13,900,000 pleasure boats, of the following types:

Outboard motor boats	7,500,000
Inboard motor boats	1,500,000
Sailboats	1,200,000
Canoes	1,800,000
Rowboats and other	1,900,000

An estimated 658,000 boats were sold in 1984, a 25% increase over 1983. The average retail cost of outboard motor boats sold was $2,500, and the average retail cost of inboard motor boats sold was $14,500.

According to the U.S. Coast Guard, there were 6,237 boating accidents in 1985 that produced 1,116 deaths.

YOUR MOTORCYCLE

In 1985, there were 5,472,000 motorcycles registered in the United States. Those two-wheeled vehicles were 3.5 times as likely to have been involved in an accident as a passenger car and a motorcycle driver was 6 times as likely to be killed in an accident as the driver of a passenger car. [29] Given those odds, it's a shame that the Federal Highway Administration found that only 65% of motorcyclists always wear a protective helmet.

YOUR RECREATIONAL VEHICLES

In 1985, Americans bought 359,200 recreational vehicles. 65% of them were motorized homes, 23% were travel trailers, 10% were folding camping trailers, and 2% were truck campers. The average retail costs of each type of vehicle was: $24,514 for a motorized home, $13,534 for a travel trailer, $3,816 for a folding camping trailer, and $6,667 for a truck camper. [30]

WHO FLIES?

In 1985, according to the Federal Aviation Administration, 311,000 Americans held private pilot's licenses and another 147,000 had student pilot's licenses. The average private pilot logged 8.9 hours of flying during the year. [31]

YOUR ELECTRONIC TOYS

We Americans have been addicted to electronics, spending a substantial $30.0 billion on televisions, radios, video cassette recorders and other consumer electronics in 1987. Our children are so enamored of these gadgets that when they were asked to name their most prized possessions, over three-quarters placed either stereo systems or television sets at the top of their lists. In the average American household, either a television set or a radio is on early 11 hours a day, or over 80% of the time someone is home and awake.

TV's and VCR's

Although we Americans made up only about 5% of the world's population in 1985, we owned about one-quarter of the world's 657 million television sets. [32] 98% of American households contained a television set, with an average of 2 sets per home. 94% of homes owned at least one color television, 60% still had a black and white set, 11% had a stereo−adaptable color TV, and 4% had a projection TV. 50% of households had two or more color TV's. Americans were expected to buy another 19,000,000 color TV sets in 1988. [33]

According to the Electronic Industries Association, 50% of American households owned video cassette recorders in October, 1987, double the number of households with a VCR in January, 1985. Projected sales of VCR's in 1988 were 12,000,000 units, which should increase the percentage of households with video re-orders to 60%. 90% of the VCR's purchased in 1985 were VHS machines, 9% were Beta format, and 1% were 8mm machines.

Radios and audio systems

You may be surprised to learn that by far more radios were purchased in 1987 than any other electronic product. Americans bought 25.3 million home radios and 29.2 million portable radio-tape player combinations. 98% of American homes owned radios, with an average of 5.5 radios per home. [34]

In October, 1987, 89% of all households had at least one audio system, and 33% had two or more systems. In the last few years, however, there has been a dramatic change in the type of systems owned, as reflected in the format of music purchases, according to the Recording Industry Association of America. In 1985, 52% of all purchases were cassette tapes, exactly double the 26% figure in 1983. Just 44% were records, down from 51% in 1983. The most dramatic decline was for 8-track tapes, which made up less than 1% of purchases in 1985, compared with 23% in 1983. The largest gain, on the other hand, was made by compact discs, a 290% increase in one year. The percentage of homes with compact disc players soared from 2% in January, 1986 to 9% in October, 1987. Americans were expected to purchase an additional 3.6 million compact disc players in 1988. [35]

A great deal of the popularity of cassette tape players has resulted from the capability of copying music from records albums, radio stations, and other tapes. In 1984, the Recording Industry Association estimated that the equivalent of 594 million albums were taped from other sources.

Telephones

According to the Federal Communications Commission, there were 58 telephones per 100 people in this country, an average of 1.6 telephones per household in 1986. 92.2% of households had telephone service in 1986, and about 53% of those had touch-tone telephone service. [36]

Since the break-up of AT&T, sales of home telephones have been soaring. In 1985, about 55% of American households owned at least one of their telephones, and 41% owned all of their phones. [37] When you shopped for a telephone, you strongly preferred no-frills instruments. According to a survey by the market research firm, the Yankee Group, 30% of your purchases were standard desk phones, and 23% were standard wall phones. Only 5% of your purchases were multi-featured models, while cordless phones accounted for 11%. In October, 1987, 17% of American households owned at least one cordless telephone. [38]

Another hot-selling item—and one that annoys a lot of people—was the telephone answering machine. The percentage of households owning an answering machine climbed from 5% in January, 1985 to 19% in October, 1987.

Computers

In 1985, according to polls by both the Roper Organization and *U.S.A. Today*, about 12% of American households owned a computer. In about three-quarters of those home, adults used the computer, half for job-related work at home, half for non-job related activities. Most popular of non-job related activities for adults were educational programs, financial management, programming, and games. Games and educational programs were by far the most popular activities for children who used home computers. [39]

Other Toys

In 1987, consumers purchased about 2 million video camcorders, about 400,000 satellite dishes, about 750,000 hand-held television sets, 300,000 car telephones, 360 million blank audio cassettes and 325 million blank video cassettes. [40]

YOUR APPLIANCES

By far the hottest product in appliance sales has been the microwave oven. According to the International Microwave Power Institute, the percentage of American households with microwave ovens soared from 16.4% in 1980 to 50% in 1986. Microwave penetration, so to speak, has been projected to reach 80% of households by 1990.

According to the U.S. Energy Information Administration, the percentage of American households with the following appliances in 1984 were:

Refrigerator	99.9%
Frost-free	63.5%
Range	99.9%
Electric	53.3%
Gas	46.6%

Oven	93.6%
Electric	51.9%
Gas	41.7%
Freezer	37.0%
Dishwasher	36.1%
Clothes washer	71.4%
Clothes dryer	59.8%
Humidifier	13.5%
Dehumidifier	9.0%
Outdoor gas grill	11.2%
Garage door opener	14.0%
Window or ceiling fan	28.0%
Whole house fan	7.8%

WHAT YOU'D LIKE TO HAVE THE MOST

According to the Roper Organization, the recreational items with the largest gap between the people who'd like to own them and the people who did own them were:

Item	% who'd like to have	% who have
Swimming pool	32%	7%
Jacuzzi	20%	1%
Hot tub	18%	1%
Sauna	14%	Under 1%

According to a study reported in the July, 1981 issue of *Psychology Today*, the things you treasured most depended on who you were. Below are the most treasured items named by children, parents, and grandparents:

Item	% treasuring
Children's list	
Stereos	45.6%
TV's	36.7%
Furniture	32.9%
Musical instruments	31.6%
Beds	29.1%
Pets	24.1%
Collectibles	17.7%

Item	% treasuring
Sports equipment	17.7%
Books	15.2%
Vehicles	12.7%
Radios	11.4%
Refrigerators	11.4%
Stuffed animals	11.4%
Clothes	10.1%
Photos	10.1%
Parents' list	
Furniture	38.1%
Visual art	36.7%
Sculpture	26.7%
Books	24.0%
Musical instruments	22.7%
Plants	19.3%
Stereos	18.0%
Appliances	17.3%
Plates	14.7%
Collectibles	11.3%
Glass	11.3%
Jewelry	11.3%
TV's	11.3%
Grandparents' list	
Photos	37.2%
Furniture	33.7%
Books	25.6%
TV's	23.3%
Plates	22.1%
Visual art	22.1%
Sculpture	17.4%
Appliances	15.1%
Plants	13.8%
Collectibles	11.6%
Musical instruments	10.5%
Silverware	10.5%
Weavings	10.5%
Whole room	10.5%

YOUR BED

When it comes to sleep, Americans like comfort. As a result, you like your beds roomy. According to a consumer survey conducted by *Better Homes and Gardens*, the types of bed you slept in were:

% of Americans owning	Size bed
41%	Full/double
31%	Queen
19%	King
6%	Twin
3%	No answer

WHO OWNS FIREARMS?

About 120 million firearms were in private hands in the United States in 1986, with about half of all homes in the country containing one or more guns. Although most people who owned firearms kept them for hunting or sport, about one-fifth of gun owners said that "self defense at home" was their more important reason for possessing a weapon. [41]

A study of gunshot deaths over a 5 year period by Arthur L. Kellerman and Donald T. Reay showed that these firearms were far more likely to endanger homeowners than protect them. For every criminal shot dead in self-protection, there were 43 accidental deaths, homicides, or suicides. Friends were 12 times as likely to be shot as strangers and members of the household were 18 times more likely to be killed by a firearm kept in the home.

YOUR PETS

About 58% of American households kept at least one pet in 1985. According to a survey of 13,000 pet owners by *Psychology Today* Magazine, those pets meant a lot to their owners. 9 out of 10 pet owners said their pet was "extremely" or "very" important to them. 75% said their pet increased the fun and laughter in the family, and nearly 80% said that at times, their pet was their closest companion. Half kept pictures of their pets in their wallets or at the office.

One indication that owners treated their pets very well was that the average supermarket devoted 240 linear feet of shelf space to pet food, the most space devoted to any product. [42]

Dogs

According to research conducted for Kal Kan Foods, Inc., about 37% of American households owned 46 million dogs in 1984. The average dog owning household had 1.44 dogs. Because so many women were entering the labor force and were reluctant to leave a dog alone all day, the percentage of dog-owning households was projected to drop to 35% by 1990.

The people who were most likely to own dogs were large households (4 or more people), high income households, and households with children.

A 1986 survey by Purina Dog Chow found that by far the largest number of people owned mixed breed dogs (31%), followed by German Shepherds (7%), golden retrievers (6%) and Labrador retrievers (6%). 30% of the pet owners polled said their dog's favorite people food was hot dogs, followed by ice cream (16%) and pizza (10%). Purina's survey found that Duke was the top dog's name, ahead of Brandy, Max, Sam, and Shadow. A survey by Kal Kan, a rival pet food company, found the traditional Rover was the favorite name, followed by Spot and Max.

What does owning a dog cost? According to estimates prepared for Psychology Today by New York veterinarian Steve Holzman, cost of an 80 pound dog over an average 11 year life span was about 9 cents an hour. By dog weight, Holzman's estimates for raising a dog to age 11 were:

	80 pound dog	40 pound dog	10 pound dog
Food	$5279	$3168	$1056
Vet expenses	$1734	$1604	$1264
Misc. (grooming, toys, license, kennels, etc.)	$1190	$980	$770

Of your pet food dollars, 61% were spent on dry food, 25% on canned food, 9% on moist food, and 5% on snacks. A 1986 survey of dog owners by *Good Housekeeping* Magazine showed that the overwhelming favorite flavor of dogs was beef (60%), followed by chicken (9%), cheese (5%), and liver (4%).

80% of dog owners took their pets to the vet at least once a year, and the visit cost an average of $37.

Cats

Americans also owned 45.3 million cats in 1984. Only 26% of households owned cats, with the average 2.03 cats per household. The percentage of households owning cats is projected to stay the same in 1990, but more cats per household will shoot the cat population up to an estimated 53.9 million. [43]

Compared with dog owning households, households containing cats were more likely to be childless, more likely to have both husband and wife working full time, and more likely to have been in a big city rather than the suburbs.

The vast majority of cats were domestic shorthair mixed breeds. According to the registration rolls of the Cat Fanciers' Association, the most common purebreds were, in order:

1. Persian

2. Himalayan

3. Siamese

4. Abyssinian

5. Burmese

6. Maine Coon

Veterinarian Steve Holzman estimated the cost of raising a cat to age 11 to be $3,957, including $1,773 for food and $1,264 for vet expenses.

About 54% of cat food dollars were spent on dry food, 36% on canned food, and 10% on moist food. *Good Housekeeping* found that cat's favorite flavors were fish (48%), chicken (16%), beef (11%), and liver (4%).

59% of cat owners took their pets to the vet in 1984, and the average visit cost $32.

Birds

About 15% of American households had pet birds, with the number of birds reaching an estimated 27 million in 1984. The national average was 2.1 birds per bird-owning household. [44]

The most common bird kept in the house was the parakeet, which has an average life span of 7 years. In December, 1985, *Money* Magazine estimated the average lifetime cost of a parakeet to be $599. About two-thirds of bird owners were women, and the majority lived in big cities.

Other Pets

About 12% of American households kept fish, with an average of 25 fish per household. That meant 250,000,000 million fish swimming away in American aquariums. [45]

Other common pets were: [46]

Pet	% of households
Raccoons	1.8%
Hamsters/gerbils	1.7%
Rabbits	1.5%
Reptiles	1.2%
Rodents	.9%
Guinea pigs	.4%

MEET MR. AND MRS. AVERAGE

If you think the glamorous men and women in the fashion ads got their modeling jobs because they were "average" consumers, you couldn't be more than wrong. According to research compiled by *U.S.A. Today*, the average American woman:

Stands 5'4" tall and weighs 143 pounds.

Wears size 10–12 dress and skirts

Wears size 7 in hats and gloves

Has a bra size of 34–36 B

Slips into 7-1/2 B shoes and a size 6 ring

Mr. American Average:

Stands 5'9" tall and weighs 173 pounds

Wears a 40 regular suit

Has a shirt size of 15-1/2 neck, 33 sleeve

Pulls on pants with a 34" waists

Takes a 7-1/2 size hat and 9-1/2 C or D shoes

Has a ring size of 9 or 10

WOMEN'S CLOTHES SHOPPING

According to the latest comprehensive Consumer Expenditure Survey, released in 1986 by the Bureau of Labor Statistics, the average woman age 16 and over spent $339 on clothes during the course of the year. As you would expect, the amount of money spent on clothes rose with household income, with women in households earning $30,000 and over spending twice the national average.

According to a 1985 study by MRCA Information Services, working women made up only 29% of the apparel market, but spent 44% of the total expenditures for women's clothing. Working women without children bought an average of 55 items of clothing during the course of the year at a total cost of $605. Working women with children bought an average of 37 items of clothing at a cost of $333, about the national average.

A study by the Market Research Corporation of American produced the following breakdown of the average woman's clothing budget:

Type of item	% of budget spent
Blouses/sweaters	27.4%
Dresses	15.5%
Skirts/suits	13.8%
Lingerie/hosiery	12.0%
Slacks	11.2%
Other	20.1%

According to the 1986 Woolite Fashion Undercover Report, the fabrics women preferred for their lingerie were

Silk	36%
Satin	26%
Silky blends	24%
Lace	15%
Cotton	15%

YOUR FANCY FOOTWEAR

A Gallup survey conducted for Scholl, Inc. and the American Podiatric Medical Association revealed that 59% of American women wore high heels regularly, even though 62% of the wearers had foot pain and other foot problems as a result. 44% of white collar women, 36% of professional women, 13% of blue collar women, and 7% of housewives wore high heels over 5 hours per day.

BIG BEAUTIFUL WOMEN

You may be pleased to discover that those thin fashion models don't represent the average American women. *American Demographics* reported that an estimated 35% to 45% of women wore a size 16 or larger. A staff member of the high fashion magazine *Vogue* admitted to a reporter that 20% of its readers wore a size 16 or larger and half wore a size 12 or larger.

MEN'S CLOTHES SHOPPING

According to the Bureau of Labor Statistic's Consumer Expenditure Survey, American men spent, on the average, a little over $200 a year on clothing—about half of what their wives spent. According to a survey by Celanese Fibers, however, men with executive or professional jobs who lived in big cities spent much more. The results of the five city survey were:

City	Spent on business clothing	Spent on leisure clothing
Atlanta	$1,014	$414
Chicago	$ 951	$560
Dallas	$1,003	$560
Los Angeles	$ 700	$728
New York	$ 900	$654

A survey by the Menswear Retailers of America revealed that half of all men bought clothing for replacement, 34% to expand their wardrobes, and only 19% bought for fashion. The survey also showed the average man's closet contained:

4 suits

4 sport coats

7–12 pairs of dress slacks

6 pairs of casual slacks

11–20 dress shirts

11–20 sport shirts

20 ties

6–15 sweaters

According to *Men's Wear* Magazine, the average man wore a 42 regular suit with a 32 inch inseam and a 15-1/2"–33" shirt. 65% of men wore regular size suits, 25% took long suits and 10% took short suits.

60% of men took their wives along when they shopped for clothes, and 75% let their wives buy all of their underwear.

YOUR COSMETICS

According to studies by *Good Housekeeping* Magazine and Simmons Market Research Bureau, the following percentages of women used these products regularly:

Mascara	82%
Blush	82%
Lipstick	75%
Eye shadow	71%
Nail polish	58%
Perfume	45%

According to the 1986 *Good Housekeeping* study, 53% of women wore make-up all the time. Cosmetic use was greater than average among women age 18–24, among working women, and among women in high income households. About 45% of women reported spending 15 minutes a day or more putting on their make-up. Half of all women reported wearing make-up and perfume to bed at times.

YOUR PURSE

Ever wonder what women keep in their purses? A 1986 *Bruskin Report* revealed the percentage of women who kept the following items in their purses:

Keys	97%
Wallet	94%
Comb	80%
Checks	76%
Make-up	69%
Address book	69%
Calculator	28%
Perfume	21%

YOUR JEWELRY

According to the *Jewelers' Circular-Keystone Directory*, 70% of women wore jewelry every day, and only 3 out of 1000 women never wore jewelry at all. The number of pieces women usually wore when they wore jewelry was:

1	6.5%
2	19.6%
3	26.7%
4	19.7%
5	27.2%

Women bought 82% of their own jewelry, with working women three times as likely to have bought pieces in the last year. About 75% of all jewelry purchases were costume jewelry. The percentage of women who purchased the following items was: [47]

Necklaces	46%
Rings	30%
Bracelets	27%
Earrings	46%

When a man did buy jewelry for a woman, however, half the time he spent over $250 for the item.

Diamonds accounted for about 6% of the total jewelry sales in the United States. The types of diamond items sold by jewelers were: [48]

Item	% of diamond sales
Men's rings	5.8%
Solitaire rings	6.7%
Other rings	24.7%
Earrings	27.2%
Pendant/necklaces	24.0%
Bracelets	4.6%
Loose stones	3.1%
Pins	1.7%
Watches	1.1%
Other	1.1%

The median price of diamond jewelry sold was: [49]

Men's solitaire rings	$ 1,350
Other men's rings	$ 1,000
Women's solitaire rings	$ 600
Other women's rings	$ 950
Pendants/necklaces	$ 550
Earrings	$ 400
Bracelets	$ 1,350
All diamond jewelry	$ 650

Nearly all first brides and 50% of "repeat" brides received engagement rings with a median purchase price of $800. 38.3% of brides wore engagement rings worth over $1,000 and 19% wore a diamond worth $2,000 or more.

Men's diamonds accounted for 14% of total diamond jewelry revenues, and 75% of men's diamond jewelry was bought by women. According to the Diamond Information Center, about one-quarter of all men 18 and over owned at least one piece of diamond jewelry.

The purchase price for all watches was: [50]

Under $ 49	39.8%
$ 50–$ 99	33.5%
$ 100–$ 299	23.5%
$ 300–$ 999	2.4%
$ 1,000+	.8%
Your watch type was:	
Quartz analog	40.9%
Digital	27.6%
Mechanical	26.4%
Other	5.1%

A watch was by far the most common type of jewelry worn by both men and women. About two-thirds of you bought your own watches. When a watch was purchased as a gift, it was 15 times more likely to be a quartz analog watch than any other type.

WHAT YOU THROW AWAY

In 1984, Americans threw away an astounding 1,547 pounds of garbage per person, twice as much trash per person as Japan, the world's second largest garbage producer. That garbage consisted of: [51]

Paper	49.4 million pounds
Yard wastes	23.8 million pounds
Glass	12.9 million pounds
Metals	12.8 million pounds
Food	10.8 million pounds
Plastics	9.6 million pounds
Wood	5.1 million pounds
Rubber/leather	3.3 million pounds
Textiles	2.8 million pounds

CHAPTER SEVEN NOTES

1. U.S. Energy Information Administration
2. U.S. Energy Information Administration.
3. USA Today
4. Integrated Automotive Resources, Inc.
5. Motor Vehicle Manufacturer's Association
6. Maaco Auto Painting & Bodyworks survey
7. SRI Research, Inc.
8. Integrated Automotive Resources, Inc.
9. Author's estimate
10. U.S. Federal Highway Administration, Cost of Owning and Operating Automobiles and Vans
11. Amoco Corp.
12. Mediamark Research Inc.
13. U.S. Federal Highway Administration, National Personal Transportation Survey
14. U.S. Federal Highway Administration, Selected Highway Statistics and Charts
15. U.S. Federal Highway Administration, National Personal Transportation Survey
16. National Safety Council, Accident Facts − 1987
17. National Safety Council, Accident Facts − 1987
18. National Safety Council, Accident Facts − 1987
19. National Safety Council, Accident Facts − 1987
20. National Safety Council, Accident Facts − 1987
21. National Safety Council, Accident Facts − 1987
22. National Safety Council, Accident Facts − 1987
23. National Highway Traffic Safety Administration
24. Insurance Institute for Highway Safety

25. National Highway Traffic Safety Administration
26. U.S. Federal Highway Administration
27. Bicycle Manufacturer's Association
28. National Safety Council
29. U.S. Federal Highway Administration
30. Recreational Vehicle Industry Association
31. U.S. Federal Aviation Administration
32. United Nations, Statistical Yearbook
33. Electronics Industries Association
34. Electronics Industries Association
35. Electronics Industries Association
36. Federal Communications Commission
37. AT&T
38. Electronics Industries Association
39. USA Today
40. Electronic Industries Association
41. American Rifle Association
42. Progressive Grocer
43. Kal-Kan Foods, Inc.
44. Pet Food Council
45. Pet Food Council
46. Pet Food Council
47. Jewelers' Circular-Keystone Directory
48. Jewelers' Circular-Keystone Directory
49. Jewelers' Circular-Keystone Directory
50. Jewelers' Circular-Keystone Directory
51. Environmental Protection Agency, World Resources, 1987

CHAPTER
EIGHT

WHAT YOU DO FOR FUN

HOW MUCH TIME
YOU HAVE FOR FUN

The amount of time Americans could devote to having fun dropped a substantial 32% between 1973 and 1985, according to a Louis
Harris survey. One major reason was that the average weekly
hours of work for the average American increased 20%, from 40.6
hours in 1973 to 48.8 hours in 1985. The two major factors in the
increase in average working hours was the large increase in the
number of working women and the boom in white-collar service
jobs.

The result: between 1973 and 1985, the number of leisure hours
available to the average American dropped from 26.2 to 17.7, a loss
of 1 hour, 12 minutes per day of free time. The average man had
19.0 leisure hours, while the average woman had just 16.4 leisure
hours. [1]

Despite the recent "fitness" craze, the Institute for Social Research of the University of Michigan found that "passive" leisure
activities (watching television, reading, listening to music, etc.)
consumed over 80% of the average person's leisure hours.
Curiously, Americans with the least time for fun, those with the
most education and the highest paying jobs, devoted the largest
number of hours to active leisure activities such as exercise, sports,
and volunteering. [2]

YOUR LEISURE TIME AT HOME

Americans have been homebodies, spending most of their leisure time with their families. According to the United Media Enterprises *Report on Leisure in America*, "More than anything, Americans are looking for companionship in their leisure time, and a person's spouse or romantic partner, children and close friends are the most important elements of that companionship."

8 of the 10 most popular leisure activities in the United Media study were home-based, including watching television, reading newspapers, listening to music, and talking on the telephone. Another poll by the Roper Organization found that adults spent 57% of their leisure hours at home, and that figure rose to 70% for Americans age 60 and over.

VISITING WITH FRIENDS, FAMILY AND NEIGHBORS

According to a 1986 poll by the Roper Organization, 36% of Americans listed talking with friends, family, and neighbors as their favorite daily activity.

What that talk consisted of varied considerably between men and women. Researchers at the State University of New York at New Paltz found that 60% of conversations between women were on personal or emotional topics, compared with just 27% of men's conversations. Sociologists Jack Levin and Arnold Arluke at Northeastern University found that 71% of women's conversations involved talking about others, compared with 64% of men's conversations. The real difference, however, was that women were much more likely to be talking about close friends and family members, while men were much more likely to be talking about sports figures, celebrities, or acquaintances.

WHO'S LONELY?

According to the United Media Enterprises *Report on Leisure in America*, about 60% of adult Americans were satisfied with the level of companionship that they had. On the other hand, 40% were dissatisfied. Based on a survey of a cross section of the U.S. population, University of Massachusetts sociologist Robert Weiss estimated that between 50 million and 60 million Americans— about one quarter of the population—felt extremely lonely at some time during any given month. Those least likely to be lonely were married adults; those most likely to be lonely were widowed, separated, or divorced.

One factor in loneliness has been personality. Based on a psychological inventory, the Myers-Briggs Type Indicator, one-half to two-thirds of Americans were classified as extroverts, with the minority classed as introverts. Introverts were likely to be lonely.

SOCIAL LIFE OF OLDER AMERICANS

8,110,000 Americans age 65 or over were living alone in 1985. [3]
Of senior citizens living alone (average age, 75): [4]

94% had talked with a relative by phone in the last 14 days

84% had seen a relative in the last 14 days

85% had talked with a close friend in the last 14 days

40% had seen a close friend in the last 14 days

40% saw one of their children at least once a week

25% saw one of their children daily

YOUR MAIL

In 1985, Americans received an average of 585 pieces of mail per person. Less than 10% of those pieces, however, was a real letter. 52% of your mail arrived first class, but 80% of that was bills. On the average, you received 44 magazines or newspapers, 3 parcels or packages, and 1 mailgram. [5]

The rest of your mail, 37%, consisted of direct mail advertising circulars or, as some people call it, "junk mail." The average household received 18 pieces of direct mail marketing per month, and "up-scale" households, those with incomes of $35,000 or higher, received an average of 35 solicitations per month. [6]

The reason you got so much junk mail was that the majority of you responded to it. A 1986 study by Simmons Market Research showed that Americans did 27% of their shopping from home, spending $171 billion a year. In the average month 48% of Americans households made at least one purchase in response to mail or telephone marketing initiatives. Because at-home shopping was more convenient for the growing number working women, the amount of money spent on mail-order purchases was estimated to increase almost 20% in 1987.

Although a lot of people complain verbally about junk mail, very few do anything to stop it. Less than 1% of Americans have taken action to get their names removed from mailing lists.

YOUR TELEPHONE CALLS

In 1985, according to the United States Telephone Association, Americans made 1,263,537,000 telephone calls every day. That total included over 102 million long distance calls, about one out of every 12 calls. Of all calls, 53% were made from home telephones, 46% from business phones, and 1% from pay telephones. [7]

97% of American homes had telephones, and those phones were used to make an average of 6 calls per day. The average household made 149 local calls and 18 long distance calls a month. Half the long distance calls were to points 500 miles away or more, and the average call lasted 8 minutes, 15 seconds. Almost 20% of long distance calls in 1986—a total of 4 billion calls—were made to toll-free "800" numbers. The average household made 2 overseas calls during the year. [8]

WHO WATCHES TELEVISION?

In 1986, 82% of adults watched television on the average day, with the average household having a set on nearly 7 hours a day. [9] The 1986 Roper Organization poll found that 25% of Americans listed watching television as their most eagerly anticipated daily activity. In 1985, A.C. Nielsen found the following average viewing hours to be:

All children	3 hours, 54 minutes per day
All teen-agers under 18	3 hours, 12 minutes per day

Age 18–34	
Men	3 hours, 40 minutes per day
Women	4 hours, 29 minutes per day
Age 45–54	
Men	3 hours, 51 minutes per day
Women	4 hours, 46 minutes per day
Age 55 and over	
Men	5 hours, 19 minutes per day
Women	6 hours, 10 minutes per day

Almost everyone turned the television on while they were doing other activities—29% read while watching TV, 22% ate, and 16% did housework. 27% of Americans did nothing else while watching TV. [10] Because Americans did so many things with their sets on, it has been very hard to determine exactly how many hours of pure leisure time have been consumed by watching television. Diary studies of the daily activities of Americans, however, have consistently shown that TV viewing has consumed over half of all available leisure time, or at least 9 hours per week. [11]

Sunday has been the most popular viewing night, followed by Thursday. Audiences have been lowest on Saturday nights. In the 1985–1986 television season, according to A.C. Nielsen, the most popular form of entertainment was the mini-series, followed by made-for-TV movies, regular series, entertainment specials, and theatrical films. Americans watched an average of 39 minutes of news per day.

Overall, time spent in front of the television set has been increasing, for two reasons. The first reason has been cable television. The percentage of households receiving 9 or more channels jumped from 8% in 1964 to 84% in 1985. In 1985, over 60 million households (68% of all households) had cable television service available to them, and 36.9 million households (41%) subscribed to basic cable service. 88% of cable households subscribed to a pay cable service, such as Home Box Office or Showtime. The average bill to subscribers was $10.25 a month for basic service and $10.53 for pay cable service. [12]

The explosion of VCR ownership has also increased time spent in front of the set. The average VCR owner rented 4 movies per month. 51% of VCR owners used their machines primarily to tape programs for TV they would otherwise be unable to watch, according to a study by the Committee on Nationwide Television Audience Measurement. One-quarter of all VCR owners taped 21 shows a month or more, many of them soap operas. According to *Adver-*

tising Age, one soap opera alone, *All My Children*, accounted for 6% of all shows taped in 1984. All together, by 1995, according to a study by the research firm of Wilkofsky Gruen Associates, 25% of America's TV viewing time will be spent watching VCR tapes.

THE ALL TIME BEST TV SHOWS

In 1985, the Screen Actors Guild asked its 54,017 members to list their favorite TV shows of all time. The results:

1. *I Love Lucy*
2. *The Dick Van Dyke Shoe*
3. *The Mary Tyler Moore Show*
4. *The Honeymooners*
5. *M*A*S*H*
6. *Cheers*
7. *Leave It To Beaver*
8. *The Twilight Zone*
9. *Hill Street Blues*
10. *Gunsmoke*

WHO'S BEEN ON TV?

According to a 1985 Roper Organization poll, 27% of men and 22% of women have been on television at least once in their lives.

WHO LISTENS TO THE RADIO

You may be surprised to discover that most Americans spent nearly as much time listening to the radio as they did watching television. According to the Radio Advertising Bureau's 1985 figures,

96% of men, 93% of women and 100% of teen-agers listened to the radio every week. 99% of you had radios in your homes, 95% of you had radios in your cars, and 57% of you listened to the radio at work. Your average listening hours a day were:

Age	Men	Women
18–24	3 hr. 56 min.	3 hr. 39 min.
25–34	3 hr. 41 min.	3 hr. 15 min.
35–49	3 hr. 17 min.	3 hr. 21 min.
50+	2 hr. 47 min.	3 hr. 53 min.

Two out of every three listeners were tuned to an FM station. If the number of radio stations playing a particular kind of music was any indication, your favorite music was country. The most popular formats of stations across the U.S. were: [13]

Format	Number of stations
Country	2,333
Adult contemporary	1,933
Top 40/rock	809
Nostalgia	687
Easy listening	524
Religious	510
Album-oriented rock	294
Black R&B	207
Golden oldies	173
Other	704

YOUR FAVORITE MUSIC

Sure enough, according to a 1986 Harris poll, more Americans liked country music than any other type. The results of the poll:

Type of music	% of adults who liked that type
Country	59%
Rock	44%

Type of music	% of adults who liked that type
Classical	35%
R&B, jazz	34%
Spirituals	30%
Folk	17%
Show tunes	15%

Comparing the 1986 poll with a similar study done in 1966 revealed striking changes in listening habits. Show tunes went from most popular in 1966 (62%) to last in 1986. Classical was second in 1966 (58%), then dropped to third place. The only category to gain over the two decades was country music.

The same 1986 Harris poll surveyed adults about the music they disliked. The results:

Type of music	% of adults who disliked that type
Rock	38%
Opera	22%
Country	10%
Classical	7%
R&B, jazz	7%
Latin American	6%

When it came to spending money to buy albums, tapes, or compact discs, however, five times as much money was spent on rock (46.6% of purchases) than country music (9.7% of purchases). Sales in other categories were pop/easy listening (14.2%), black/disco (10.1%), classical (5.9%), jazz (3.9%), and gospel (3.0). [14]

WHO GOES TO THE MOVIES?

In their report "Movie Going in the United States," the Newspaper Advertising Bureau found that the average American went to the movies 5 times, compared with 29 times in 1946. 85% of moviegoers were age 12–39. About one-quarter of Americans had been to the movies in the last month. The average cost of a movie ticket was $3.54.

Surprisingly, people who owned VCR's went to the movies an average of 9 times a year. Three out of five VCR owners rented movies, an average of nine rentals a month.

Who didn't go to the movies? The Motion Picture Association of America, Inc. found the following percentages of Americans didn't attend a movie show:

Single adults	34%
Men	36%
Women	44%
Married couples	45%

One reason people listed for not attending movies was that some movies offended them. Of 6,685 pictures rated by the Motion Picture Association of American through 1985, 44% had been rated "R," 37% had been rated "PG" or "PG-13,", 13% had been rated "G," and 5% had been rated "X." In 1985, however, 58% of all pictures rated earned an "R," giving some credence to the claim that movie makers were including more violence and sex.

THE FAVORITE ALL-TIME MOVIES

In 1984, *TV Guide* asked program directors at local TV stations to name the movies their viewers requested most frequently. The results:

1. *Casablanca*

2. *King Kong*

3. *The Magnificent Seven*

4. *The Maltese Falcon*

5. *The Adventures of Robin Hood*

6. *The African Queen*

7. *The Birds*

8. *Citizen Kane*

9. *Miracle on 34th Street*

10. *Girls! Girls! Girls!*

Casablanca also topped the list of the favorite movies of the members of the Screen Actors Guild. Their favorites in 1985 were:

1. *Casablanca*

2. *Gone With The Wind*

3. *It's a Wonderful Life*

4. *On The Waterfront*

5. *The Lion in Winter*

6. *The African Queen*

7. *A Streetcar Named Desire*

8. *The Godfather*

9. *Some Like It Hot*

10. *Manhattan*

Finally, a nationwide poll of movie critics and professors in 1986 produced the following top 10 list of their favorite movies:

1. *Citizen Kane*

2. *Gone With The Wind*

3. *Casablanca*

4. *It's a Wonderful Life*

5. *On the Waterfront*

6. *The Searchers*

7. *The Godfather*

8. *Birth of a Nation*

9. *Wizard of Oz*

10. *City Lights*

WHO ARE FOLLOWERS OF THE ARTS?

Two nationwide surveys of attendance at arts performances and museums have painted very different portraits of the importance of the arts in American lives.

The first survey, "Public Participation in the Arts," was conducted by the Census Bureau for the National Endowment for the Arts. That survey produced the following percentages of Americans who had attended at least once during the year:

Event/institution	% of adults attending at least once
Jazz performance	10%
Classical music performance	13%
Opera	3%
Musical play	19%
Play	12%
Ballet	4%
Art museum	22%

A second survey was conducted by Louis Harris and Associates and sponsored by Philip Morris Inc. This survey showed much broader yearly attendance, as follows:

Event/institution	% of adults attending at least once
Play/musical comedy/pantomime other theater	67%
Popular singer/band/rock group	60%
Opera/musical theater	35%
Ballet/modern/folk/ethnic dance	34%
Art museum	58%

The best explanation for the difference is that the broader categories of activities in the Louis Harris survey stimulated Americans to remember attending a broader range of arts performances—

concerts in a local park, school plays, entertainment at shopping malls, etc. In either case, however, it is clear that a majority of American adults attend some sort of art exhibit or performance over the course of a year.

WHO READS?

Researchers Larry Mikulecky and Nancy Leavitt Shanklin of Indiana University found that the average woman read 164 minutes a day and the average man read 150 minutes a day. These figures included all reading—books, magazines, newspapers, work-related material, recipes, instructions on packages, etc. They found that 99% of jobs required some reading, with the average being 113 minutes per day. Ithiel de Sola Pool of the Massachusetts Institute of Technology found that the number of printed words read by the average American each day was 8,500.

The requirement of reading on the job meant that people who didn't read well or at all had trouble finding employment. The Ford Foundation estimated that 25 million American adults, 14% of the population, were illiterate, meaning they couldn't read and understand sentences. Another 35 million Americans, 20% of the population, were functionally illiterate, meaning they couldn't read beyond a fifth grade level.

WHO READS BOOKS

In 1985, Americans bought over 2 billion books, 1.3 billion paperbacks and 766 million hardcovers. They paid over $9 billion for their reading pleasure. [15]

According to research sponsored by the Book Industry Study Group and conducted by the Gallup Organization in 1985, 66% of American women and 54% of American men were classified as "book readers," having read a book in the last three months. It's no surprise that book reading increased with both income and education. According to a 1985 Gallup poll, 37% of college graduates had spent some time reading a book the day before the poll, compared with 20% of Americans with a high school diploma and 16% of high school dropouts. Book readers included 70% of people with incomes of $40,000 or above, 68% of Americans with some college, and 75% of college graduates.

Of the book readers, two-thirds had read 1–5 books in the last three months, 17% had read 6–10 books, and 17% had read 11 or more books. The approximately 35% of all readers who were frequent readers accounted for 75% of all books read and 55% of all books purchased.

According to the 1985 Gallup Poll on Book Buying, 42% of readers bought the last book they read, 27% received it as a gift, 18% borrowed it from the library, 8% borrowed a book from a family member, and 2% borrowed one from a friend. The average book buyer had purchased about 6 books every three months, with the purchases being split evenly between fiction and non-fiction.

Most popular fiction categories were mystery (19%), romance (18%), popular fiction (12%), historical fiction (11%), action and adventure (11%), and science fiction (10%). Most popular non-fiction categories were reference and instructional books (16%), history (16%), biography (15%), religious (9%), and diet and health (7%).

To meet the appetite of readers in 1985, 17,000 American publishing houses produced 40,929 new titles. [16]

WHO USES THE LIBRARY?

According to a 1985 Gallup survey, 28% of Americans went to the library at least once a month, 45% said they went every three months or less often, and 27% said they never went to the library. 64% of those who visited a library had library cards. Those with library cards checked out over 1 billion books.

WHO READS THE NEWSPAPER?

On the average, 60.5% of adult Americans read at least one newspaper on the average weekday and 65.6% read the newspaper on an average Sunday in 1986. [17] Newspaper readership was highest (70%) for Americans with a college degree and those who earned over $50,000 per year. In 1986, average daily newspaper circulation was 62.8 million and average Sunday circulation was 58.8 million. [18]

According to a 1984 survey of 19,000 adults by the Newspaper Advertising Bureau, 62% of newspaper readers went through the entire newspaper, page by page. Of all readers, 92% usually read the general news pages, 80% usually read the entertainment sections, 79% usually read the sports section, and 78% read the editorial pages. After the general news section, the sports pages were the most popular with male readers (86% readership), while the home furnishings/improvement section were the least popular (69% readership). After general news, the entertainment and cooking sections were the most popular with women (84% readership), while sports were the least popular section (72% readership).

WHERE YOU GET YOUR NEWS

In 1982, 65% of Americans said they received most of their news about world events from television; in 1959, 57% received most of their news from newspapers. At the other end of the spectrum were about 9% of Americans, over 15 million adults, who absolutely refused to read, watch or listen to any news at all. [19]

WHO READS MAGAZINES?

In 1985, about 9 out of every 10 Americans read at least one magazine during the course of a month, according to the Magazine Publishers Association. Americans purchased about 6 billion copies of 1,553 domestic consumer magazines. The number of magazines published increased 66% between 1974 and 1985.

The most-read magazines were: [20]

Magazine	Per issue circulation
Reader's Digest	17,866,798
TV Guide	17,115,233
Modern Maturity	10,770,688
National Geographic	10,392,548
Better Homes & Gardens	8,058,839

WHO READS
IN THE BATHROOM?

According to studies done by Alexander Kina for his book, *The Bathroom: Criteria for Design*, 40% of you read in the bathroom, 20% smoked, 14% listened to the radio, and 8% of you talked on the telephone. On the average, you visited the bathroom 5 or 6 times a day.

For those of you who really wondered: 34% of you flushed while still sitting and 64% of you stood up before you flushed.

WHO PARTICIPATES
IN THE ARTS AS
A LEISURE ACTIVITY?

Louis Harris and Associates found the following levels of participation in 1985:

Activity	Number of Americans participating
Photography	80,000,000
Needlework/handwork	75,000,000
Play musical instrument	53,000,000
Paint/draw/other graphic arts	50,000,000
Write stories/poems	43,000,000
Sing in choir/choral group	38,000,000
Ballet/modern dance/other dance	36,000,000
Pottery/ceramics	29,000,000
Sculpt/work with clay	15,000,000
Perform/work with theater groups	12,000,000

WHO PLAYS
MUSICAL INSTRUMENTS?

In 1986, according to the American Music Conference, 51% of all households included at least one amateur musician:

20,600,000 Americans played the piano

18,900,000 played the guitar

6,300,000 played the organ

4,000,000 played the flute

4,000,000 played the clarinet

WHO BELIEVES IN THE OCCULT?

A survey conducted by *Psychology Today* for its September, 1986 issue revealed that only 10% of Americans were complete non-believers in the occult. 83% believed in extra-sensory perception (ESP), 47% believed in re-incarnation, and 43% of women and 24% of men believed in astrology.

YOUR RECREATIONAL ACTIVITIES

Americans have always loved sports and outdoor recreation. Only 8 to 11% of all adults never participated in any kind of active leisure time activity.

A number of major studies have been conducted to determine the number of Americans who participate in different activities. The following National Recreation Survey of Americans age 12 and over was conducted by the Census Bureau for the National Park Service:

Activity	% participating in last 12 months
Walking for pleasure	53%
Swimming	53%
Visiting zoos, fairs, etc.	50%
Picnics	48%
Driving for pleasure	48%
Sightseeing	46%
Attending sports events	40%

Activity	% participating in last 12 months
Fishing	34%
Bicycling	32%
Boating	28%
Canoeing/kayaking	8%
Sailing	6%
Motorboating	19%
Running/jogging	26%
Attending concerts, plays, etc.	25%
Camping	24%
Backpacking	5%
Outdoor team sports	24%
Tennis	17%
Day hiking	14%
Golfing	13%
Birdwatching	12%
Hunting	12%
Off-road vehicle driving	11%
Sledding	10%
Waterskiing	9%
Snow skiing	9%
Horseback riding	9%
Ice skating	6

Another study, this one of adults 18 and over conducted in 1984 by the Gallup Organization for the National Gardening Association, included some different activities:

Activity	% participating in last 12 months
Flower gardening	47%
Swimming	41%
Vegetable gardening	40%
Bicycling	33%
Fishing	30%
Camping	23%
Jogging	22%
Bowling	21%
Aerobics	20%
Weight-lifting	19%
Billiards/pool	18%
Softball	18%
Calisthentics	15%
Motorboating	14%

Activity	% participating in last 12 months
Volleyball	14%
Basketball	13%
Hunting	13%
Golf	12%
Ping pong	12%
Baseball	11%
Tennis	11%
Canoeing/rowing	10%
Roller skating	9%
Horseback riding	8%
Target shooting	8%
Snow skiing	7%
Waterskiing	7%
Racquetball	6%
Sailing	6%
Touch/flag football	6%

Most obsessive of sports participants, according to the Gallup study, were joggers, who hit the pavement an average of 67 times a year. Swimmers got wet an average of 40 times, golfers teed up 28 times, sailors hoisted sail 17 times, and skiers hit the slopes an average of 14 times.

The people most likely to have participated in sports and recreation activities, according to Gallup, were the well-educated and the wealthy. College-educated Americans had the highest level of participation in every activity, and participation rates of households with incomes of $40,000 a year or more were double the national average.

A final study worth noting surveyed adults 18 and over in 1985 for President's Commission on Americans Outdoors. This study found the following percentages of Americans who participated in outdoor activities not just once but "often" during the year:

Activity	% participating often in 1985
Spectator outings	76%
Sightseeing	34%
Driving for pleasure	43%
Picnicking	28%
Visiting historic sites	14%

Activity	% participating often in 1985
Visiting zoos, fairs, etc.	17%
Walking for pleasure	50%
Attending outdoor concerts	11%
Water and golf	48%
Sailing/windsurfing	4%
Swimming in ocean/lake	28%
Swimming in pool	30%
Golf	10%
Ball games and running	41%
Basketball	10%
Softball/baseball	16%
Football	6%
Running/jogging	17%
Attending sports events	22%
Soccer	3%
Fishing, hunting, motor sports	37%
Fishing	25%
Hunting	11%
Motorboating	15%
Recreational vehicle camping	8%
Off-road vehicle driving	11%
Observing nature	31%
Backpacking	5%
Day hiking	12%
Tent camping	9%
Other camping	5%
Canoeing/kayaking/rafting	5%
Nature/birdwatching	15%
Winter sports	11%
Ice skating	3%
Downhill skiing	5%
Cross country skiing	3%
Sledding	4%
Other activities	
Bicycling	17%
Horseback riding	3%
Tennis	10%

WHO EXERCISES?

A 1986 Gallup poll, conducted for *American Health* Magazine, revealed that 69% of Americans were exercising. Half of those who exercised admitted they were working out primarily because their doctor told them it would be a good idea. 30% of the men and 19% of the women exercised because they wanted to lose weight. Only 13% of those polled said they exercised for "the fun of it."

27% of those who exercised (19% of adults) spent 5 hours a week or more on fitness activities, 25% (17% of adults) exercised between 2 and 4.5 hours per week, and 48% (33% of adults) worked out 1.5 hours a week or less.

In terms of type of exercise, walking was in and jogging showed a marked decline. Nearly half of all Americans walked for exercise in 1986. A Gallup poll showed the number of Americans who jogged dropped from 30.2 million in 1984 to 25.5 million in 1986 (14% of adult population). At the same time, the number of joggers who reported that they ran every day or nearly every day was cut in half in that two year period. Gallup found only 7 million "lifestyle" joggers, those who ran at least one out of every three days over the course of a year.

One reason for the decline in jogging may have been the injury rate. A study by the Centers for Disease Control found that 1 out of 3 joggers could expect to suffer an injury every year. The rate of injury during the course of a year went from 3 out of 10 joggers who ran less than 10 miles per week to 7 out of 10 joggers averaging 40 miles per week or more. Half of all injuries involved a knee or foot. On a more positive note, the CDC found that the average jogger could expect to be hit by a thrown object only once every 12 years, to be bitten by a dog every 26 years, and to be hit by a car every 135 years.

Many Americans looking for more vigorous exercise turned to aerobics—20% of adults participated in 1985. A study presented to the 1985 International Dance-Exercise Association did show that 1 out of every 2 participants in aerobics were injured during the course of a year, but the overwhelming number of injuries were minor complaints such as shin splints. Only 9% of those injured were treated by a physician. The study found a correlation between frequency of exercise and injury, with those who did aerobics more than three times a week increasing their chances of injury significantly.

WHO BENEFITS FROM EXERCISE?

According to the Gallup Poll for American Health, Americans who exercised regularly were 2.5 times more likely to report that they were happy than Americans who didn't exercise at all.

People who exercised a lot also lived longer. One of the most comprehensive studies every conducted looked at the relationship between exercise and longevity of 16,936 men who graduated from Harvard between 1916 and 1950. The study found men who burned 2,000 or more calories per week through exercise had a 30% lower death rate than non-exercisers. Benefits for exercise began to be statistically noticeable at 500 calories burned per week and were the greatest for those who burned over 3,000 calories per week. Researchers reported that for every hour men exercised, they added that hour to the length of their lives—and maybe two or three more.

Burning 2,000 calories took a lot of effort, however. To burn those calories in a week, you'd have to:

Walk for 5 hours at 5–6 mile per hour pace

Run for 4 hours, 20 minutes at an 8.5 minute mile pace

Do aerobics for 5 hours

Swim 4 hours at 2 miles per hour

Bicycle 4 hours, 20 minutes at 10 miles per hour

Play vigorous racquetball or squash for 3 hours, 40 minutes

By these standards, 80% to 90% of American adults did not get enough exercise each week.

WHO ARE SPORTS FANS?

"Sports Poll '86," conducted for *Sports Illustrated* by Lieberman Research, Inc., revealed that 71% of American men and women consider themselves sports fans. 84% of those polled said they watched sports on TV at least once a week, with the average viewing time 6.8 hours of sports per week. 49% of those polled had attended at least one live sporting event in the past 12 months.

The poll found the following percentages of Americans who said they were "interested" in the following sports:

Sport	% of Americans interested
Pro football	60%
Baseball	59%
Fishing	43%

Sport	% of Americans interested
College football	42%
Bowling	35%
Pro basketball	32%
Pro boxing	32%
Auto racing	31%
College basketball	30%
Hunting	26%
Pool/billiards	26%
Ice skating	25%
Tennis	22%
Horse racing	20%
Hockey	18%

WHO GOES TO THE GAME?

In 1985, Simmons Market Research Bureau found that the following numbers of Americans had attended at least one live sporting event for the following sports:

Sport	Number of Americans attending at least once
Major league baseball	21,000,000
Professional football	9,500,000
College football	9,300,000
College basketball	7,600,000
Professional basketball	6,400,000
Ice hockey	3,900,000
Boxing	3,600,000
Wrestling	3,600,000
Golf	3,200,000
Tennis	2,500,000

WHO WATCHES SPORTS ON TV?

According to an August, 1985 survey by Simmons Market Research Bureau, Inc., professional football and baseball attracted by far the largest number of television viewers. The number and percentage of adult Americans who "frequently" or "almost always" watched televised sports in 1985 were:

Sport	Number of viewers	% of adults
Pro football	63,200,000	37%
Baseball	62,700,000	37%
College football	48,900,000	29%
Boxing	37,200,000	22%
College basketball	36,200,000	21%
Pro basketball	34,700,000	21%
Pro wrestling	28,800,000	17%
Bowling	28,600,000	17%
Tennis	26,300,000	16%
Auto racing	25,800,000	15%
Golf	25,800,000	15%
Drag racing	18,400,000	11%
Thoroughbred horse racing	18,100,000	11%
Hockey	16,600,000	10%
Track and field	16,100,000	10%
Rodeo	13,200,000	8%
Weight lifting	12,900,000	8%
Harness horse racing	9,800,000	6%
Pro soccer	8,100,000	5%
Roller derby	6,600,000	4%

In every one of these 20 sports, more men than women were regular viewers. The sports with the lowest percentage of female fans were drag racing and boxing; those with the highest percentage were tennis and thoroughbred horse racing. More single men were regular viewers than married men. The sports with the highest income audiences were tennis, hockey, golf, pro football, and college basketball. The sports with the lowest income audiences were roller derby, harness horse racing, pro wrestling, and bowling.

YOUR VACATIONS

In 1986, according to the annual Travel Poll conducted by the Hertz Corporation, 104.8 million adult Americans took vacations in this country or abroad. The average person took 6.8 trips and spent 23.4 nights away from home. He or she traveled a total of 8,644 miles, 78% by car, van or truck, 17% by airplane, and 5% by other means of transportation. The average total expenditure per person was $2,339, $835 on transportation, $698 on lodging, $806 on food, and $1,335 on clothes, luggage and entertainment.

Weekend trips were increasingly popular, with the average family taking three such trips during the course of the year. According to the American Automobile Association, 54% of weekend travelers stayed at hotels or motels, 22% stayed with friends or relatives, 17% camped, and 7% stayed at their vacation home. Total cost for the weekend jaunt for a family of two adults and two children in 1986 was $165.

Although a 1985 poll by AT&T revealed that more Americans would like to take a winter vacation than a summer vacation, summer trips outnumbered winter trips 7 to 1. Preferred destinations in the summer were the beach, then major cities. In the winter, the majority of vacationers headed toward the sun, with 2 million Americans going on cruises.

In 1984, the average vacation trip by car, truck or van was 114 miles one way. According to the U.S. Travel Data Center, 44% of all trips were taken to visit friends or relatives, with the rest for various leisure activities. On the average summer vacation, the average family spent either 6 or 7 nights away from home.

According to a study by the Airport Transit Association in 1986, 72% of American adults had flown on an airplane during their lives. Despite widespread fears of flying, airplane travel has proved to be by far the safest method of transportation. In 1985, scheduled airlines flew 5,600,000 flights with 7,831,000 hours in the air. There were 4 fatal accidents among those 5.6 million flights, taking the lives of 197 people out of approximately 350,000,000 passengers. For those of you who want to compare the costs of air travel with the costs of driving, the average fare for domestic airline travel in the U.S. in 1985 was 12.8 cents per mile. [21]

In 1984, 3,000 intercity bus lines carried 362 million passengers on scheduled runs and 214 million passengers on charters and tours. Average cost to the passenger of all bus transportation was 8.4 cents per mile. Buses were involved in 305 fatal accidents, but only 53 bus passengers died. [22]

In 1984, AMTRAK carried 20.9 million rail travelers at a cost to the passenger of 12.2 cents per mile. 3 train passengers were killed in accidents. [23]

Overall, according to the National Safety Council, the fatality rates for types of transportation in 1986 were:

Type of transportation	Fatalities per 100 million passenger miles
Bus (school, intercity)	.03
Scheduled airline flights	.04

Type of transportation	Fatalities per 100 million passenger miles
Railroad passenger trains	.07
Passenger autos and taxis	.99

Although Americans were 25 times safer flying than driving, an estimated 10% of them were afraid to fly.

WHAT YOU LIKE TO DO ON VACATION

According to a Louis Harris & Associates poll, the top five activities Americans liked to do on vacation were:

Golfing/skiing	43%
Tennis	21%
Scuba/skin diving	19%
Casino gambling	14%
Sailing	5%

YOUR FAVORITE VACATION SPOTS

Heading the favorite list of tourist spots was Niagara Falls. According to an R.H. Bruskin Associates poll, 35% of American adults have been to that fabled honeymoon location. 34% had visited the Statue of Liberty, 31% had seen the White House, 31% had seen the Grand Canyon, and 30% had been to Yellowstone Park. Leading the list of favorite tourist states in 1985 was California, followed by Florida, New York, and Texas.

In 1985, over 12 million Americans traveled to foreign countries. 53% of those trips were to Europe or the Mediterranean, 28% were to the Caribbean or Central America, 4% were to South America, and the rest were to other locations, including Canada. The average foreign trip lasted 17 days. [24]

In 1985, 7.5 million foreign visitors came to the United States. 39% were from Western Europe, 13% were from the Caribbean or Central American, 10% were from South America, and 10% were from Japan. [25]

HOW YOU CELEBRATE THANKSGIVING

About 28.5 million Americans traveled 100 miles or more to eat their Thanksgiving dinner in 1987. [26] According to a 1986 R.H. Bruskin Associates poll, here's where you ate that dinner:

Your own home	45%
Someone else's home	42%
Restaurant	4%
No special dinner	2%
Don't know	7%

And what did you have for dinner? You guessed it. On Thanksgiving Day, 1987, Americans ate 45 million turkeys. [27]

HOW WE CELEBRATE CHRISTMAS

In 1987, The Conference Board estimated that Americans spent a whopping $35 billion on Christmas gifts, an average of $380 per household. According to research by U.S.A. Today, the average household wrapped 30 gifts. Nationwide, Americans used over 320,000 miles of wrapping paper costing $500,000,000.

Those gifts were placed under 32 million live Christmas trees and 3.2 million artificial trees. Of the live trees, our favorites were Scotch pines (24% of trees purchased), Douglas fir (16.4%), Balsam fir (12.4%), and White pine (10%). On the trees we hung $800,000,000 worth of lights.

For our holiday cheer, we bought about $1 billion in liquor and $2 billion in food. 85 million people made an overnight trip of at least 100 miles from home.

YOUR GARDENING

According to the National Gardening Survey conducted by the Gallup Organization, gardening was America's number one outdoor leisure activity. According to the study:

82% of households gardened

63% did lawn work

50% grew flowers outside

46% had indoor plants

40% had a vegetable garden

18% had fruit trees

11% grew berries

4% had nut trees

The five favorites in your flower gardens were:

Flower	% of all gardens
Iris	63.0%
Chrysanthemum	59.9%
Peony	46.0%
Lily	42.6%
Day lilies	41.9%

Those of you who had indoor plants had a lot of them. 86% had 6 or more plants, 61% had 11 or more, and a quarter had more than 20 plants inside the house.

Half the vegetable gardens were smaller than 550 square feet. The average investment in gardening materials was $32, and the average harvest was produce worth $356. The average gardener worked 1 to 4 hours a week in the vegetable patch.

The top vegetable-patch crops were, according to a *Better Homes and Gardens* survey:

Crop	% of all gardens
Tomatoes	92.2%
Beans	62.6%
Cucumbers	58.8%
Peppers	56.8%
Onions	54.7%
Carrots	44.9%
Lettuce	44.9%

WHO'S FOR THE BIRDS?

In 1985, an estimated 21 million Americans were avid bird-watchers. The Audobon Society estimated that in 1986, bird watchers spent $34.7 million on cameras, $739.4 million on film, $79.3 million on binoculars, $98.5 million on special clothing for birding, and a large chunk of the $4.1 billion Americans spent on travel to observe wildlife.

On top of these expenditures, an estimated 62.5 million Americans, one-third of the adult population, spent $517 million feeding birds. They also spent $54.7 million on bird feeders, $25.8 million on bird baths, and $20.2 million on bird houses.

FISHING

According to the Bass Anglers Sportsman Society, 65 million Americans put a line in the water in 1986. They spent a total of 710.6 million days fishing, an average of 20 days per fisherman. The average fisherman spent $214 on angling, making the total national expenditure a tidy $7.8 billion.

YOUR PHOTOGRAPHY

According to a nationwide study by the Photo Marketing Association International, America has been a nation of shutterbugs. In 1985, 93.2% of American households had a conventional still camera, 36.3% had an instant print camera, 27.5% owned a movie camera, and 2.8% owned a video camera.

In terms of camera types, 49% of households owned a 110 type camera, 26% owned a 126 type camera, 18% owned a disc camera, 16% owned a 35mm camera, 17% owned a single lens reflex automatic camera, and 26% owned a single lens reflex manual camera. In term of new cameras purchased in 1985, however, 35mm cameras led the way at 36% of units sold. Next came disc cameras (28%), instant cameras (19%), and instamatic cameras (15%).

The average American used a camera at least once a month, and about a quarter of all camera owners took pictures on at least 36 occasions during the year. Fewer than 10% of Americans used a camera less than 3 times during the year. The average amateur expenditure on film and developing was $38.31, and the number of pictures taken was 50.

Christmas topped the list of picture-taking occasions (88% of Americans using a camera). Next came travel/vacations (82%), birthdays (79%), photographing children (59%), family (53%), and weddings (53%).

WHO GAMBLES?

In 1984, according to *Gaming and Wagering Business Magazine*, Americans wagered $177 billion—that's 15 times what they donated to churches, twice as much as they spent on higher education, and over half of what they spent on food. In 1985, the gambling industries revenues were about $25 billion. Of that total, state lotteries made about $10 billion, illegal gambling and casinos made about $5 billion each, race tracks and off track betting took in about $3 billion, and bingo and charitable games earned over $1 billion.

In terms of religious affiliations, Catholics were most likely to take a flyer on a game of chance. 80% of Catholics, 77% of Jews, and 74% of Presbyterians and Episcopalians placed a bet in the course of a year. Least likely to have wagered were those on the extremes of the spectrum of religious belief—fundamentalists (33%) and atheists (40%). And of all Americans, a 1986 ABC News/Washington *Post* poll found that only 18% said buying a lottery ticket was morally wrong.

Who played the lottery? About 7 out of 10 adults in the typical state had bought at least one lottery ticket. A survey conducted in California by the Field Institute found that just 18% of adults had purchased 71% of all lottery tickets. On the average, these heavy players had lower incomes and less education than the average Californian. Missouri State Lottery researchers found 4 out of 5 buyers were over age 35. In Missouri, 20% of people with incomes under $35,000 regularly buy tickets, 17% of those with incomes between $35,000 and $50,000, and just 1% of people with incomes of $50,000 or more.

In terms of betting dollars per person, Massachusetts led the way in 1985, with its citizens wagering $160.57 apiece. Next were Maryland ($158.22), New Jersey ($129.22), and Pennsylvania ($117.28).

About 24 million Americans visited casinos in 1986. According to the report *Gambling in America* by the Commission on the Review of the National Policy Toward Gambling, 40% preferred slot machines, 33% liked bingo, 17% liked blackjack, and 6% preferred craps. Craps players had the highest incomes, blackjack players were the best-educated. In 1984, the average visitor to Las Vegas had a gambling budget of $737. The same year, a survey of players at Atlantic City casinos by Arbor, Inc. showed that table game players (those who prefer craps, roulette, blackjack, etc.) made an average of 4 trips to the city and had an average gambling budget of $360 per trip. Slot machine players made an average of 2.5 trips with an average gambling budget of $105.

The magazine *Gambling Times* found that "high rollers," the term for heavy gamblers, spent an average of 11 days a year on gambling vacations, with a gambling budget of $3,605 per trip. 96% of them were men, their average household income was $75,000, and they preferred craps and blackjack by a wide margin over other games.

An estimated 60% of adult Americans made an illegal bet, most commonly on sports, in 1984, producing an estimated $3–$5 billion dollar profit for organized crime.

Next most popular of legal games was bingo, with 50 million Americans (29% of adult population) having played the game. According to statistics compiled by the *Bingo Bugle*, 57% of bingo players were women, 60% had incomes over $16,000, and two-thirds were under age 45. The heaviest players, however, were women over age 65.

About 24 million Americans played the horses. In 1985, they wagered over $12 billion dollars on over 13,000 days of racing. The average horseplayer wagered $129 on his trip to the track. On the average, he or she lost 62% of that money, going home with just $49. [28]

WHO VOLUNTEERS?

According to a survey by the Independent Sector, a coalition of non-profit groups, 89,000,000 Americans 14 and older did some volunteer work in 1985, averaging 3.5 hours per week of volunteer time worth $110 billion to non-profit organizations.

51% of women and 45% of men volunteered some time. Volunteering increased with education and income. 65% of college graduates and 60% of those with incomes of at least $40,000 gave some time in 1985, compared with 46% of high school graduates and 40% of those earning less than $10,000.

CHAPTER EIGHT NOTES

1. The Harris Survey, Louis Harris and Associates
2. Institute for Social Research, "Time, Goods, and Well-being"
3. U.S. Bureau of the Census, Current Population Reports
4. National Center for Health Statistics, National Health Survey
5. U.S. Postal Service, Annual Report of the Postmaster General
6. U.S. Postal Service, Annual Report of the Postmaster General
7. United States Telephone Association, Statistics of the Telephone Industry
8. United States Telephone Association, Statistics of the Telephone Industry
9. Mediamark Research
10. USA Today survey
11. Institute for Social Research, "Time, Goods, and Well-being"
12. Television Digest, Inc. and Paul Kagan Associates, Inc.
13. Radio Advertisers Bureau
14. Recording Industry Association of America
15. Book Industry Study Group
16. R.R. Bowker Co.
17. Mediamark Research
18. Editor & Publisher Co., Inc.
19. The Roper Organization
20. The Audit Bureau of Circulation
21. U.S. Federal Aviation Administration
22. American Bus Association
23. U.S. Federal Railroad Administration
24. U.S. Bureau of Economic Analysis
25. U.S. Bureau of Economic Analysis
26. American Automobile Association
27. National Turkey Federation
28. American Racing Manual

CHAPTER
NINE

WHAT YOU EAT
AND DRINK

WHAT YOU EAT

According to the U.S. Department of Agriculture, the average American consumed 1,431 pounds of food in 1984, an average of nearly 4 pounds a day. About 22% of that weight was dairy products, 21% was vegetables and potatoes and 15% was meats and poultry.

The percentage of nutrients we received from that food were, by food type:

Food type	% of food energy	% of protein	% of fats
Diary products	9.9%	20.2%	11.2%
Meat and poultry	21.0%	42.9%	36.1%
Eggs	1.8%	4.9%	2.7
Fat, oil, butter	18.2%	.1%	43.0%
Fruits	3.3%	1.3%	.4%
Potatoes, vegetables	5.4%	6.0%	.5%
Grain products	19.9%	18.8%	1.3%
Sugar, sweeteners	17.0%	—	—
Misc.	3.6%	5.8%	2.6%

The Department of Agriculture found that the average American received more than enough nutrients, including vitamins and minerals. The exceptions were American women, who came up

12% short on calcium, 25% low in magnesium, and 33% low in iron. Although the Agriculture Department found that almost all Americans got enough vitamins, a *Better Homes and Gardens* study found that 70% of Americans took vitamin supplements. The most common types of supplements were:

Vitamin C	43.4%
Multiple vitamins with iron	43.1%
Multiple vitamins with minerals	34.9%
Multiple vitamins	28.5%
B complex vitamins	27.8%
Vitamin E	26.1%

YOUR MEAT AND SEAFOOD EATING

Purchases of meat accounted for about 25% of the average food budget in 1984. [1] In 1985, Americans consumed, on the average: [2]

79.2 pounds of beef

70.1 pounds of poultry (chicken and turkey)

62.0 pounds of pork

14.5 pounds of seafood

1.8 pounds of veal

1.4 pounds of lamb

Between 1970 and 1985, per capita consumption of beef dropped by about 5 pounds, while consumption of poultry increased by 22 pounds per person. [3] According to projections in the April, 1986 issue of *American Demographics* magazine by Patricia Guseman and Stephen Sapp, beef consumption was expected to rebound, increasing about 25% by the year 2000. Fish consumption was projected to increase over 30%, while consumption of poultry and pork was expected to remain relatively constant.

What main courses have been your favorites when dining out? The Gallup Report on Eating Out revealed that 22% of you preferred fish, 19% voted for steak, 17% wanted shellfish, 12% liked roast beef, 11% named chicken, 3% liked ham or pork, another 3% preferred veal, and 1% opted for lamb.

How did you like your beef? The "Taste In America" report found that 29% of you liked it rare, 42% preferred it medium, 16% ordered beef medium well or medium rare, and 13% liked it well done.

How did you like your chicken? A Gallup poll revealed that 31% of you preferred fried chicken, 22% liked baked chicken, 18% named barbecued chicken, 12% liked chicken cordon bleu, 4% named chicken cacciatore, 2% said chicken divan, 2% said chicken fricassee, and 7% of you didn't like chicken at all.

A word on turkey: 86% of you told R.H. Bruskin Associates that you ate turkey all year round, not just on Thanksgiving Day.

HOT DOGS AND HAMBURGERS

According to the National Hot Dog and Sausage Council, the average American wolfed down 80 hot dogs in 1984. Hot dogs were served in 95% of U.S. homes, with adults having consumed more than children and women having eaten more than men. Approximately 580 hot dogs were consumed every second of every day.

Even more popular was the hamburger. The average American ate over 200 hamburgers in 1984. McDonald's alone sold 140 hamburgers a second in 1986, for a total of 4.5 billion hamburgers during the year.

PIZZA

According to MRCA Information Services, American ate pizza an average of 30 times in 1986. 48% of Americans liked pizza with thin crust and 45% voted for pizza with thick crust.

VEGETABLES

According to the Department of Agriculture, the average U.S. resident ate 197 pounds of vegetables in 1985, up 27% from 1970.

Of those, 89 pounds (45%) were fresh, 90 pounds were canned (46%), and 18 pounds were frozen (9%). On the average, we consumed: **[4]**

Lettuce	27.4 pounds
Tomatoes	13.4 pounds
Onions	13.4 pounds
Cabbage	9.0 pounds
Celery	7.8 pounds
Corn	7.2 pounds
Carrots	6.3 pounds
Cucumbers	4.3 pounds
Peppers	3.6 pounds
Broccoli	1.8 pounds

87% of American households consumed fresh vegetables at least 3 times per week, although the total bill for those vegetables was only $1.74. **[5]**

According to *Taste in America*, the top vegetables we ordered when we ate in restaurants were:

Broccoli	30%
Mixed vegetables	14%
Asparagus	13%
String beans	6%
Zucchini	6%

What did we like on our salads? A Gallup poll found that we were most likely to add tomatoes (72%), iceberg lettuce (60%), cucumbers (55%), bacon bits (48%), and grated cheddar cheese (46%).

VEGETARIANS

A 1986 Gallup poll found that 3.7% of American adults, or 6.2 million people, said they were strict vegetarians, although many admitted sampling an occasional bit of poultry or fish.

FRUITS

Americans ate an average of 89 pounds of fresh fruits. 8.8 pounds of canned fruit, and 2.9 pounds of dried fruits in 1984, according to the Department of Agriculture. The percentage of households who purchased the following fruits were: [6]

Apples	90%
Bananas	86%
Oranges	82%
Strawberries	67%
Peaches	65%
Grapes	63%
Grapefruits	61%
Watermelons	60%
Cantaloupes	60%
Lemons	53%
Pears	53%
Tangerines	43%
Cherries	40%
Plums	37%
Pineapples	37%
Nectarines	33%
Honeydew melons	31%
Avocados	29%
Blueberries	25%
Cranberries	21%
Limes	20%
Apricots	17%
Raspberries	17%

In 1987, according to the "Fresh Trends: 1987" survey, our favorite fruits were, in order, bananas, apples, seedless grapes, oranges, and peaches. [7]

SOUPS

According to *Taste in America*, the most popular soups ordered in restaurants were:

Minestrone/vegetable	23%
Seafood/fish	23%
Creamed soups	8%

Onion	8%
Chicken	8%

POTATOES

Americans consumed 121 pounds of potatoes per person in 1985.
[8]

DAIRY PRODUCTS

Per capita milk consumption dropped 9% between 1960 and 1985, primarily due to public attention to cholesterol. Health concerns were also the reason why low fat and skim milk made up 46% of milk consumption in 1985, compared with just 5% of consumption in 1960.

In bread spreads, Americans used 2.2 times as much margarine as butter in 1985. Americans ate 22.4 pounds of cheese per capita in 1985, 2.7 times as much as they consumed in 1960. Yogurt consumption soared 1330% from 1960 to 1985. [9]

WHAT YOU DON'T LIKE

According to a 1985 Gallup poll, the foods we hated the most were:

Snails	43%
Brains	41%
Squid	34%
Shark	34%
Tripe	32%

Also receiving a lot of mention were beef kidneys, beef tongue, oxtail, squab and mussels. Contrary to popular belief, only 5% of Americans wouldn't eat liver.

A smaller proportion of people were allergic to one or more foods. According to a 1986 R.H. Bruskin study, 4% of you were allergic to dairy products, 3% to vegetables, 2% to fruits, wheat products or spices, and 1% to shellfish or meat.

YOUR BREAKFAST

According to a study by the Wheat Industry Council, 25% of you regularly skipped breakfast. For the rest of you, however, breakfast was an important meal that has been increasingly consumed outside your home. According to the National Restaurant Association, eating breakfast out increased 47% between 1978 and 1984. The percentage of you who ate breakfast out by age was:

18–24	16%
25–34	26%
35–49	29%
50–64	19%
65+	10%

What you ordered most often when you ate out were coffee (56%), eggs (39%), breads (32%), bacon/sausage (23%), juice (19%), and breakfast sandwiches (18%). [10]

What about those breakfasts at home? Some facts about what you eat in the morning:

- In 1985, Americans consumed 255 eggs per capita, down from 403 eggs per person in 1945. [11]

- According to the Gallup Report on Eating Out, our favorite baked goods were:

Pastries/danish	63%
Biscuits	47%
Muffins	46%
Hard rolls	34%
English muffins	34%
Doughnuts	29%
Croissants	26%
Bagels	19%

Although Americans consumed 6 million bagels in 1984, 75% of you didn't know what a bagel was.

- Americans consumed 41.6 billion servings of cold cereal in 1986, an average of over 11 million servings a day. **[12]**

- The Gallup Report on Eating Out found your favorite breakfast meats were:

Bacon	70%
Sausage	70%
Ham	68%
Steak	19%
Beef hash	13%

- The Coca-Cola Co. estimated that $237 million in Coke was sold for breakfast in 1986.

YOUR COFFEE DRINKING

Coffee drinking has been on the decline in America, primarily because far fewer young people have been acquiring the habit. In 1962, 81% of Americans in their twenties drank coffee every day. By 1985, that figure had been cut in half, to 41%. The figures for all age groups in 1985 were: **[13]**

Age	% drinking coffee
10–19	7%
20–29	41%
30–59	71%
60+	79%

The heaviest coffee drinkers were those age 50–59, who consumed an average of 3.3 cups per day. As people got older, however, they tended to switch to decaffeinated coffee. 35% of Americans 60 years or older drank decaffeinated coffee, compared with just 7% of people in their twenties.

YOUR LUNCHES

According to MRCA Information Services, about 15.2 million American adults skipped lunch at least 9 out of every 10 days in 1985. Of the rest of you, 39% of men and 24% of women "brown bagged" their lunches. According to a 1986 Roper Organization survey, your favorite brown bag foods were:

Sandwiches	26%
Fresh fruit	19%
Leftovers	18%
Cake/cookies/candies	12%
Salty snacks	7%
Raw vegetables	7%

According to the "Sandwiches Across America" 1987 survey, 99% of Americans ate sandwiches, and 31% had sandwiches two or three times a week. America's favorite meat sandwiches were: [14]

Ham	30%
Bacon, lettuce, tomato	28%
Corned beef	10%
Pastrami	8%
Salami	5%
Bologna	5%
Submarine	5%
Liverwurst	4%

What did you like on those sandwiches? According to the 1985/86 Gallup Annual Report on Eating Out, 57% of you liked a slice of tomato, 54% added lettuce, 52% spread mayonnaise, 24% used onion, 24% used mustard, and 11% added healthy alfalfa sprouts. When asked to vote for an ideal sandwich, Americans voted most often for roast beef, Swiss cheese and tomatoes on whole wheat bread.

YOUR DINNERS

In 1986, *U.S.A. Today* polled nearly 1,000 American households on a midweek evening to find out what people were actually eating. They discovered that 88% of people were having dinner at home, 8% were eating in a restaurant, and 4% were consuming take-out food. In 92% of the households eating at home, everyone ate the same thing.

At home, 73% were eating a fresh main course, 18% were eating frozen food, 4% were eating canned food, and 4% were eating a meal prepared from a box. In 29% of the cases, the main course was beef, 15% was chicken, 5% pork, 4% fish, and 4% soup or sandwiches.

Salads were the side dish in 21% of households, 19% served potatoes, corn was on the table in 8%, peas and broccoli were served in 5% of households each, and beans and carrots were each eaten in 4% of households.

Milk was served with dinner in 27% of households. Other beverages were:

Soft drinks	15%
Tea	15%
Water	14%
Coffee	10%
Wine	4%
Beer	3%
Other alcohol	4%

58% of households didn't serve dessert after the meal.

YOUR SWEET TOOTH

Americans love sweets. In 1985, the average American consumed 169.4 pounds of sweeteners, just a little less than the total weight of all the meat consumed. According to the *Nutrition Action Health Letter*, the primary sources of that sugar in 1985 were:

Soft drinks	21.9%
Candy	20.5%
Bakery goods	13.3%
Breads and cereals	10.8%
Milk products	9.6%
Fruit	4.6%

According to MRCA Information Services, the average American consumed the following treats most often for dessert at home in 1986:

Fruit	72 meals
Cookies	33 meals
Cakes	32 meals
Ice cream	22 meals
Pies	20 meals

According to a 1986 Gallup poll, 52% of you rarely or never ordered desserts at a restaurant. When you did order dessert, however, your favorites were:

Apple pie	24%
Cheesecake	24%
Ice cream/sherbert	17%
Chocolate mousse	10%
Rice pudding	6%

THE SCOOP ON ICE CREAM

According to the Human Nutrition Information Service, nearly 25% of all Americans ate ice cream at least once in the last three days. According to the International Association of Ice Cream Manufacturers, 98% of U.S. households purchased ice cream during the course of the average year, and 84% bought ice cream at least once a month. A third of all households were "heavy users," going through a gallon every two weeks.

What were your favorite flavors? According to the International Association of Ice Cream Manufacturers, they were:

1.	Vanilla	35.1%
2.	Chocolate	12.4%
3.	Neapolitan	7.4%
4.	Chocolate chip	5.9%
5.	Strawberry	5.6%
6.	Vanilla fudge	4.2%
7.	Butter pecan	2.7%
8.	Cherry	2.5%
9.	Butter almond	1.6%
10.	French vanilla	1.4%
	Others	21.2%

Your favorite sherbert flavors were:

1.	Orange	32.6%
2.	Rainbow	22.0%
3.	Lime	13.4%
4.	Raspberry	11.5%
5.	Pineapple	10.7%
	Others	9.8%

All that ice cream added up to 53 billion scoops produced in America in 1984, enough to give every person on earth 12 ice cream cones.

CANDY

According to the National Confectioners Association, Americans ate an average of 17.7 pounds of candy per person in 1985. By type, that candy was:

Chocolate	57%
Hard candy	13%
Soft candy	12%
Chewy candy	7%
Other	11%

COOKIES

According to a 1984 poll by Sunshine Biscuits, 63% of Americans preferred chocolate chip cookies, 16% favored sandwich cookies (such as Oreos), and 10% voted for butter cookies. 49% of those polled liked to eat cookies with milk, 15% liked them with coffee, and 9% ate them with ice cream.

SNACKS

A comprehensive survey of adult Americans conducted by the *New York Times* in 1987 revealed that 83% of Americans snacked, and 47% had snacked the day before the survey. American's favorite snacks were, in order of preference:

Sweets, ice cream	46%
Fruits, juice, vegetables	22%
Pretzels, chips, nuts,	21%
Bread, crackers	10%
Yogurt, cheese, milk	7%
Soft drink	6%
Cereal	3%
Pizza	1%

YOUR CHIP AND POPCORN CONSUMPTION

Americans consumed an average of 4.19 pounds of potato chips and 3.24 pounds of corn chips in 1984. Popcorn consumption has been increasing fast, however, doubling in the 15 year period between 1970 and 1984. The average American consumed 42 quarts of popcorn in 1984. You also munched on an average 6.7 pounds of peanuts in 1984. **[15]**

WHAT YOU SPEND FOR FOOD

The average American household spent $3,391 for food in 1984, according to the most recent Consumer Expenditure Survey. That was 15.5% of spending, a huge drop from the 50% of income spent on food in the 1930's. The exact percentage varied considerably by household income. Households with incomes under $12,000 spent 23% of income on food, while households with incomes of $60,000 and over spent only 9% on food. **[16]**

How much do you spend at the grocery store? The Food Marketing Institute found that in 1985, a single person spent $41 a week, a family of two spent $62 a week, a family of three spent $69 a week, a family of four spent $92 a week, and families of five spent $98 a week.

According to the 1985 Department of Agriculture figures, our grocery expenditures by product type were: **[17]**

Meat	29%
Fruits and vegetables	21%
Dairy products	15%
Bakery products	10%
Poultry	5%
Flour and cereal	2%
Eggs	2%
Other	15%

In 1983, of all the money you paid for food, only 27% went to the farmer.

To cut costs, according to A.C. Nielson, 83% of women and 57% of men clipped coupons. American manufacturers issued 208 billion coupons in 1986, according to *Advertising Age*, but only 8.75 billion, or 4.2%, were actually redeemed. The likelihood of a coupon being redeemed ranged from 3% for coupons appearing in newspapers, magazines or advertising supplements to 10% for coupons received in the mail to 15–20% for coupons printed on the actual packages you purchased.

YOUR GROCERY SHOPPING HABITS

In 1985, according to the Food Marketing Institute, almost half of all shoppers preferred to go to the grocery store on Fridays or Saturdays, while only 3% favored Mondays.

According to a nationwide study sponsored by the Campbell Soup Co. and *People* Magazine, men spent 42% of all food shopping dollars in 1986. While a poll by the Roper Organization revealed that 80% of women still did most of the major grocery shopping, 77% of men at least occasionally did major shopping and 83% did "fill-in" shopping. 47% of men at least occasionally went shopping with their wives.

At the store, shoppers had a choice of an average of 17,469 items. To help them shop, 67% of men used a shopping list, though only 12% prepared the list themselves. About 30% of both men's and women's purchases were impulse items not on lists. During a major shopping trip, men spent an average of $72.40 and women spent $74. Men spent an average of 61 minutes in the store and women spent an average of 71 minutes. Men tended to select grocery stores on the basis of low prices and good variety; women tended to look for good meat and produce departments.

When you finished shopping in 1987, 30% of your purchases were packed in plastic bags, up from just 1.7% of purchases in 1980.

COOKBOOKS

According to Vance Research Services, American households owned an average of 15 cookbooks, tried between one and two new recipes a month, and looked through cookbooks for recipe ideas 12 times a year.

MEALS AWAY FROM HOME

Of the meals we ate that weren't prepared at home, we consumed 61% in restaurants, 18% at someone else's home, 8% in our cars, 6% at work, and 7% in other locations. [18]

YOUR RESTAURANT MEALS

According to the National Restaurant Association, 37% of Americans ate at least one meal away from home on the average day in 1986. On the average, you consumed 19% of your meals away from home, spending a record 40% of your total food dollars. Those most likely to eat out were young people age 18–24, who consumed 250 meals a year away from home.

About 40% of the food purchased was take-out food that wasn't consumed where it was purchased. 11% of you bought food in a take-out restaurant on the average day. According to a Gallup Poll, you were most likely to take out hamburgers (30%), beverages (24%), French fries (21%), chicken (14%), and pizza (11%).

Nationally, you spent an average of $526 per person in bars and restaurants in 1986, according to the Food Institute. Expenditures ranged from an average of $673 per person in the Pacific states to a low of $441 per person in the West North Central states.

Americans ate dinner in a restaurant an average of 5 times per month in 1986. According to the National Restaurant Association, 55% of you preferred restaurants specializing in American cooking. Your favorite ethnic foods were:

Italian	36%
Chinese	23%
Mexican	20%
French	8%
German	6%
Greek	2%
Japanese	2%
Other	3%

After you finished your meals, about 12% you charged them on a credit card, according to the Gallup Report on Eating Out. And if you took a doggie bag home, only 13% of the time did you actually feed the leftovers to a dog.

WHAT YOU DRINK

According to studies done by *Impact*, a beverage industry newsletter, the average American consumed 182 gallons of liquid in 1985. That liquid was:

Soft drinks	50 gallons
Water	47 gallons
Bottled water	5 gallons
Tap water	42 gallons
Coffee	25 gallons
Beer	24 gallons
Milk	21 gallons
Fruit juice	11 gallons
Wine	2 gallons
Hard liquor	2 gallons

SOFT DRINKS

In 1983, for the first time, the average American consumed more gallons of soft drinks than water over the course of the year. Beverage industry experts project that by the year 2000, you'll be drinking 65 gallons of soft drinks a year, up 30%, while cutting down on your water intake by 13%.

According to the trade publication *Beverage Industry*, your favorite soft drink flavors in March, 1986 were:

Cola	63.3%
Lemon-lime	13.5%
Dr. Pepper	7.0%
Orange	5.5%
Root beer	4.1%
Other	6.6%

Your soft drink consumption in 1985 came to 237 twelve ounce servings. 56% of your soft drinks were consumed from cans.

HARD LIQUOR

The average adult American purchased 2.83 gallons of distilled spirits or "hard liquor" in 1984. Leading the list of the nation's drinkers were residents of Nevada, who purchased 6.27 gallons apiece, while the citizens of West Virginia bought only 1.17 gallons. [19] According to a 1984 Simmons Market Research Bureau study, 57% of American men and 50% of American women drank hard liquor, with men drinking 80% of the total amount of distilled spirits consumed. It probably will come as no surprise that men made up the overwhelming percentage of whiskey drinkers, and that 9 out of 10 women preferred mixed drinks to drinking liquor on the rocks, with water, or with club soda.

On the average, hard liquor purchases made up 26% of a household's expenditures on alcohol, but that figure rose to 38% of purchases for households with incomes of $50,000 or greater. [20]

The type of liquor you ordered most often was: [21]

Type	Age 18–24	Age 25–34	Age 35–39	Age 40+	$25,000 + income
Vodka	16%	25%	23%	19%	22%
Bourbon	16%	8%	15%	19%	18%
Rum	28%	17%	12%	9%	7%
Scotch	2%	6%	16%	16%	17%
Can/Whis	6%	9%	6%	13%	5%
Gin	14%	11%	8%	6%	11%
Blnd. whis.	4%	7%	6%	10%	9%
Cordials	10%	7%	6%	2%	6%
Brandy	4%	6%	5%	5%	3%
Tequila	2%	4%	3%	2%	2%

These preferences changed among what the liquor industry calls "the premium liquor buyers"—that is, the people that buy the most expensive brands. Their favorites, in order, have been Scotch, Canadian Whiskey, bourbon, rum, and imported gin.

In 1985, according to *Advertising Age*, the best selling individual brands of liquor were:

Bacardi rum

Smirnoff vodka

Seagram 7-Crown whiskey

Canadian Mist whiskey

Jim Beam bourbon

The most popular mixed drinks have been, in order, Bloody Mary, Whiskey Sour, Margarita, Daiquiri, and Tequila Sunrise. The most popular flavors for after-dinner drinks were: [22]

Coffee	14.6%
Peppermint	13.3%
Whiskey	7.6%
Blackberry	5.3%
Sloe gin	4.8%
Triple sec	4.3%
Apricot	4.1%
Mint	3.5%
Ginger	2.6%
Chocolate	2.4%

WINE

In 1984, 44% of men and 48% of women drank wine, with women accounting for 58% of all wine consumed. The average American adult bought 3.12 gallons of wine. Residents of Washington, D.C. bought over 9 gallons, while residents of Mississippi averaged less than one gallon per person. [23]

Wine accounted for 22% of the average household's alcohol purchases, but 35% of the purchases of households with incomes over $50,000 per year. Those households spent an average of $163 a year on wine, almost triple the $59 spent by households with incomes of $30,000–$50,000 per year. [24]

If you drank wine, your favorite types were: [25]

Red wine	22%
White wine	62%
Rose wine	16%

YOUR BEER DRINKING

58% of men and only 28% of women drank beer in 1984, with men downing 80% of the suds consumed in the U.S. Beer and ale accounted for 51% of the liquor expenditures in the average household, but only 25% of expenditures for households with incomes of $50,000 a year or more. Over half of all people age 18–34 drank beer, but only 23% of those age 60 and over. [26]

About 22% of men were considered "heavy drinkers," consuming, on the average, more than 1 beer a day. Light beer accounted for 19% of U.S. beer sales, while imports made up only 4% of American consumption. 61% of the domestic beer sold was standard priced, 32% was low-priced, and 7% was premium priced. About 7% of U.S. adults drank ale. [27]

ARE BEER DRINKERS HEALTHIER?

A study of 17,000 adult Canadians funded by the Alcoholic Beverage Medical Research Foundation based at the Johns Hopkins University School of Medicine revealed that beer drinkers were sick 13% less often than the population as a whole. Wine drinkers were sick only 2% less often than average, while teetotalers were sick 1% more often.

CHAPTER NINE NOTES

1. U.S. Bureau of Labor Statistics, Consumer Expenditure Survey
2. U.S. Department of Agriculture, Food Consumption, Prices, and Expenditures
3. U.S. Department of Agriculture, Food Consumption, Prices, and Expenditures
4. U.S. Department of Agriculture, Food Consumption, Prices, and Expenditures
5. Vance Research Services
6. U.S. Department of Agriculture, Food Consumption, Prices, and Expenditures
7. Vance Research Services
8. U.S. Department of Agriculture, Food Consumption, Prices, and Expenditures
9. U.S. Department of Agriculture, Food Consumption, Prices, and Expenditures
10. USA Today Research
11. U.S. Department of Agriculture, Food Consumption, Prices, and Expenditures
12. U.S. Department of Agriculture, Food Consumption, Prices, and Expenditures
13. International Coffee Organization
14. Edelman Public Relations
15. U.S. Department of Agriculture, Food Consumption, Prices, and Expenditures
16. U.S. Bureau of Labor Statistics, Consumer Expenditure Survey
17. U.S. Department of Agriculture, Food Consumption, Prices, and Expenditures
18. Gallup Report on Eating Out
19. U.S. Bureau of Alcohol, Tobacco and Firearms
20. The Conference Board

21. Simmons Market Research Bureau
22. The Liquor Handbook
23. Business Trends Analysts, "The U.S. Wine Market"
24. The Conference Board
25. The Wine Institute
26. The Conference Board
27. U.S. Brewers Association

Index